CompTIA

Security+

& A+

Shawn Walker

THIS BUNDLE INCLUDES:

CompTIA A+ 220-1101 (Core 1)

+

CompTIA A+ 220-1102 (Core 2)

+

CompTIA Security+ SY0-701

Certification kit

Study Guide + Practice Tests

COPYRIGHT

CompTIA A+ 220-1101 (Core 1)

Introduction

Welcome to your journey toward CompTIA A+ certification. This book is designed to be a comprehensive guide for anyone aspiring to become CompTIA A+ certified. Whether you are just starting in information technology or looking to solidify your skills with formal certification, this book aims to equip you with the knowledge and tools necessary to pass the CompTIA A+ exams. The primary goal of this guide is to provide you with a clear and thorough understanding of all the topics covered in the CompTIA A+ 220-1101 and 220-1102 exams. These range from basic computer systems and networking to more complex security and operational procedures. Each chapter is structured to build upon the previous one, ensuring a cohesive and comprehensive mastery of all necessary skills.

For those of you new to the field, this book aims to explain complex technical concepts in layman's terms. It's crafted to prepare you for the exam and give you a solid foundation for your career in IT. For the more experienced technicians, it will serve as an excellent refresher and a structured way of preparing for the exam. Moreover, this guide is meant to be practical. It includes hands-on examples and real-world scenarios you might encounter in your daily work or on the exam. Through these examples, you'll learn not only to understand the theoretical aspects of the material but also to apply them in practical settings.

What can you expect from CompTIA A+ certification? CompTIA A+ certification is recognized globally as the starting point for a career in IT. It validates understanding of the most common hardware and software technologies in business and certifies the skills necessary to support complex IT infrastructures. CompTIA A+ is a powerful credential that helps IT professionals worldwide ignite their IT careers. Holding a CompTIA A+ certification signifies that you possess the essential knowledge and skills to troubleshoot and solve problems ranging from networking and operating systems to mobile devices and security. The certification not only opens doors to a vast range of IT jobs, such as support specialist, field service technician, desktop support analyst, and help desk tier 2 support, but it also serves as a springboard to more specialized paths. The CompTIA A+ exams (220-1101 and 220-1102) cover five major domains, starting with hardware, networking, and ending with operational procedures. In these domains, you will encounter a variety of questions that test your ability to problem-solve across multiple technologies, helping you to prepare for a diverse range of challenges in the IT world.

In this guide, you will find all the resources, tips, and guidance needed to navigate the path to certification. By the end of this book, you will feel confident not only in taking the exam but also in your capability to handle real-world IT challenges. Let's embark on this educational journey together, with the end goal of not only passing the CompTIA A+ exams but also propelling your IT career forward.

Overview of CompTIA A+ Certification

The CompTIA A+ certification is more than just an entry-level credential for IT technicians; it is a globally recognized standard that validates your foundational skills in IT and can significantly enhance your professional trajectory.

Professional Recognition and Credibility In the IT industry, credibility is paramount. For many employers, a CompTIA A+ certification is not just a bonus; it's a requirement. Holding this certification demonstrates that you have the knowledge and skills necessary to support complex IT infrastructures. This includes a wide range of devices and operating systems, making you a versatile and invaluable member of any IT team. By showcasing this credential, you signal to potential employers that you are committed to your career and have invested in your professional development.

Job Market Advantages The job market in information technology can be highly competitive. With the CompTIA A+ certification, you differentiate yourself from other candidates who lack formal recognition of their skills. This certification opens doors to numerous job opportunities that might otherwise be out of reach, including roles such as support specialist, field service technician, desktop support analyst, and help desk tier 2 support. Each of these roles requires the reliable and verified ability to handle IT operations effectively, and your certification is proof of your capabilities.

Foundation for Further Specialization CompTIA A+ is not only about proving your competency in basic IT functions; it also lays the groundwork for further specialization. Whether your interests lie in cybersecurity, cloud computing, or network management, A+ serves as the cornerstone upon which you can build a more focused and advanced skill set. It provides the essential knowledge that will help you grasp more complex concepts and technologies as you advance in your career.

Enhanced Earning Potential Investing in your professional development invariably affects your earning potential. Studies and surveys consistently show that certified professionals earn significantly more than their non-certified peers. The CompTIA A+ certification can be a stepping stone to higher-paying jobs within the IT field. As you gain experience and add more specialized certifications, your value in the job market increases, thereby enhancing your career earnings over time.

Professional Network Expansion When you become CompTIA A+ certified, you join a community of professionals with similar qualifications and career aspirations. This network can be an invaluable resource for collaborative learning, job opportunities, and professional mentoring. Networking events, online forums, and CompTIA-sponsored meetups allow you to connect with other IT professionals who can provide support and insight throughout your career.

Personal Satisfaction and Confidence Beyond the professional benefits, achieving CompTIA A+ certification brings personal satisfaction. The preparation process involves significant learning and personal growth, and successfully passing the exam is a testament to your dedication and effort. This achievement can boost your confidence, reinforcing your problem-solving abilities and technical knowledge in real-world scenarios.

Exam Tips and Study Strategies

Approaching the CompTIA A+ exams requires not only a solid understanding of IT fundamentals but also strategic preparation. The tips provided in this section are designed to optimize your study and exam performance, ensuring you are well-equipped to tackle the diverse array of questions you will encounter.

Understanding the Exam Structure The CompTIA A+ certification is comprehensive, covering a wide range of topics to ensure you have a rounded understanding of IT systems. Each of the two exams — 220-1101 and 220-1102 — consists of up to 90 questions, which need to be completed within 90 minutes. This means you have an average of one minute per question, a fact that underscores the importance of efficient time management.

Types of Questions: You will face multiple types of questions on the exams:

Multiple-choice questions are straightforward and require you to select the correct answer from several options.

Drag-and-drop activities assess your ability to organize information or complete a task by placing items in a specific order or location.

Performance-based questions are interactive and simulate real-world scenarios. You might be asked to solve a problem or complete a task within a simulated environment.

Strategies for Different Question Types

Multiple-Choice Questions: Always read the question carefully and try to answer it before looking at the available options. Eliminate clearly wrong answers first, which will increase your chances of selecting the correct answer from the remaining options.

Drag-and-Drop Activities: These questions test your understanding of how things fit together, so it's crucial to understand processes and hierarchies within IT systems. Reviewing flowcharts and diagrams can be particularly helpful in preparing for these questions.

Performance-Based Questions: These require more time, so manage your time wisely. It's often beneficial to skip these at the beginning of the test and return to them after completing the multiple-choice questions, ensuring that you don't rush through them under time pressure.

Time Management Managing your time effectively during the exam is crucial. Consider these tips:

Prioritize Quick Wins: Answer the questions you find easiest first to secure quick points and build confidence.

Mark and Review: If you encounter a difficult question, mark it for review and move on. This prevents you from spending too much time on one question and running out of time for others.

Keep an Eye on the Clock: Regularly check the time to ensure you are on track to complete all questions. Aim to have at least 10-15 minutes towards the end to go back to marked questions.

CHAPTER 1

Mobile Devices

Smartphones

In today's tech-centric world, smartphones have become ubiquitous tools integral to personal and professional life. Their complex nature, which combines both hardware and software elements in a compact form, makes understanding them essential for IT professionals, especially those pursuing the CompTIA A+ certification.

Hardware Components

Central Processing Unit (CPU): The CPU in a smartphone function similarly to the brain in the human body. It processes instructions, performs calculations, and manages the operations of other components within the system. Modern smartphones typically use multi-core CPUs, which means they can process several tasks simultaneously, enhancing the device's ability to perform multiple functions at once.

Memory: There are two primary types of memory in smartphones:

RAM (Random Access Memory): This is the short-term memory of a smartphone. It is used to store the operational data of apps that are currently in use, which allows for quick access and smooth multitasking.

Storage: This refers to the long-term memory of the phone, where everything from the operating system to apps, and personal data like photos and music are stored. Most smartphones come with a fixed amount of storage, though some allow expansion via microSD cards.

Battery: The battery supplies power to the smartphone. Its capacity is critical as it determines how long the device can operate before needing a recharge. Battery life is influenced by the phone's activities, with more intensive processes consuming more power.

Display: Smartphone screens vary widely in size and technology, featuring LCD (Liquid Crystal Display) and OLED (Organic Light-Emitting Diode) panels. The display is not just an output device but often functions as an input device with touchscreen capabilities.

Software Components

Operating System (OS): The OS is crucial as it manages the smartphone's software and hardware. It allows other applications to run over it, providing a user interface that enables users to interact with the device. The two dominant operating systems in today's market are Android and iOS, each with its ecosystem and interface.

Applications: Apps are software designed to help users perform various tasks. This could be anything from managing their calendar and emails to playing games and checking the weather. Apps utilize the hardware capabilities of the smartphone to perform their tasks and provide practical functionality to the user.

Connectivity and Sensors

Smartphones are equipped with a range of connectivity options and sensors that enhance their usability:

Wi-Fi, Bluetooth, and NFC (Near Field Communication) allow for connecting to the internet, other devices, and contactless payment systems, respectively.

GPS (Global Positioning System) enables location tracking and location-based services.

Sensors such as accelerometers, gyroscopes, and proximity sensors help the phone understand its orientation and proximity to other objects, enhancing user interaction.

Understanding smartphones requires a blend of knowledge about both hardware and software components. For IT professionals, this knowledge is critical not only for troubleshooting and maintaining these devices but also for optimizing their performance to ensure the best user experience.

Tablets

Tablets represent a unique category within the mobile device spectrum, combining the portability of smartphones with the enhanced functionality often associated with laptops. This fusion makes tablets highly versatile devices, ideal for everything from casual web browsing and media consumption to complex professional tasks that require more screen real estate and processing power. Understanding the distinct characteristics of tablets is crucial for IT professionals, especially in environments where tablets serve as primary tools for business operations.

Larger Screen Size and Display Technology

The most noticeable feature distinguishing tablets from smartphones is their size. Typically, tablets feature screens ranging from about 7 inches to upwards of 12 inches, measured diagonally. This larger size offers more workspace, which is beneficial for tasks such as reading documents, participating in video calls, and multitasking with multiple apps. The screen technology may vary, with higher-end tablets boasting displays that feature high resolution, vibrant colors, and sharp visuals, making them suitable for design and video editing tasks.

Hardware Capabilities

While the core hardware components such as CPUs and GPUs in tablets are similar to those found in smartphones, they often are more powerful to handle more demanding tasks. This can include better graphics handling, faster processing speeds, and increased RAM, which facilitate smoother performance under heavier loads. Many tablets also offer considerable storage capacity, with some models providing options for expansion via microSD cards, a feature that is increasingly rare in smartphones.

Operating Systems and Software

Tablets generally run on the same operating systems as smartphones, namely iOS or Android, but they are increasingly being seen with desktop-class operating systems, such as Windows in convertible or hybrid models. This allows them to run a broader range of software applications previously restricted to desktop environments, effectively bridging the gap between mobile and traditional computing. The application ecosystem for tablets is robust, with many developers creating apps specifically optimized for the tablet's larger screen.

Connectivity and Portability

Despite their larger size, tablets remain highly portable. They are designed to be light enough to be carried in a handbag or backpack without the bulk typically associated with laptops. In terms of connectivity, tablets offer similar options to smartphones, including Wi-Fi, Bluetooth, and often cellular options, allowing them to access the internet and perform data operations on the go. Additionally, many tablets are equipped with various ports, such as USB-C or Lightning, supporting a range of peripherals including keyboards, mice, and external displays, further extending their functionality.

Usage Scenarios

The versatility of tablets allows them to serve a wide range of use cases, from personal entertainment devices to powerful tools for professional workflows. They are particularly popular in industries such as education, where they are used as interactive textbooks, and in the business sector for presentations and fieldwork where a laptop would be cumbersome.

Understanding tablets and their capabilities allows IT professionals to better manage and support these devices within various settings, ensuring optimal performance and integration into broader IT systems.

Laptops

Laptops, also commonly referred to as notebook computers, represent a pivotal category in mobile computing, blending the portability of tablets with the robust performance capabilities traditionally associated with desktop PCs. As an IT professional, understanding the nuances of laptop technology is crucial, as these devices frequently form the backbone of corporate and personal computing solutions.

Key Hardware Components

Processor (CPU): The central processing unit in a laptop serves as the brain of the device, executing instructions from computer programs. Laptops typically use processors that are powerful enough to handle complex tasks, yet energy-efficient enough to conserve battery life. Unlike desktops, which can handle larger, more power-intensive CPUs, laptops require a balance between power and thermal management to avoid overheating in a compact space.

Memory (RAM): Random Access Memory in laptops is crucial for multitasking and running applications smoothly. Laptop RAM varies significantly, from basic models starting around 4GB to high-performance models boasting 32GB or more. This component is often upgradeable, allowing users to expand memory as their needs grow.

Storage: Laptops feature a range of storage options, including traditional hard disk drives (HDDs) and solid-state drives (SSDs). SSDs are more prevalent in newer models due to their faster read and write speeds, durability, and reduced power consumption. Many high-end laptops now feature NVMe SSDs, which offer even faster data transfer speeds.

Display: Laptop displays vary widely based on their intended use. Sizes typically range from 11 to 17 inches, measured diagonally. Resolution, color accuracy, and panel technology (such as IPS, OLED, and TN) also vary, affecting everything from casual viewing to professional graphic design and gaming.

Battery Life: One of the most critical features of a laptop is its battery life. Effective power management is key, as battery capacity directly influences the device's portability and usability in mobile settings. Modern laptops can offer anywhere from 4 to over 18 hours of operation on a single charge, depending on the model and usage.

Software and Operating Systems

Laptops run full desktop operating systems, such as Windows, macOS, or various distributions of Linux. This capability allows them to run complex software applications, including professional-grade design software, development environments, and more, which are often too resource-intensive for tablets or smartphones.

Connectivity Options

Connectivity is another area where laptops excel. With multiple USB ports, HDMI outputs, and often Ethernet ports, laptops are well-equipped to handle a range of peripherals from external displays to gaming controllers. Many also include Wi-Fi and Bluetooth as standard features, and some business models come with built-in cellular connectivity to maintain data connections on the go.

Portability and Durability

Despite their performance capabilities, laptops are designed to be portable. Their compact form factor, which integrates the keyboard and pointing device (such as a touchpad), is ideal for use in a variety of settings, from coffee shops to corporate offices. Durability is also a consideration, with many business-oriented models built to withstand drops, spills, and other potential mishaps.

In conclusion, laptops bridge the gap between the portability of mobile devices and the performance of desktop computers, making them indispensable in today's mobile-first world. They are versatile enough to accommodate a wide range of computing needs, from everyday browsing to intensive computational tasks.

Wearables

Wearable technology, often referred to as "wearables," encompasses a wide range of electronic devices that are designed to be worn on the body. Unlike traditional mobile devices that you might carry in your pocket or a bag, wearables are integrated into clothing or worn on the skin, providing hands-free operation that enhances everyday activities with digital intelligence. Understanding the functionalities and technical components of wearables is essential for IT professionals as these devices continue to intersect more deeply with both consumer electronics and healthcare industries.

Common Types of Wearables

Smartwatches and Fitness Trackers: Perhaps the most recognizable wearables, these devices are worn on the wrist and offer a range of features from timekeeping and basic fitness tracking to in-depth health monitoring and mobile connectivity. Smartwatches can sync with smartphones, providing notifications, music controls, and even call capabilities directly from the wrist. Fitness trackers focus more on health aspects, tracking steps, heart rate, sleep patterns, and various other physical activities.

Smart Eyewear: Devices such as smart glasses incorporate augmented reality (AR) or simple heads-up displays to overlay digital information onto the physical world. These can be used for navigation, capturing video, or receiving notifications in a format that allows the user to interact with the environment naturally.

Wearable Medical Devices: These specialized wearables monitor health conditions in real-time, providing critical data directly to healthcare providers. Examples include devices that monitor blood sugar levels, heart rate monitors, and advanced prosthetics that respond to neural commands.

Functionality and Integration

The primary appeal of wearable technology is its ability to integrate seamlessly into daily life and routines. For instance:

Fitness Integration: Wearables can collect data that helps users understand their physical activities and tailor workouts to optimize health and performance outcomes.

Communication Enhancement: Smartwatches allow users to stay connected with less dependency on their smartphones, ideal for situations where carrying a phone is impractical.

Health Monitoring: Continuous health monitoring enables early detection of potential health issues, facilitating timely medical responses.

Technical Specifications

Wearable devices incorporate a variety of sensors to perform their functions, including accelerometers, gyroscopes, GPS, and biometric sensors. These components allow wearables to track movement and provide location-based services, along with monitoring physiological data.

Battery Life: Since wearables are designed for continuous use, battery life is a crucial aspect. Manufacturers strive to balance functionality with battery efficiency, often resulting in devices that require frequent charging cycles.

Connectivity: Most wearables are equipped with Bluetooth and Wi-Fi capabilities, allowing them to connect to other devices and the internet to sync data and access cloud services.

Software and Data Management

Wearables run on compact operating systems designed for low-power, high-efficiency tasks. Wearable OSs, such as Wear OS by Google and watchOS by Apple, provide a platform for developers to create apps that enhance the functionality of the devices. Data security and privacy are particularly important in the context of wearables due to the personal and sensitive nature of the data collected. Ensuring data is securely transmitted and stored is a paramount concern, one that IT professionals must adeptly manage. As wearables continue to evolve, they integrate more deeply into everyday life, illustrating the convergence of fashion, technology, and personal data. of Things (IoT). The horizon is vast, and the integration of such technologies promises a future where our physical and digital worlds become increasingly interconnected.

Installing and Configuring Mobile Devices

OS Installation

The ability to install and configure operating systems on mobile devices is a critical skill for any IT professional, especially those aiming for CompTIA A+ certification. This section provides a comprehensive guide on how to approach the installation of operating systems across a variety of mobile devices, including smartphones, tablets, and other connected devices.

Understanding OS Installation on Mobile Devices

Unlike traditional desktops where operating systems can be installed from external media like DVDs or USB drives, mobile devices typically require different methods. The installation or updating of a mobile operating system is often managed through over-the-air (OTA) updates, which are delivered directly to the device via Wi-Fi. However, there are situations where a manual installation may be necessary—such as when restoring a device to solve software issues or upgrading/downgrading to specific versions for testing purposes.

Step-by-Step Guide to OS Installation

Preparation:
Backup Data: Always begin by backing up the device's data to prevent loss. Use cloud services or local storage according to the device's ecosystem.

Charge the Device: Ensure the device is fully charged or connected to a power source to avoid interruptions during the installation process.

Check Compatibility: Verify that the hardware of the device supports the operating system version you intend to install.

Downloading the Appropriate Firmware:
For devices that need manual installation, downloading the correct firmware version from the manufacturer's official website is crucial. Ensure the firmware matches the specific model number of the device.
Using Manufacturer Software:

Many manufacturers provide software tools (like Apple's iTunes for iPhones or Samsung's Odin for their Android devices) that facilitate the OS installation process on computers connected to the mobile device via USB.

Initiating Installation:
Connect the device to your computer and open the installation software.

Follow the software's prompts to begin the installation process. This typically involves selecting the downloaded firmware and starting the update procedure.

Monitoring the Installation Process:
Keep the device connected and avoid using it during the installation. Power interruptions or disconnects can lead to a failed install, which might require additional steps to recover the device.

Post-Installation:
Once the installation is complete, the device will typically restart automatically.
Follow on-screen instructions to configure initial settings, restore data, and re-install apps.

Testing:
After installation, ensure all functionalities are working as expected. Check connectivity, app functionality, and user interface responsiveness.

Troubleshooting Common Issues:
Installation Failures: If the installation process fails, consider repeating the process or using a different version of the firmware.
Device Not Recognized: Ensure that all drivers are up-to-date and the cable connection is secure.
Post-Installation Errors: Factory resetting the device can resolve many issues that arise after a new OS installation.

Future Updates and Configuration:
Once a new OS is installed, keeping the device updated with the latest software patches is essential for security and performance. Most devices allow you to set up automatic updates, ensuring that you always have the latest features and security enhancements.

Software Configuration: Optimizing Performance

Once the operating system is successfully installed on a mobile device, the next crucial step is configuring the software settings to optimize performance and enhance the user experience. Proper software configuration not only ensures the device operates efficiently but also helps in securing the device from potential threats and enhances functionality tailored to user needs.

Understanding Software Configuration
Software configuration involves adjusting the settings and options within the device's operating system and installed applications to achieve optimal performance, security, and personalized usage. This process is vital in both personal and enterprise scenarios where devices must be configured to specific standards to meet security protocols or functional requirements.

Steps for Configuring Software on Mobile Devices

Updating the Operating System and Apps:

Ensure that the latest version of the operating system is installed. Updates often include performance improvements, security patches, and new features that can significantly enhance device operation.

Regularly update all apps to their latest versions. App updates, similar to OS updates, can resolve known issues and vulnerabilities.

Adjusting Settings for Optimal Performance:
Battery Optimization: Adjust settings such as screen brightness and background data usage to extend battery life. Utilize built-in battery saver modes when necessary.

Memory Management: Clear cache frequently and uninstall unnecessary apps to free up memory and improve device responsiveness.

Storage Management: Use tools to monitor and clean up storage space regularly, ensuring that the device does not run out of space, as this can severely affect performance.

Configuring Security Settings:
Screen Locks: Set up a strong authentication method, such as a password, PIN, fingerprint, or facial recognition, to secure access to the device.

Encryption: Enable encryption settings to protect the data stored on the device, making it inaccessible to unauthorized users.

Remote Wipe and Find My Device: Activate these features to locate a lost device or erase its data remotely if it is lost or stolen.

Network Configuration:
Wi-Fi Settings: Configure connection preferences, set up VPNs for secure access, and manage Wi-Fi networks to ensure secure and stable connections.

Bluetooth Configuration: Manage Bluetooth connections and ensure that the device is not discoverable when not in use to prevent unauthorized access.

Accessibility and Personalization:
Customize user interface options such as themes, fonts, and colors to suit personal preferences or accessibility needs.

Configure accessibility settings like text size, color correction, or voice control to accommodate users with specific needs.

Testing and Monitoring
After configuring the software settings, it is crucial to test the device to ensure that all configurations are functioning as expected. Monitor the performance of the device over time to determine if any adjustments are needed based on usage patterns and software updates.

Ensuring Continuous Improvement
Configuring a mobile device is not a one-time task. Continuous monitoring and adjustments are necessary to maintain optimum performance as new updates and apps are installed and as user needs evolve. Keeping abreast of new developments and features in software can also provide opportunities to further enhance device functionality.

Application Management

In the landscape of mobile devices, applications—or apps—are the tools through which users interact with their devices to perform various tasks, from productivity and entertainment to communication and lifestyle management. Effective application management is crucial for maintaining device performance, security, and user satisfaction. This segment explores the best practices for managing apps, including their installation, updates, and permissions settings, providing a comprehensive guide tailored to both novice and experienced IT professionals.

Installing Applications

The process of installing apps might seem straightforward—simply selecting an app from a digital store and clicking 'install.' However, as an IT professional, ensuring the secure and efficient installation of apps involves several considerations:

Source Verification: Always install applications from reputable sources, such as official app stores or directly from trusted developers' websites. This minimizes the risk of introducing malware into the device.

Storage Considerations: Before installation, check the storage requirements. Ensure that the device has enough free space not only for the initial installation but also for future updates which may require additional space.

Compatibility Checks: Verify that the app is compatible with the device's operating system version to avoid performance issues or crashes.

Managing Updates

Keeping applications updated is vital for security, functionality, and performance:

Automating Updates: Most modern devices offer the option to automate app updates, ensuring that you always have the latest features and security patches without having to manually initiate updates.

Reviewing Update Logs: Occasionally review what changes have been made in an update. Update logs can provide insights into new features or adjustments that might affect how the app interacts with device resources.

Balancing Updates with Performance: In environments where device performance is critical, test updates on a single device before rolling them out universally, ensuring they do not disrupt essential services or degrade overall system performance.

Configuring Permissions

Applications often require certain permissions to function correctly—access to your camera, contacts, location, etc. Managing these permissions is essential for protecting user privacy and securing data:

Understanding Permissions: Educate users about the implications of app permissions. Understanding why an app requests certain permissions can inform decisions about whether to grant them.

Minimizing Permissions: Apply the principle of least privilege by default—only grant permissions that are essential for the app's functionality.

Regular Reviews: Periodically review the permissions granted to each app and adjust them as necessary, especially if an app's usage role within the organization or its operational context has changed.

Monitoring and Maintenance

Regular monitoring and maintenance of applications ensure that they continue to serve their intended purpose without compromising the device's performance or security:

Audit Apps Regularly: Conduct regular audits of installed applications to ensure they are still in use, supported by the developer, and compliant with corporate standards.

Removing Unused Apps: Uninstall apps that are no longer needed to free up resources and reduce security risks associated with outdated software.

Troubleshooting: Be prepared to troubleshoot issues as they arise, from crashes to performance lags, which can often be resolved through basic actions like clearing the app's cache or reinstalling the application.

As we refine our approach to application management, ensuring each app serves its purpose without compromising the integrity or performance of the mobile device, we pave the way for more advanced device management practices. These foundational skills are not only crucial for immediate operational efficiency but also prepare us for future challenges in mobile device management, where complexity and user demands continue to evolve. Our exploration of mobile devices will next transition into broader connectivity issues and network management, where the seamless operation of these applications often plays a critical role.

Synchronization and Connectivity Issues

Wi-Fi Connectivity: Troubleshooting Common Issues

Wi-Fi connectivity is essential for mobile devices, serving as the primary method for accessing the internet, syncing data, and performing online activities. Ensuring reliable Wi-Fi connectivity is therefore a crucial skill for IT professionals. This section offers detailed steps for diagnosing and resolving common Wi-Fi issues that can affect mobile devices.

Basic Troubleshooting Steps

Ensure Wi-Fi is Activated:
Confirm that the Wi-Fi option is turned on in the device's settings. It's easy to overlook this basic setting, especially if the device has been in Airplane Mode, which disables all wireless functions.

Reboot the Device:
Restarting the mobile device can resolve many connectivity issues. This action refreshes the operating system and network connections without altering any saved settings.

Inspect Network Availability:
Check if the device recognizes and displays available networks. If the desired network isn't listed, the issue might be with the network's visibility or the device's Wi-Fi antenna.

Intermediate Troubleshooting Steps

Re-establish Network Connection:
Forget the Wi-Fi network in the device's settings and reconnect. This process involves selecting the problematic network from the Wi-Fi list, choosing "Forget this Network," and then reconnecting by entering the network password again. This can clear any errors in previous connection attempts.

Reduce Wireless Interference:

Move the device closer to the Wi-Fi router or access point to minimize distance and physical barriers, which can impede signal strength. Also, turn off other devices that might be causing interference, such as microwaves or Bluetooth-enabled devices.

Check for Software Updates:
Ensure that the device's operating system is up-to-date. Manufacturers frequently release updates to improve functionality and rectify existing bugs, including those related to connectivity.

Advanced Troubleshooting Steps

Adjust Router Settings:
Access the router's settings via a connected computer or the router's app. Changing the broadcast channel can often reduce interference from other nearby networks. Most routers perform best on channels 1, 6, or 11.

Renew IP Address:
Sometimes, connectivity issues arise from IP conflicts. Renew the device's IP address by turning off Wi-Fi and then re-enabling it, or use the network settings to manually release and renew the IP address.

Network Settings Reset:
As a last resort, reset the device's network settings. This will erase all saved Wi-Fi passwords and other network information, restoring network configurations to their default settings. This is typically done through the system settings under "Reset" options.

Utilizing Diagnostic Tools

Wi-Fi Analyzer Tools: These apps can be downloaded onto a mobile device or computer and are useful for examining the Wi-Fi environment. They help identify the best channel by showing which channels are most congested.

Contact Support: If issues persist after all other troubleshooting steps have been exhausted, contact the device manufacturer or network provider for further assistance. There might be a hardware issue with the Wi-Fi antenna or other internal components.

By following these steps, you can effectively troubleshoot and resolve most Wi-Fi connectivity issues encountered on mobile devices. Mastering these techniques will not only enhance user satisfaction but also bolster your capabilities as an IT professional.

Bluetooth Connectivity: Setup and Troubleshooting

Bluetooth technology has become a staple in mobile devices, facilitating wireless communication over short distances. This capability allows devices to connect to a wide array of accessories, from headphones and speakers to keyboards and health-tracking devices. Understanding how to set up and troubleshoot Bluetooth connections is crucial for ensuring these devices can interact seamlessly.

Setting Up Bluetooth Connections

Enable Bluetooth: First, ensure that Bluetooth is enabled on both the device and the accessory you wish to connect. This is usually found in the device's settings under the Bluetooth menu, where you can toggle it on.

Pairing the Devices: Once Bluetooth is activated, put the accessory into pairing mode. This process varies by device— some have a dedicated button, while others require holding a power button. Your mobile device should then discover and list available devices within range under the Bluetooth settings menu.

Connecting: Tap on the desired device in the list on your mobile device to initiate a connection. You may need to enter a PIN code, typically provided with the accessory's documentation, to complete the pairing.

Confirmation and Testing: After pairing, your device will confirm that the Bluetooth accessory is connected. Test the connection by playing audio or using the accessory's features to ensure functionality.

Troubleshooting Common Bluetooth Connectivity Issues

Even with a proper setup, you may encounter issues with Bluetooth connectivity. Here are steps to diagnose and resolve common problems:

Check Battery Levels: Low power on either the mobile device or the Bluetooth accessory can cause connection issues. Ensure both devices are adequately charged.

Re-establish the Connection: If the devices were previously paired but aren't connecting, try forgetting the device on your mobile and then reconnecting as if setting up for the first time. This clears old connection data that might be causing issues.

Reduce Interference: Other wireless devices can interfere with Bluetooth signals. Try to minimize the number of active devices in the vicinity, or move to a different location to see if the connection improves.

Update Software: Ensure that both the mobile device and the Bluetooth accessory have the latest firmware updates installed. Manufacturers often release updates to fix bugs or improve performance.

Reset Network Settings: If problems persist, try resetting the network settings on your mobile device. This will revert all network configurations like Wi-Fi and Bluetooth to their default states and might resolve underlying issues.

Range and Obstacles: Bluetooth technologies typically work over short distances. Ensure that there are no significant obstacles between the connected devices and that they are within the effective range, usually around 10 meters (30 feet) without obstructions.

Consult Documentation: Some devices have specific connection instructions. Review the user manual for both your mobile device and the Bluetooth accessory for any particular steps or settings.

Bluetooth connectivity, when functioning correctly, can greatly enhance the usability of mobile devices by linking them with an array of peripheral devices that extend their capabilities. Mastering the setup and troubleshooting of Bluetooth can markedly improve the user experience.

GPS Functionality: Troubleshooting Common Issues

Global Positioning System (GPS) technology is critical for a wide array of mobile device functions, from navigation and location tracking to geotagging in apps. Despite its broad utility, GPS can sometimes behave unpredictably, leading to errors and issues that can impair functionality. Below, we delve deeper into some of the most common GPS issues encountered on mobile devices, providing detailed explanations and specific steps to resolve these issues effectively.

Common GPS Issues and How to Resolve Them

Weak or No GPS Signal:
Cause: GPS signals are microwave signals that can be weakened by obstructions such as buildings, heavy tree cover, or even cloud cover. Indoor environments particularly disrupt GPS connectivity.

Resolution: To improve GPS signal strength, move to a more open space with fewer overhead obstructions. If indoors, positioning yourself near windows can help. In settings, ensure that GPS is set to high accuracy mode, which uses a combination of the satellite, Wi-Fi, and mobile networks to pinpoint location.

GPS Drift:
Cause: GPS drift occurs when the GPS shows the location moving even when the device is stationary. This can be due to reflections of the GPS signal, particularly in urban areas with high buildings (a phenomenon known as "Urban Canyon").

Resolution: Utilize apps designed to stabilize GPS coordinates or switch to a device with better GPS hardware if persistent drift is an issue. Calibration of the GPS from device settings may also help.

Slow GPS Lock:

Cause: A slow GPS lock can occur when the device's GPS receiver takes time to lock onto the signal of satellites overhead, common in areas with signal interference.

Resolution: Activate 'Assisted GPS' (AGPS), which uses network resources to provide an initial location estimate and speed up satellite locking. Ensure that AGPS data is updated regularly in device settings.

Inaccurate Location:

Cause: Factors such as outdated maps, incorrect software calibration, or degraded GPS hardware can lead to inaccurate location readings.

Resolution: Regularly update your mapping software and operating system. If inaccuracies persist, recalibrate the GPS. For Android users, this might involve using apps that can reset the GPS and clear cache. For iOS, toggling location services off and on can help recalibrate settings.

GPS Stops Working:

Cause: This could be due to a software glitch, faulty GPS hardware, or temporary disruptions caused by software conflicts.

Resolution: Restart the device to reset the GPS module. If the issue persists, try resetting network settings which will also reset all location settings. If these steps fail, consult the manufacturer for a potential hardware issue.

Additional Tips for Managing GPS Functionality

Environmental Considerations: Be mindful of environmental conditions that might affect GPS accuracy, such as atmospheric conditions or geographic locations prone to signal disruption.

Hardware Checks: Periodically check the device's hardware for any damage, particularly if the device has been dropped or exposed to moisture, as this could affect the internal GPS antenna.

Software Updates: Keep all related apps and your device's operating system up-to-date to benefit from the latest GPS improvements and bug fixes released by developers.

By thoroughly understanding these common GPS-related issues and their solutions, users and IT professionals alike can enhance the reliability and performance of mobile devices' location-based services

Cellular Data Management

In today's highly connected world, cellular data plays a pivotal role in ensuring mobile devices stay connected to the internet, especially when traditional Wi-Fi networks are out of reach. Managing cellular data effectively is crucial for maintaining connectivity, optimizing data usage, and minimizing costs associated with data overages. This section delves into the essentials of managing cellular data settings and troubleshooting common connectivity problems, providing clear guidance to help users and IT professionals alike maintain robust and efficient mobile communications.

Cellular data settings on mobile devices allow users to control how their devices connect to cellular networks for internet access. These settings are vital for managing how apps and services use data, which can be particularly important when considering the limitations and costs associated with data plans.

Key Cellular Data Settings:

Data Roaming: This setting should be managed carefully, as enabling data roaming can lead to significant charges when traveling abroad. Data roaming allows your device to connect to the internet through other carriers' cellular networks when your main carrier's network is unavailable.

Data Limit and Warning: Setting a data limit on your device can prevent data overages. Most devices allow users to set specific limits and warnings when nearing those limits, ensuring you don't exceed your data plan's allowance.

App Data Usage: Modern mobile operating systems allow users to see which apps are using how much data. This can be crucial for identifying apps that use excessive background data or for restricting certain apps to Wi-Fi only, preserving your cellular data for more critical tasks.

Troubleshooting Cellular Data Connectivity:

Check Network Coverage: Poor network coverage is a common cause of cellular data issues. Verify that you are within your network provider's coverage area, especially if you experience sudden connectivity issues without apparent reason.

Restart Your Device: As with many technical issues, a simple restart can often resolve cellular data connectivity problems. This action refreshes your network settings and re-establishes a connection to your service provider.

Re-Insert SIM Card: If restarting doesn't help, try re-inserting your SIM card. Sometimes, connectivity issues can stem from a poorly seated SIM card in its tray.

Enable Airplane Mode Briefly: Toggling airplane mode on and then off can also help reset your device's connections to cellular networks.

Update Carrier Settings and OS: Ensure that your device's operating system and carrier settings are up to date. Carriers may release updates to improve connectivity or resolve bugs affecting cellular data.

Check for Physical Damage: If problems persist, inspect your device for any physical damage that might affect its antenna or other cellular components. Such damage may require professional repair.

Contact Your Carrier: If all else fails, contact your carrier. There might be a network outage, maintenance, or an issue with your account that only your carrier can resolve.

Preparing for Future Connectivity Needs

As mobile technology evolves, understanding and managing cellular data settings becomes increasingly important. Whether it's ensuring seamless connectivity while on the move, optimizing data usage to avoid overages or troubleshooting connectivity issues, effective cellular data management is key to a smooth mobile experience.

With a firm grasp on managing cellular data, our journey through mobile device connectivity issues continues to unfold, bringing us closer to mastering the comprehensive network management skills needed in today's connected world. As we transition seamlessly into more complex networking topics, our understanding deepens, preparing us to tackle even the most challenging aspects of modern IT environments.

Test Your Knowledge (C

1. Which of the following is a common feature of a tablet compared to a smartp

A) Smaller screen size

B) Cellular connectivity

C) Larger screen size

D) No touchscreen

2. Which type of memory is used for primary storage in modern smartphones?

A) HDD

B) SSD

C) SD card

D) NVMe

3. What is the primary use of NFC in mobile devices?

A) High-speed data transfer

B) Network connectivity

C) Contactless payment

D) GPS enhancement

4. Drag and drop the following mobile operating systems to the corresponding devices they are most commonly installed on.

Devices: [Smartphone, Tablet]

Operating Systems: [iOS, Android]

5. What wireless technology enables devices to perform contactless payments?

A) Bluetooth

B) NFC

C) Wi-Fi Direct

D) LTE

6. Which component is essential for a smartphone to connect to a cellular network?

A) SIM card

B) SD card

C) NFC module

D) Bluetooth adapter

7. Which sensor is essential for orientation detection in mobile devices?

A) Accelerometer

B) Gyroscope

C) GPS

D) NFC

8. Which feature differentiates a phablet from a smartphone?

A) Smaller screen

B) Larger screen

C) No touchscreen

D) Uses only WiFi

9. What technology

A) Bluetooth

B) NFC

C) Wi-Fi Di

D) LTE

10.

... allows a device to emulate a credit card and make contactless payments?

... rect

... ill in the blank: An _____ is typically required to increase storage capacity in mobile devices.

1. What type of display technology is used in high-end smartphones?

A) LCD

B) OLED

C) Plasma

D) TFT

12. What is the primary function of the gyroscope sensor in mobile devices?

A) Measure atmospheric pressure

B) Orientation detection

C) Enhance sound quality

D) Increase battery efficiency

13. What is the primary function of GPS in smartphones?

A) Navigation

B) Fitness Tracking

C) Gaming

D) Social Media

14. Which technology allows smartphones to connect to peripherals like keyboards and headphones?

A) NFC

B) Bluetooth

C) Wi-Fi Direct

D) LTE

15. Which of the following is NOT a common feature of all smartphones?

A) Touchscreen

B) Internet connectivity

C) Physical keyboard

D) Operating system

Please refer to the "Test Your Knowledge A+ (Answers)" chapter for the answers.

CHAPTER 2

Network Types and Technologies

LAN (Local Area Network)

A Local Area Network (LAN) is essential to most organizational and home computing environments, facilitating the connection of various devices like computers, printers, and servers within a limited geographical area such as a single building or a campus.

What is a LAN?

A LAN is designed for small geographic areas, providing high-speed connectivity and enabling devices within close proximity to share resources and communicate efficiently. Unlike Wide Area Networks (WANs), which cover broader geographic distances, LANs operate with minimal latency due to the shorter travel distance for data, enhancing the speed and reliability of network communications. LANs can be configured in various ways depending on the network's specific needs and the scale of the environment. Here are the most common network topologies used in LAN configurations:

Star Topology:

In a star topology, each device on the network connects to a single central hub or switch. This setup is highly favored in modern networks due to its robustness and ease of troubleshooting. If one connection fails, it does not affect the others. Adding or removing devices is straightforward and does not disrupt the entire network, making it highly scalable.

Bus Topology:

Once prevalent in early Ethernet networks, bus topology connects all devices via a single backbone or communication line. Each device is directly connected to this backbone. This setup has fallen out of favor due to its limited scalability and difficulty in troubleshooting—any fault in the main cable can bring down the entire network.

Ring Topology:

In a ring topology, each device is connected to two other devices, forming a ring. Data travels in one direction around the ring, passing through each device. While not as common as star topology, it offers simplicity and can perform well in smaller settings. However, like bus topology, a break in the network can disrupt the entire system unless redundant connections are established.

Mesh Topology:

Mesh topology is where devices are interconnected with many redundant interconnections between network nodes. In a full mesh topology, every node has a connection to every other node in the network. This setup provides high redundancy and reliability but can be expensive and complex to implement, making it more common in environments where communication availability is critical.

Hybrid Topology:

It is a network topology that combines two or more different network topologies, such as star, ring, bus, or mesh. It integrates these various topologies into a single unified network system that leverages the strengths and mitigates the weaknesses of each individual topology. For example, a hybrid topology might include a main star-configured backbone with each star point connecting to a tree configuration.

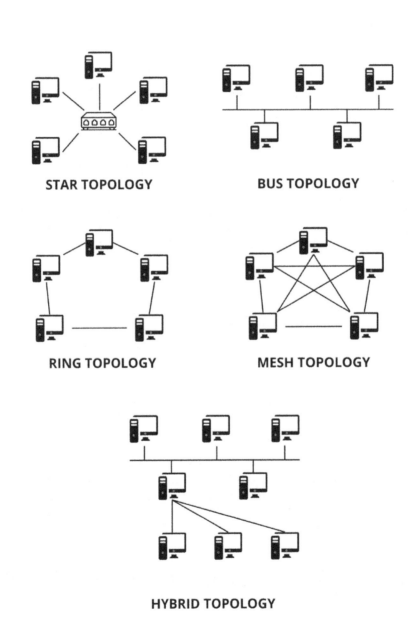

STAR TOPOLOGY

BUS TOPOLOGY

RING TOPOLOGY

MESH TOPOLOGY

HYBRID TOPOLOGY

Key Devices in LANs

To set up and maintain a LAN, several critical devices are used:

Routers: These connect different networks, managing data entering and leaving the LAN as well as data moving within the network.

Switches: Vital in networks with a star topology, switches connect devices within a LAN and manage the data traffic to ensure smooth network operation.

Network Interface Cards (NICs): Every device on a LAN needs a NIC to connect to the network, whether through wired Ethernet or wireless Wi-Fi connections.

Access Points (APs): In wireless LANs (WLANs), APs act as the central transmitter and receiver of wireless signals.

Optimizing LAN Performance

Effective LAN management involves regular firmware updates for routers and switches, setting Quality of Service (QoS) to prioritize essential traffic, and robust security protocols to protect the network. Keeping the network's hardware and software updated and monitoring for unauthorized access is crucial for maintaining a secure, fast, and reliable LAN.

LANs are the foundation upon which businesses and homes operate digitally. As we conclude our exploration of LAN configurations and their implementations, we move toward understanding more complex networking setups that extend beyond basic configurations, preparing us for broader network management challenges that lie ahead. This journey enhances our ability to design and manage networks that are not only efficient but also scalable and secure, ready for the future of digital communications.

WAN (Wide Area Network)

A Wide Area Network (WAN) is a telecommunications network that extends over a large geographical area, distinguishing it from Local Area Networks (LANs) that typically span a single building or campus. WANs are essential for connecting multiple LANs, enabling businesses and organizations to communicate and share resources across cities, countries, or even continents. This section provides a detailed explanation of WANs, their key components, and their practical applications.

The Concept of WAN

WANs are designed to cover broad areas, making it possible for distant nodes to communicate as if they were locally connected. Unlike LANs, which are restricted to a smaller, more controlled area, WANs traverse public networks and private leased lines to connect dispersed users and networks. The internet is the largest example of a WAN, connecting millions of networks and devices worldwide.

Components of a WAN

Routers: These are crucial for WAN operations as they direct data packets across different networks, choosing the optimal path for data to travel to its destination.

Switches: While switches are more commonly associated with LANs, they also play roles in WANs, especially at aggregation points where multiple LANs connect to the WAN.

Modems: These devices modulate and demodulate the signals sent over telephone lines, cable systems, or satellites to connect LANs to WANs.

WAN Optimizers: These specialized devices enhance WAN efficiency by reducing latency, minimizing traffic, and increasing data transfer speeds across the network.

Applications of WAN

Enterprise Networking: Businesses use WANs to connect their various offices and branches, enabling them to share resources, communicate efficiently, and maintain cohesive operations across multiple locations.

Telecommunications: WANs are used by telecommunications companies to provide long-distance telephony, internet services, and television transmission services.

Education and Research: Universities and research institutions use WANs to connect with each other, share resources, and collaborate on projects, regardless of geographical distances.

Government Services: WANs enable governmental bodies to connect different departments and agencies, facilitating data sharing and inter-departmental communication essential for public services.

Benefits of WAN

Resource Sharing: WANs allow organizations to share IT resources and data among employees, regardless of their locations, leading to cost savings and enhanced collaboration.

Centralized Infrastructure: Instead of maintaining servers, storage, and backups at multiple locations, companies can centralize these resources, simplifying IT management and potentially reducing costs.

Flexibility and Scalability: WANs provide the flexibility to grow and expand the network without significant infrastructure changes. New branches or remote users can be added to the network as business needs evolve.

Challenges in Managing WAN

Complexity: The management of WANs is inherently complex due to their scope and the diversity of technologies involved. This complexity requires sophisticated network management tools and skilled IT professionals.

Cost: Deploying and maintaining WANs can be costly. Infrastructure expenses, including lease lines and equipment, as well as ongoing operational costs, can be significant.

Security Risks: Given that WANs often traverse public network segments, they are exposed to higher security risks. Implementing robust security measures, including encryption, firewalls, and intrusion detection systems, is crucial.

As WAN technology continues to evolve, understanding its foundational concepts and practical applications remains critical for IT professionals. This knowledge not only supports effective network design and management but also empowers businesses to leverage connectivity for strategic advantage.

PAN (Personal Area Network): Technology and Usage

A Personal Area Network (PAN) is a network arranged within an individual person's workspace, primarily designed to connect personal devices within a range of about 10 meters (approximately 30 feet). Unlike LANs or WANs, PANs focus on the interconnectivity of devices centered around a single user's daily environment, including smartphones, laptops, tablets, wearables, and peripheral devices like printers and webcams. This section explores the core technologies behind PANs, their applications, and how they integrate into our digital lives.

Core Technologies Behind PAN

PAN technology is primarily wireless, leveraging short-range communication protocols to facilitate connectivity between devices. The most prevalent technologies include:

Bluetooth: This is the most ubiquitous form of PAN technology found in millions of devices worldwide. Bluetooth allows for quick, secure connections between devices without the hassle of wires. It is ideal for connecting headphones and computer peripherals and transferring small amounts of data between devices.

Wi-Fi Direct: Similar to Bluetooth, Wi-Fi Direct provides a method for devices to connect directly to each other without a central wireless router. It supports a higher data transfer rate compared to Bluetooth and can be used for streaming video content from a smartphone to a television or for printing documents from a computer to a printer directly.

Infrared: Although less common today, infrared technology was once widely used for PANs, particularly in remote controls for various devices. It requires a direct line of sight between devices and operates over very short distances.

Near Field Communication (NFC): NFC is used for making transactions, exchanging digital content, and connecting electronic devices with a touch. NFC is highly effective for tasks like contactless payments or setting up more complex communications like Wi-Fi or Bluetooth without manual configuration.

Applications of PAN

The versatility of PANs allows them to serve various personal and business needs:

Device Synchronization: Easily sync data across multiple personal devices, such as contacts, emails, calendar entries, and documents, ensuring information continuity across your digital environment.

Internet Sharing: Use a PAN to share internet access from a mobile device to other devices via tethering, which can be particularly useful when Wi-Fi is unavailable.

File Transfers: Quickly transfer files between devices, such as photos from a smartphone to a computer or documents between tablets in a meeting.

Health Monitoring: Connect health-related devices like fitness trackers, heart rate monitors, or smartwatches to your smartphone to monitor physical activities and health metrics.

Optimizing PAN Performance

To ensure optimal performance and security of your PAN, consider the following:

Regularly update device software to patch any security vulnerabilities and improve functionality.

Maintain device proximity within the effective range to ensure reliable connectivity.

Use secure pairing methods to protect against unauthorized access, especially when handling sensitive data.

Monitor connection stability and interference, particularly in environments crowded with multiple wireless devices.

PANs significantly enhance the flexibility and utility of personal devices, making digital interaction more seamless and integrated into daily activities. As technology advances, the applications and capabilities of PANs will continue to expand, further blurring the lines between our physical and digital worlds.

Key Networking Protocols

Networking protocols are essential rules and standards that dictate how data is transmitted across networks, ensuring that communications between diverse devices and platforms are consistent and reliable. This section explores several pivotal networking protocols, describing their roles in detail and illustrating their applications with practical examples.

TCP/IP (Transmission Control Protocol/Internet Protocol)

Function: TCP/IP is the foundational suite of the internet, comprising two main protocols. TCP manages the direct connections between devices, ensuring data packets are sent and received reliably. IP deals with routing and addressing, making sure data packets find the correct path to their destination.

Example: When you stream a video on YouTube, TCP ensures the video data packets arrive in sequence and without error, while IP ensures these packets travel from YouTube's servers to your device.

HTTP (Hypertext Transfer Protocol) and HTTPS (HTTP Secure)

Function: HTTP facilitates the transmission of web pages from servers to browsers, allowing users to view and interact with web content. HTTPS encrypts this data exchange using SSL or TLS, enhancing security by protecting the integrity and privacy of the exchanged data.

Example: When you log into your online banking account, HTTPS secures your login credentials and banking information, preventing eavesdroppers from stealing your sensitive data.

FTP (File Transfer Protocol)

Function: FTP enables the transfer of files between a client and a server on a network, supporting large file transfers with mechanisms for secure exchange via FTPS or SFTP.

Example: A graphic designer uploads finalized artwork files to a print company using FTP, ensuring large file sets are transferred quickly and intact.

SMTP (Simple Mail Transfer Protocol)

Function: SMTP is used to send emails over networks. It interacts with protocols like POP3 or IMAP, which retrieve incoming emails from the server.

Example: When you send an email through services like Gmail or Outlook, SMTP handles the sending of your email from your device to the recipient's email server.

DHCP (Dynamic Host Configuration Protocol)

Function: DHCP assigns IP addresses dynamically to devices on a network, along with other network configuration parameters, facilitating easy and efficient network management.

Example: When you connect your laptop to a coffee shop's Wi-Fi, DHCP assigns your laptop an IP address so you can browse the internet without manual network configuration.

DNS (Domain Name System)

Function: DNS converts human-friendly domain names into machine-friendly IP addresses, which is crucial for routing user requests to the correct website or server.

Example: When you type www.google.com into your web browser, DNS translates this into an IP address like 192.168.1.1, directing your request to Google's servers.

Understanding these protocols is crucial for anyone involved in IT, network administration, or cybersecurity. These protocols underpin virtually all digital communications, from sending an email to streaming movies.

Configuring Networking Hardware

Routers: Setup and Configuration Steps

Routers are critical components in both home and enterprise networks, directing traffic between multiple devices and facilitating Internet connections. Understanding how to properly set up and configure routers is essential for ensuring efficient network operation and security. This section provides a detailed guide to configuring routers, breaking down the process into manageable steps and explaining key settings that need attention.

Setup and Configuration of Routers

Physical Setup:
Connect the router to the modem using an Ethernet cable, typically from the modem's output port to the router's internet input port. Then, connect the router to a computer using another Ethernet cable for initial configuration. This connection is necessary for accessing the router's configuration settings through a web interface.

Accessing the Router Interface:
Open a web browser on the connected computer and enter the router's IP address into the address bar. Common default IP addresses for routers are 192.168.1.1 or 192.168.0.1. You will be prompted to enter a username and password, which are often set to 'admin' by default for initial setup.

Basic Configuration Settings:
Change Default Credentials: For security purposes, change the default username and password to something more secure. This step is critical to prevent unauthorized access to your router settings.
Set up Wi-Fi Networks: Configure your wireless network name (SSID) and password. Choose WPA2 or WPA3 encryption for better security. You may also set up multiple networks, such as a guest network if your router supports it.

Advanced Configuration:

Firmware Update: Check for the latest firmware updates from the router's manufacturer and update if necessary. Firmware updates can fix bugs, patch security vulnerabilities, and improve performance.

DHCP Settings: Ensure DHCP (Dynamic Host Configuration Protocol) is enabled if you want the router to automatically assign IP addresses to devices on your network.

NAT (Network Address Translation): Enable NAT to allow multiple devices to share a single IP address when accessing the internet, conserving IP addresses and enhancing security.

Port Forwarding: Configure port forwarding if you need to direct traffic from the internet to a specific device within your network, useful for hosting servers or gaming applications.

Network Security Settings:

Firewall: Ensure the router's built-in firewall is enabled to provide an additional layer of security by blocking unauthorized incoming connections.

MAC Address Filtering: Optionally, you can enhance security by setting up MAC address filtering, which restricts network access to only those devices whose MAC addresses are listed as allowed.

Monitoring and Maintenance:
Regularly check the router's logs to monitor for unusual activities, such as unauthorized access attempts or unfamiliar devices connecting to your network.

Keep the router's software up to date and periodically review your security settings to ensure they meet your current needs.

Testing and Troubleshooting

After configuring your router, test the network connections to ensure devices can connect to the internet and communicate with each other effectively. If issues arise, revisit the relevant settings, checking especially for common pitfalls like incorrect IP addresses or subnet masks, and encryption settings that might be causing connection issues.

Configuring routers effectively lays a foundation for robust, secure network environments. As network demands grow, the ability to adeptly manage and configure routers will remain an essential skill for any IT professional.

Switches: Roles and Configuration

Network switches play a crucial role in modern networks, acting as the central hub through which all data flows within a Local Area Network (LAN). Unlike routers that direct data between different networks, switches manage data across devices within the same network. This detailed guide will explain the fundamental roles of network switches and provide step-by-step instructions on their configuration, ensuring even beginners can understand and apply this knowledge effectively.

Roles of Network Switches

Traffic Management: Switches control the flow of network traffic by receiving incoming data packets and redirecting them to their appropriate destination within the LAN. This is achieved through the use of MAC addresses that uniquely identify each device on the network.

Network Segmentation: Switches can segment a network into smaller, more manageable sections, reducing the overall traffic on each segment and improving performance. This is often accomplished using VLANs (Virtual Local Area Networks), which logically separate network devices without requiring separate physical switches.

Performance Enhancement: By delivering messages only to the connected devices intended to receive them, rather than broadcasting to all network devices as hubs do, switches reduce unnecessary network traffic and enhance security.

Configuration of Network Switches

Configuring a network switch involves several key steps that ensure it operates efficiently and securely within your network infrastructure:

Initial Setup:
Connect the switch to a power source and to one or more devices using Ethernet cables. For initial configuration, connect a computer to the switch using an Ethernet cable to access the management interface.

Access Management Interface:
Most modern switches have a web-based interface or a command-line interface (CLI). To access the web interface, enter the switch's IP address into a web browser. The default IP address and login credentials are typically provided in the switch's manual.

Basic Configuration Tasks:

Change Default Password: To secure your switch, change the default administrator password to a strong, unique password.

Update Firmware: Check for firmware updates from the manufacturer and apply them to fix bugs, patch vulnerabilities, and improve functionality.

Configure VLANs:

VLANs help organize a network into logical groups to improve efficiency and security. To create a VLAN:

Navigate to the VLAN settings in the switch's management interface.

Assign a VLAN ID and name.

Add ports to the VLAN by selecting from available ports on the switch.

Set Up Quality of Service (QoS):

QoS prioritizes traffic to ensure that high-priority services like VoIP and streaming video are not negatively affected by high traffic load.

Configure QoS by defining which devices or services are prioritized higher in the network traffic queue.

Security Settings:

Implement port security to limit the number of valid MAC addresses that can access each port, preventing unauthorized devices from connecting to the network.

Enable IEEE 802.1X authentication to use a central authentication server, ensuring that only authorized users can access the network.

Testing and Monitoring

After configuring the switch, conduct tests to ensure that all devices are communicating correctly and that VLANs and QoS settings are functioning as expected. Regular monitoring of network traffic and switch performance can help identify potential issues before they affect network integrity.

Switches are foundational to the efficiency and security of LANs. Proper setup and configuration help maintain optimal network performance and protect sensitive data.

Access Points: Installation and Management

Wireless Access Points (APs) are pivotal devices in extending the reach and capacity of a wireless network. They act as bridges, connecting wireless clients to a wired network infrastructure in a secure and efficient manner. Proper installation and management of APs are crucial to ensure optimal network performance, security, and scalability. This guide provides detailed instructions on setting up and managing wireless access points, tailored for both beginners and seasoned IT professionals.

Installation of Wireless Access Points

Selecting Optimal Locations:
Place APs in central locations to maximize coverage and minimize signal obstructions caused by walls, furniture, or other physical barriers. The goal is to provide uniform wireless coverage throughout the desired area.

Avoid locations near microwaves, cordless phones, and large metal objects, which can cause interference and degrade signal quality.

Physical Setup:
Mount the AP on the wall or ceiling to increase the signal range and reduce the likelihood of physical tampering. Most APs come with mounting kits and detailed instructions on how to secure the device properly.

Connect the AP to the network using an Ethernet cable. Ensure the cable is plugged into a PoE (Power over Ethernet) port on your network switch or router if the AP is powered via PoE. Otherwise, connect it to a power source using the adapter provided.

Configuring Network Settings:
To configure the AP, connect to it directly through a computer via Ethernet or wirelessly using the default network SSID mentioned in the AP's manual.

Access the AP's web-based setup page by entering its IP address in a web browser. Login with the default credentials (typically 'admin' for both username and password).

Change the default network name (SSID), enable encryption (preferably WPA2 or WPA3 for enhanced security), and set a strong password to secure your wireless network.

Management of Wireless Access Points

Updating Firmware:
Regularly check for firmware updates provided by the AP manufacturer. Firmware updates can enhance functionality, patch vulnerabilities, and improve performance. Update the firmware using the administration interface of the AP.

Adjusting Radio Settings:
Optimize radio settings such as channel selection and transmission power. Selecting the right channel can minimize interference with other nearby APs. Adjusting transmission power can help manage the AP's coverage area, preventing overlap with other APs and minimizing interference.

Monitoring and Troubleshooting:
Use network management tools to monitor the performance and status of your APs. Pay attention to metrics like signal strength, client connectivity, and bandwidth usage.

Troubleshoot connectivity issues by checking AP and client logs, verifying network configurations, and assessing physical and RF (radio frequency) interference issues.

Implementing Advanced Features:
Consider setting up multiple SSIDs to segregate network traffic, such as creating a separate network for guests.

Implement VLANs (Virtual Local Area Networks) to further segment the network and enhance security.

Security Practices:

Regularly update passwords and monitor network access. Employ MAC address filtering to control device connections and use network segmentation to protect sensitive data.

Ensuring Optimal Network Health

Regular maintenance, such as restarting APs periodically and reevaluating site coverage based on changing environmental conditions or network demands, ensures a healthy wireless network. Effective AP management enhances user satisfaction by providing stable and robust wireless connectivity.

Configuration and Troubleshooting

IP Addressing Techniques: Assignment and Management

IP addressing is a fundamental aspect of network design and management, enabling the identification and location of devices on both local and global networks. Effective IP address management (IPAM) is crucial for ensuring reliable network performance, efficient troubleshooting, and optimal security. This section delves into the techniques for assigning and managing IP addresses, making it accessible even for those new to networking concepts.

Understanding IP Addresses

An IP address is a unique identifier assigned to each device connected to a network. It serves two main purposes: network interface identification and location addressing. There are two types of IP addresses:

IPv4: Consists of four sets of numbers separated by periods (e.g., 192.168.1.1). It is the most widely used IP address format.

IPv6: Developed to address IPv4 depletion, it consists of eight groups of four hexadecimal digits, separated by colons (e.g., 2001:0db8:85a3:0000:0000:8a2e:0370:7334).

Assignment of IP Addresses

IP addresses can be assigned in two primary ways:

Static IP Addressing:

Description: A static IP address is manually assigned to a computer by an administrator and remains constant unless changed manually.

Use Case: Ideal for servers, network printers, or any device that needs to maintain a constant IP address.

Example: A network printer within an office may be assigned a static IP address to ensure devices can consistently locate the printer without configuration changes.

Dynamic IP Addressing:

Description: Dynamic IP addresses are assigned by a DHCP (Dynamic Host Configuration Protocol) server, which allocates IP addresses from a defined pool of addresses as devices connect to the network.

Use Case: Suitable for devices that do not require permanent IP addresses, such as employee laptops and mobile phones.

Example: An employee's laptop connecting to the company's Wi-Fi network receives an IP address from the DHCP server that may change each time the device reconnects to the network.

Management of IP Addresses

Effective management of IP addresses is critical for network efficiency and security. Here are key strategies for managing IP addresses:

IP Address Planning: Organize and plan IP addresses and subnets to avoid conflicts and ensure efficient use of IP space. Consider future growth and the potential need for additional addresses.

Using Subnetting: Divide larger networks into smaller, more manageable subnets to enhance performance and security. Subnetting involves segmenting the network into groups of IP addresses that are easier to manage and can isolate network traffic.

Implementing DHCP: Set up a DHCP server to automate the IP address configuration process. This reduces administrative overhead and minimizes configuration errors.

Maintaining IP Address Documentation: Keep detailed records of IP address assignments, including static IP addresses and DHCP configurations. This documentation is vital for troubleshooting and tracking purposes.

Regular Audits: Conduct regular audits of IP address usage to ensure that all addresses are accounted for and correctly assigned. Look for unused addresses, address conflicts, and adherence to IP address policies.

Security Considerations

Monitoring IP Addresses: Monitor network traffic based on IP addresses to detect unusual activities or unauthorized access.

Securing DHCP Servers: Protect DHCP servers from attacks by securing network access and monitoring for unauthorized changes.

Effective IP address management not only supports seamless network operation but also enhances security and scalability.

Subnetting Basics: Introduction to Concepts and Practices

Subnetting is a fundamental networking technique used to optimize the efficiency and security of a network by dividing a larger network into smaller, more manageable logical segments, called subnets. This section introduces the basic concepts of subnetting, providing a step-by-step guide to understanding and implementing subnetting in various network environments. This approach will help demystify subnetting for beginners while offering practical insights for more experienced IT professionals.

What is Subnetting?

Subnetting involves segmenting a single network into multiple smaller networks. It allows network administrators to control traffic flow, enhance security, and improve network performance by limiting broadcast domains. By doing so, subnetting helps in better managing limited IP address spaces and reduces network congestion.

Why Subnet?

Improved Network Management: Smaller networks are easier to manage and troubleshoot.
Enhanced Security: Subnetting can help isolate network segments, limiting the spread of security breaches within a network.
Optimized Performance: By reducing the size of broadcast domains, subnetting decreases unnecessary traffic on the network, enhancing performance.
Efficient Use of IP Addresses: Subnetting allows for the efficient allocation of IP addresses within networks that don't need a large number of IP addresses.

Basic Concepts of Subnetting

IP Address: Consists of two parts: the network part and the host part. With subnetting, you extend the network part to include bits from the host part, effectively creating a subnetwork.
Subnet Mask: A 32-bit number that masks an IP address and divides the IP address into network and host parts. The subnet mask is used to determine the subnet to which an IP address belongs.
Steps to Subnet a Network

Determine the Network Requirements:
Assess how many subnets and hosts per subnet are needed. This will depend on the size of the organization and the different departmental needs within the business.

Choose a Suitable Subnet Mask:
Based on the requirements, select a subnet mask that accommodates the necessary number of subnets and hosts. For instance, changing the subnet mask from 255.255.255.0 to 255.255.255.192 creates smaller subnets.

Divide the IP Address Range:
Apply the subnet mask to your network's IP address range to divide it into subnets. Each subnet will have a specific range of IP addresses, a broadcast address, and a network address.

Assign IP Addresses:

Assign IP addresses to devices within each subnet, ensuring that IP addresses are unique within the entire network.

Configure Routing Between Subnets:

Since each subnet is essentially a separate network, configure routers to enable communication between subnets. This involves setting up routing tables that direct traffic between subnets.

Example of Subnetting

Imagine a business that requires three separate subnets: one for management, one for sales, and one for the production department. Each department's network devices and computers need to communicate within the same subnet but can be isolated from the others for security and performance reasons.

If the main network has an IP address range of 192.168.1.0 with a standard subnet mask of 255.255.255.0, you might assign:

Subnet Name	IP Address Range	Subnet Mask	Supports Hosts	Department
Subnet 1	192.168.1.0/25	255.255.255.128	Up to 126	Management
Subnet 2	192.168.1.128/26	255.255.255.192	Up to 62	Sales
Subnet 3	192.168.1.192/26	255.255.255.192	Up to 62	Production

Subnetting is a powerful tool for organizing a network into more practical and efficient segments. As we continue exploring networking configuration and troubleshooting techniques, we'll delve deeper into advanced subnetting practices and other crucial network management strategies, preparing you to handle complex networking scenarios efficiently. This knowledge lays the groundwork for our next discussion on advanced IP management techniques, further enhancing your network configuration skills.

Network Troubleshooting Tools and Their Use

Effective network management isn't just about setting up configurations; it also involves diagnosing and resolving network issues quickly and efficiently. Network troubleshooting tools are essential for diagnosing network problems, verifying connectivity and routing, and ensuring that data flows smoothly through a network. This section introduces some of the most widely used networking tools like ping and traceroute, explaining their functions and practical applications in real-world scenarios.

Ping

Function: Ping (Packet Internet Groper) is a diagnostic utility that tests connectivity between two nodes or devices across a network. It operates by sending Internet Control Message Protocol (ICMP) echo request packets to the target host and listens for ICMP echo response replies. Ping measures the time it takes for the packets to go from the originating host to the destination and back, indicating how long it takes for data to travel the round trip.

Usage:

- **Checking Network Connectivity:** Ping is commonly used to check the general status of a network connection. Administrators can see if a device is reachable and how well it's responding.
- **Network Performance Assessment:** By reviewing the time taken for a response, ping helps assess how fast or slow the network or specific connections are.

Example: If you're unsure whether a server is up and running, you can ping its IP address from your command prompt or terminal. A successful ping will show reply messages with the time taken for the round trip, while a failure might indicate that the device is offline or there are network issues preventing connectivity.

Traceroute

Function: Traceroute is another essential network diagnostic tool used to trace the path data packets take from one computer to another on a network. It identifies each "hop" (points like routers or switches) along the route to the target destination. Traceroute sends a sequence of Internet Control Message Protocol (ICMP) packets addressed to the destination. By increasing the "time-to-live" (TTL) value of each successive batch of packets, it discovers each router on the route.

Usage:
- **Identifying Network Path Issues:** Traceroute is particularly useful for identifying where delays or failures occur in the network path.
- **Optimizing Network Performance:** By understanding the path, network admins can reconfigure routes to optimize performance.

Example: To diagnose a slow connection to a remote server, you can use traceroute to see if there are any unusually long delays at any hop or if the data is taking an inefficient path, possibly requiring rerouting.

Practical Application of These Tools

Network Maintenance: Routine checks with ping and traceroute can help maintain optimal network performance and preemptively identify potential issues.

Troubleshooting: In the event of network issues, these tools can quickly pinpoint problems, significantly reducing downtime.

Network Mapping: Regular use of traceroute can help in creating detailed maps of network pathways, which can be critical in large scale networks for planning and management.

As network environments grow increasingly complex, mastering these tools and understanding their output becomes crucial. Practicing with ping and traceroute, interpreting their outputs, and combining them with other diagnostic tools like network analyzers or SNMP monitoring tools, provides a robust set of skills for any network administrator.

Test Your Knowledge (Chapter 2)

1. Which of the following is considered a WAN?

A) A network within a single office floor

B) A network spread across a city

C) A network within a single room

D) A network in a single building

2. Which protocol is essential for assigning IP addresses automatically?

A) SMTP

B) FTP

C) DHCP

D) SNMP

3. Drag and drop the following to the correct order to configure a basic home router:

1. Change default administrator password
2. Log into the router's web interface
3. Update the router's firmware
4. Set up Wi-Fi with WPA2 security

4. Which type of network is typically used to connect devices over a short distance, such as Bluetooth devices?

A) LAN

B) WAN

C) PAN

D) MAN

5. What is the function of a switch in a network?

A) Distribute wireless signals

B) Connect multiple devices on a network providing communication between them

C) Connect a local network to the internet

D) Provide a secure gateway to external networks

6. In a network diagram, place these components in the correct location: Router, Switch, PC, and Modem.

7. Which of the following is a valid IPv4 address?

A) 192.168.1.1

B) 192.168.300.1

C) 256.100.50.25

D) 123.456.78.90

8. What tool would you use to verify your connection to a website without opening a web browser?

A) nslookup

B) tracert

C) ping

D) netstat

9. Match the following terms with their definitions:

1. Subnet Mask
2. Gateway
3. DNS

    A) Translates domain names to IP addresses

    B) Divides network into subnetworks

    C) Device that routes traffic from a local network to other networks

10. Which cable type is used to connect a PC to a switch in a typical wired LAN?

A) Coaxial

B) Fiber optic

C) HDMI

D) Ethernet

11. Fill in the blank: To view all network connections on your device, you would type _____ in the command line interface.

12. What does VPN stand for and what is its primary use?

A) Variable Path Network; used for dynamic routing

B) Virtual Private Network; used to establish a secure connection over the internet

C) Visual Public Network; used for creating public network access

D) Volatile Path Network; used for temporary network setups

13. Which OSI layer does a router operate on?

A) Layer 1

B) Layer 3

C) Layer 5

D) Layer 7

14. Drag and drop the correct tool next to its use:

1. Cable tester
2. Crimper
3. Multimeter

   A) Measures electrical current

   B) Tests connectivity in network cables

   C) Attaches connectors to Ethernet cables

15. What is the typical role of a firewall in a network?

A) To serve web pages

B) To store files

C) To manage print jobs

D) To block unauthorized access

Please refer to the "Test Your Knowledge A+ (Answers)" chapter for the answers.

CHAPTER 3

Hardware

Motherboards: Functions and Components

The motherboard is the central hub of a computer, a crucial component that connects all other components and devices together, allowing them to communicate with each other. Understanding the functions and various components of a motherboard is essential for anyone preparing for the CompTIA A+ certification, as it forms the foundation of any computer system. This section breaks down the motherboard's key roles and its essential components in a way that is accessible to beginners but also detailed enough for more advanced learners.

Primary Functions of a Motherboard

Communication Hub: The motherboard facilitates communication between all of the computer's components, including the CPU, RAM, storage devices, and peripherals. It acts as a data channel provider for all these components to work in harmony.

Power Distribution: It distributes power received from the power supply unit to various components of the computer.

System Regulation and Control: The motherboard hosts the system's firmware (BIOS or UEFI), which initializes the computer at startup and provides the interface for system management.

Key Components of a Motherboard and Their Functions

CPU Socket: The socket that holds the CPU (Central Processing Unit), the brain of the computer, which executes program instructions. The type of socket determines the compatibility with different types of CPUs.

RAM Slots: Slots for Random Access Memory (RAM) modules, where the system stores data being used by the CPU. More slots allow for more RAM, which can enhance system performance.

Chipset: Acts as a control center that manages data flow between the CPU and other components of the system, including memory, graphics cards, and storage devices. The chipset is divided into two parts: the Northbridge, which handles communications between the CPU, GPU, and RAM, and the Southbridge, which manages input/output functions and slower peripherals.

Expansion Slots (PCIe, PCI, AGP): Provide expansion capabilities for additional cards like graphics cards, sound cards, and network cards. PCI Express (PCIe) slots are the most common in modern systems, providing high-speed interfaces for advanced graphics cards and SSDs.

Storage Connectors (SATA, M.2): Connectors for storage devices such as hard drives and solid-state drives. SATA connectors are standard for external drives, while M.2 slots are used for integrating compact, high-speed SSDs directly onto the motherboard.

I/O Ports and Connectors: These include USB ports, audio jacks, Ethernet ports, and display outputs (HDMI, DisplayPort, VGA). These ports allow the connection of external devices like monitors, keyboards, mice, and networking cables.

Power Connector: Supplies power to the motherboard from the power supply unit. The main power connector is typically a 24-pin connection, with an additional 4 or 8-pin connector near the CPU for supplementary power.

BIOS/UEFI Chip: A non-volatile ROM chip that houses the system's BIOS or UEFI firmware. It provides the basic instructions for initializing the hardware and loading the operating system.

Practical Application

When assembling a computer or upgrading components, it's crucial to understand the compatibility and configuration settings of the motherboard. For instance, upgrading the CPU requires checking the motherboard's CPU socket and chipset compatibility to ensure the new processor will work with the existing motherboard. Similarly, adding more RAM or a new graphics card requires knowing the types and speeds supported by the motherboard's expansion slots and memory slots.

With a solid understanding of motherboards, we pave the way for deeper dives into specific hardware components like CPUs, RAM, and storage solutions. Each component's role and optimization are crucial for building and maintaining efficient, reliable computer systems. This foundational knowledge is not only crucial for the CompTIA A+ exam but also forms the bedrock for advanced studies in computer hardware engineering and troubleshooting.

Processors: Types and Specifications

Processors, or central processing units (CPUs), are the brains of any computer system. They are responsible for executing instructions that operate the computer and its programs. This section explores the various types of processors, their specifications, and what makes them different. Understanding these differences is crucial for anyone involved in computer hardware selection, system assembly, or maintenance, providing foundational knowledge for CompTIA A+ certification candidates.

Single-Core Processors:
Description: Early CPUs had a single core, meaning the physical chip contained only one processing unit. It could handle one task at a time sequentially, switching between tasks if multi-tasking was necessary.

Use Case: These processors are now largely obsolete for modern applications but were once standard in basic computing tasks.

Multi-Core Processors:

Description: Modern processors generally contain multiple cores, allowing them to perform multiple processes simultaneously. Common configurations include dual-core, quad-core, hexa-core, and octa-core processors.

Use Case: Multi-core processors are suitable for a wide range of applications, from personal computing to intensive gaming and professional graphic design or video editing, where multitasking performance is crucial.

Hyper-Threading/Simultaneous Multithreading:

Description: Some processors can use hyper-threading technology, where a single core is divided virtually to handle multiple threads simultaneously. This technology essentially allows each physical core to function as two logical cores.

Use Case: Ideal for tasks that require significant multitasking and applications that can take advantage of parallel processing, like video rendering and complex calculations in scientific computing.

Key Processor Specifications

Clock Speed: Measured in gigahertz (GHz), this is the speed at which the processor executes instructions. Higher clock speeds translate to faster processing capabilities, although real-world performance also depends on other factors like the number of cores and the workload type.

Cache Memory: CPUs have small amounts of cache memory to store frequently used data and instructions. More cache generally improves performance, as the processor can quickly access essential data without retrieving it from the slower main RAM.

Thermal Design Power (TDP): Indicates the maximum amount of heat generated by the processor that the cooling system is required to dissipate under any workload. TDP is crucial for building systems as it impacts the choice of cooling solutions and overall system stability.

Integrated Graphics: Some CPUs come with integrated graphics, which are built into the processor. This setup is sufficient for everyday graphics needs, like web browsing and basic video streaming, and eliminates the need for separate graphics cards.

When choosing a processor, consider the intended use of the computer. High-performance tasks like gaming, 3D rendering, and video editing may require processors with higher clock speeds, more cores, and extensive hyper-threading capabilities. For general office work and web browsing, a mid-range processor might suffice, balancing cost and performance efficiently.

Memory Types: RAM and Their Applications

Memory, particularly Random Access Memory (RAM), plays a critical role in a computer's performance by providing space for your computer to read and write data to be accessed by the CPU quickly. RAM is directly linked to the speed and efficiency of the system, affecting everything from system boot times to multitasking capability. This section will delve into various types of RAM, exploring their characteristics, uses, and implications for system performance.

Understanding RAM

RAM is volatile memory, which means it requires power to maintain the stored information and loses its content when the computer is turned off. It provides short-term data access, serving as a working area where the CPU can process data and execute programs. The speed, capacity, and type of RAM in a system can significantly impact performance.

DRAM (Dynamic RAM):

Description: The most common type of memory in personal computers, DRAM, stores each bit of data in a separate capacitor. This design makes it relatively slow and inexpensive but requires the memory to be refreshed thousands of times per second.

Use Case: DRAM is used as the main memory in most computers and is suitable for tasks that do not require high-speed memory access.

SRAM (Static RAM):

Description: Faster and more expensive than DRAM, SRAM uses multiple transistors for each memory cell, allowing it to operate without the need for frequent refreshing. This makes it faster and more reliable.

Use Case: Due to its speed, SRAM is used in the CPU's cache memory and for certain real-time applications where speed is crucial.

SDRAM (Synchronous DRAM):

Description: An improvement on traditional DRAM, SDRAM can synchronize with the CPU's clock, allowing quicker access to the memory. It waits for the clock signal before responding to control inputs and is therefore more efficient than conventional DRAM.

Use Case: SDRAM is widely used in computers for more efficient and faster access to data, suitable for general computing, gaming, and multimedia tasks.

DDR SDRAM (Double Data Rate SDRAM):

Versions: Includes DDR, DDR2, DDR3, DDR4, and the latest DDR5, each an improvement over the last with higher transfer rates and lower voltage requirements.

Description: DDR SDRAM achieves greater bandwidth by transferring data twice per clock cycle—both on the rising and falling edges of the clock signal.

Use Case: DDR4 and DDR5 are commonly used in modern desktops and laptops, ideal for high-performance gaming, video editing, and server applications, where speed and capacity are critical.

Selecting the Right Type of RAM

Choosing the right RAM involves considering several factors:

Capacity: More RAM allows a system to run more applications simultaneously and handle more data at once.

Speed: Higher speed RAM can process more data per second, improving overall system responsiveness.

Compatibility: Ensure the RAM is compatible with the motherboard in terms of type and generation (e.g., DDR4, DDR5).

Practical Example

For a standard office computer used for tasks like word processing and internet browsing, 8 GB of DDR4 RAM would typically suffice. However, for a high-end gaming PC or a workstation used for 3D rendering or video production, 32 GB of DDR5 RAM might be necessary to achieve optimal performance.

Storage Devices: HDDs, SSDs, and Other Options

Storage devices are essential for data retention in any computer system, responsible for preserving information even when the device is powered down. Different types of storage—Hard Disk Drives (HDDs), Solid State Drives (SSDs), hybrid drives, and various forms of external and portable storage—offer diverse benefits and are suited to specific applications. This section explores these technologies in depth to help you understand their mechanisms, uses, and how they fit into the broader landscape of computer hardware.

Hard Disk Drives (HDDs)

Hard Disk Drives utilize spinning magnetic disks, known as platters, to store data. A read/write head on an arm accesses the data while the platters are spinning, in a mechanism similar to a record player but at a much faster pace. This method, though reliable for long-term storage and cost-effective per gigabyte, is slower compared to solid-state technologies due to the mechanical movement involved. HDDs are particularly prone to damage from physical shocks. Despite these drawbacks, their high storage capacity makes them ideal for use in servers or for archival purposes where speed is less critical.

Solid State Drives (SSDs)

In contrast, Solid State Drives employ flash memory to store data, eliminating moving parts and significantly enhancing data access speeds. SSDs are more durable and less susceptible to physical shock, consume less power, and operate more quietly than HDDs. Although they cost more per gigabyte, their price has been steadily decreasing, making them a popular choice for primary storage in personal computers and laptops. Users who require fast system boot-ups and application loading times will find SSDs especially beneficial.

Hybrid Drives (SSHDs)

Hybrid Drives, or SSHDs, combine the mechanical architecture of HDDs with the flash memory technology of SSDs. An SSHD typically uses its SSD component as a cache for storing frequently accessed data, which enhances the overall speed of data retrieval while providing the large storage capacity of the traditional hard drive portion. SSHDs represent a compromise between the high speed of SSDs and the economical storage capacity of HDDs, suitable for users who need a balance of speed and storage without the higher cost of large-capacity SSDs.

External and Portable Storage Options

Beyond internal storage options, external and portable storage devices such as external HDDs, SSDs, USB flash drives, and SD cards offer additional flexibility and convenience. These devices are crucial for expanding storage capacity, performing backups, and transferring data between devices. For instance, external HDDs are often used for large-scale backups and data transfers, while USB flash drives and SD cards offer portability for moving files easily between locations.

Integrating Storage Devices into Computer Systems

Integrating these storage technologies into computer systems involves understanding their connection interfaces, such as SATA for HDDs and SSDs, PCIe for high-speed SSDs, and USB for external devices. This knowledge is vital for building, upgrading, and maintaining computer systems to ensure optimal storage performance.

The next chapter will delve deeper into the specific interfaces and connection standards that facilitate the communication between storage devices and computer motherboards. Understanding these connections is critical for configuring and troubleshooting storage-related issues and for ensuring that all components in a computer system function harmoniously. This continuation will reinforce the practical skills needed for hardware management and expand your expertise in creating efficient, reliable computing environments.

Purpose and Uses of Peripheral Types

Input Devices

Input devices are essential for interacting with computer systems, translating user actions into data that computers can process. This comprehensive overview explores a wide range of input devices, from the ubiquitous keyboards and mice to more specialized equipment like scanners and graphics tablets, detailing their functionalities and practical applications.

Keyboards

Keyboards are one of the most fundamental input devices, used in nearly every computer setup. They come in various designs to meet different needs:

Mechanical Keyboards: Known for their tactile feedback and durability, each key has its own switch, which can vary in feel and sound. These are preferred by gamers and professionals who require precision and longevity.

Membrane Keyboards: These feature keys that are not separate moving parts but are part of a single membrane layer. They are quieter and typically more affordable but may lack the tactile response of mechanical models.

Ergonomic Keyboards: Designed to minimize user strain, these keyboards may feature a split design or additional rests and vary in angle to promote a natural hand position.

Mouse

A mouse converts the physical motion of the user's hand into cursor movement on the screen. Various types of mice cater to different uses:

Optical Mouse: Uses an LED light to detect surface movement, suitable for most everyday computing tasks.

Laser Mouse: Employs a laser to achieve more precise detection, effective on a wider range of surfaces including glossy and transparent ones.

Wireless Mouse: Offers the freedom of movement without a cable and connects via Bluetooth or a USB receiver.

Gaming Mouse: Typically includes additional buttons and features for enhanced functionality, designed for high-intensity gaming.

Scanners

Scanners convert physical documents and images into digital formats, making them accessible for electronic manipulation and storage:

Flatbed Scanners: Suitable for a variety of documents, these scanners have a glass pane where items are placed for scanning.

Sheet-fed Scanners: Ideal for quick scanning of multiple pages, these pull documents through the scanner.

Other Input Devices

The range of input devices extends beyond the traditional keyboard and mouse:

Graphics Tablets: Allow precise control for digital art creation, using a stylus or pen on a touch-sensitive surface.

Touch Screens: Enable direct interaction with display content through touch, commonly found on mobile devices and some laptops.

Game Controllers: Such as joysticks and gamepads, provide immersive interaction for video games.

Microphones: Convert sound into digital data, useful for voice commands or digital recording.

Webcams: Capture real-time video and images for online communication.

Barcode Scanners: Streamline data entry in retail and inventory management.

Digital Cameras: Can serve as input devices when connected to a computer, allowing direct transfer of photos and videos.

Biometric Sensors: Offer security through fingerprint or facial recognition.

Motion Sensing Devices: Used in gaming and virtual reality, these detect physical movements and translate them into digital input.

Voice Recognition Devices: Enable interaction through voice commands, essential for virtual assistants and hands-free control.

Understanding the wide array of input devices available helps users and IT professionals alike choose the right tools for specific tasks, whether for general use, professional environments, or specialized applications. This knowledge not only prepares you for practical IT scenarios but also enriches your understanding for CompTIA A+ certification, ensuring you are well-equipped to handle and optimize the use of various input devices in any computing environment.

Output Devices

Output devices are essential for conveying information from a computer to the user in a perceivable form such as visual, printed, or auditory outputs. This section covers the most common types of output devices—monitors, printers, and speakers—and explains their functions, uses, and how they enhance user interaction with computer systems. Understanding these devices is critical for anyone involved in computer configuration, support, or any IT-related tasks, ensuring a well-rounded knowledge base for the CompTIA A+ certification.

Monitors

Monitors are perhaps the most critical output device for any computer system, providing a visual display of the user interface and data. Types of Monitors:

LCD (Liquid Crystal Display): Utilizes a liquid crystal solution sandwiched between two polarizing materials. LCDs are energy-efficient and offer excellent color reproduction, making them suitable for general use and professional graphic design.

LED (Light Emitting Diode): An advancement of LCD technology, LED monitors use light-emitting diodes for backlighting, which allows for thinner panels, better energy efficiency, and more accurate color contrast.

OLED (Organic Light Emitting Diode): Displays deep black levels and high contrast ratios by using a film of organic compounds that emit light in response to an electric current. OLEDs are used in high-end monitors and portable devices where image quality and color depth are crucial.

Specifications to Consider:

Resolution: The number of pixels that can be displayed on the screen, directly affecting the clarity and detail of the image.

Refresh Rate: Measured in hertz (Hz), indicating how many times per second the screen refreshes its image. Higher rates are crucial for activities where motion is displayed, such as gaming or video editing.

Aspect Ratio: The ratio of the width to the height of the display screen, affecting how content is scaled and displayed.

Printers

Printers convert digital documents into physical copies, an essential function in many business and home environments. Types of Printers:

Inkjet Printers: Spray tiny droplets of ink directly onto paper. They are capable of producing high-quality color prints with great detail and are suitable for home users and small offices.

Laser Printers: Use toner and static electricity to transfer images and text onto paper. Known for their speed and efficiency, they are ideal for environments that require high volume printing.

Thermal Printers: Commonly used in receipt printing, they use heat-sensitive paper and are valued for their speed and low maintenance costs.

Considerations for Selecting Printers:

Print Speed and Quality: Determined by the printer type and the intended use—higher quality and speed generally increase the cost.

Ongoing Costs: Including toner or ink replacements and paper, which can vary widely based on the printer model and usage patterns.

Speakers and Other Audio Output Devices

Speakers transform audio signals into sound, allowing users to hear music, system sounds, or audio from multimedia content. Types of Audio Outputs:

External Speakers: Range from simple desktop speakers to complex surround sound systems, providing higher quality and volume than built-in speakers.

Headphones and Earbuds: Personal audio devices that deliver sound directly to the user, suitable for private listening or in environments where noise minimization is necessary.

Connecting these devices involves various interfaces, such as HDMI, DisplayPort, USB, and wireless technologies like Bluetooth. The choice of connection impacts the quality and speed of the data transmitted, thus affecting the overall performance of the output device.

Storage Peripherals: External Storage Devices

In today's digital age, the need for data storage extends beyond the internal capabilities of standard computer systems. External storage devices, such as USB drives and external hard disk drives (HDDs), play a crucial role in data mobility and security, offering flexible and portable solutions for data backup, transfer, and archiving. This section provides an in-depth exploration of these devices, detailing their types, uses, advantages, and considerations for optimal use.

USB Drives (Flash Drives)

USB drives, commonly referred to as flash drives or thumb drives, are compact, portable devices that store data on flash memory. Equipped with a USB interface, they are universally compatible with almost any modern computer system, providing a convenient and swift means of transferring files between devices.

Capacity: Ranging from a few gigabytes to 1 TB or more, allowing for the storage of anything from simple documents to large media files.
Portability: Small enough to be carried on a keychain or in a pocket, making them ideal for personal or professional use when frequent travel or data transport is involved.
Speed: Modern USB drives support USB 3.0 or USB 3.1 standards, offering significantly faster data transfer rates compared to their USB 2.0 predecessors.
Use Case: Perfect for quick data transfers between computers in different locations, sharing presentations or class materials, and as a bootable device for system recovery tasks.

External Hard Disk Drives (HDDs)

External HDDs provide a higher-capacity storage solution compared to USB drives, making them suitable for more extensive data storage needs.
Capacity: Typically ranges from about 500 GB to 10 TB or more, catering to substantial data backup requirements.
Portability: While larger and heavier than USB drives, many external HDDs are still compact enough to be easily transported in a laptop bag or briefcase.
Speed: Connection interfaces like USB 3.0, USB-C, or eSATA allow for fast data transfer speeds that facilitate efficient handling of large data volumes.
Use Case: Ideal for regular backups of large datasets, such as video collections, extensive software libraries, or system backups for small businesses.

Advantages of External Storage

Data Security: Keeping a backup of critical data on an external device can protect against data loss due to system failures, malware, or hardware damage.

Flexibility: Easily add storage capacity without opening a computer's case or needing specialized tools or knowledge.

Portability: Move data physically between locations without network dependencies, which can be crucial in environments with limited or insecure internet access.

Choosing the Right Storage Peripheral

Selecting the right external storage involves considering several factors:

Data Needs: Assess the type and volume of data you need to store. Larger files, such as video or scientific data sets, may require the higher capacities of an external HDD.

Speed Requirements: For tasks involving large file transfers or frequent access to stored data, choose devices with faster data transfer rates.

Portability and Durability: If frequent transportation of data is necessary, prioritize devices that offer robustness and compact form factors.

Budget: USB drives are generally less expensive for lower capacities, while external HDDs offer a better cost-per-gigabyte ratio for larger capacities.

Network Connectivity

Networking peripherals are integral components that facilitate communication between computers and other devices within a network. These devices, which include network interface cards (NICs), routers, and switches, are essential for building and maintaining robust network infrastructures. By understanding the specific functions and applications of each type of networking peripheral, IT professionals can optimize network performance, reliability, and security. This section provides a detailed examination of these crucial devices, their operational mechanisms, and their roles within different network environments.

Network Interface Cards (NICs)

A Network Interface Card (NIC) is a hardware component that allows computers to connect to a network. NICs can be either integrated into the motherboard or installed as an add-on card.

Functionality: NICs are responsible for converting data into a format suitable for transmission over a network, handling both incoming and outgoing data. They manage data conversion, signal integrity, and data traffic control, ensuring that data packets are transmitted and received correctly according to network protocols.

Types and Features:

Wired NICs: These NICs connect to networks via Ethernet cables. They are known for providing reliable, high-speed connections and are commonly used in stationary setups where security and speed are priorities, such as in server rooms or desktop PCs in offices.

Wireless NICs: These provide connectivity through Wi-Fi signals. They offer the convenience of mobility and are ideal for devices where direct cabling is impractical, such as in laptops and mobile devices used in flexible work environments.

Key Specifications:

Speed: Wired NICs commonly support 10/100 Mbps or 1 Gbps, while advanced models may support 10 Gbps for ultra-high-speed requirements. Wireless NIC speeds depend on the Wi-Fi standard they support, such as 802.11ac or 802.11ax, which can significantly impact performance.

Bandwidth Handling: The ability of NICs to handle bandwidth efficiently affects network performance, especially in environments with high data transmission rates.

Compatibility: Compatibility with the computer's motherboard, operating system, and network standards is crucial to ensure that the NIC operates correctly within the system.

Routers

Routers are sophisticated devices that direct data packets between different networks, ensuring that information reaches its intended destination across interconnected networks.

Functionality: Routers analyze data packets, determine their optimal paths, and forward them accordingly. They can be programmed to prioritize traffic, which is essential in managing network load and optimizing performance for critical applications.

Applications:

Home Use: In home networks, routers typically provide both wired and wireless connectivity, connecting multiple devices to the internet and facilitating communication between them.

Business Use: In more complex networks, routers manage traffic not only to external networks but also between different segments of internal networks, implementing advanced security protocols to protect data integrity.

Switches

Switches are pivotal in creating networks by connecting multiple devices on the same network segment, facilitating the efficient transfer of data within local networks.

Functionality: Unlike routers, switches operate primarily within local networks (LANs). They direct data specifically to devices within the network based on MAC addresses, enhancing speed and efficiency by reducing unnecessary data broadcasts.

Usage Considerations:

Scalability: Switches are scalable, allowing networks to expand seamlessly by adding more switches or connecting larger ones.

Performance: High-performance switches are capable of handling significant amounts of data and are crucial in environments with high transaction volumes, such as data centers.

Integrating Networking Peripherals

Effective integration and configuration of NICs, routers, and switches are crucial for setting up and maintaining efficient and secure networks. Understanding how these devices interact and complement each other helps in designing network infrastructures that meet specific organizational needs, from small home offices to large enterprise environments.

Building on the foundation of networking peripherals, the subsequent discussions will delve into advanced network configuration strategies, including setup, security enhancements, and troubleshooting practices. This progression will equip IT professionals with the comprehensive skills required to manage modern network challenges, ensuring optimal performance and security across all computing platforms. This knowledge is indispensable for both practical applications and preparation for the CompTIA A+ certification.

Troubleshooting Hardware Components

Identifying and Resolving Hardware Issues

Troubleshooting hardware is a critical skill for any IT professional. Accurately diagnosing and resolving hardware issues is essential for maintaining the reliability and efficiency of computer systems. This section outlines systematic diagnostic procedures for identifying common hardware problems, providing a structured approach that can be followed to minimize downtime and ensure a swift resolution. Understanding these steps is crucial for anyone preparing for the CompTIA A+ exam or working in IT support roles.

Step 1: Initial Assessment

The troubleshooting process begins with a thorough initial assessment, which helps define the problem's scope and nature.

Interviewing the User: Engage with the user to get a comprehensive understanding of the issue. Key questions might include: What exactly happens when the problem occurs? What were you doing when the problem first appeared? Have there been any recent changes to the system such as new installations or updates? These questions can help pinpoint the circumstances that trigger the issue.

Observing the Problem: Direct observation can offer critical insights that user descriptions might not capture. Attempt to replicate the issue by following the user's normal operations. This approach can sometimes reveal problems that occur intermittently or under specific conditions that are not obvious during standard diagnostic tests.

Step 2: Systematic Isolation

Isolating the problem involves several checks to narrow down the cause of the issue.

Checking All Connections: Begin by ensuring that all internal and external connections are secure. This includes power cables, USB connections, network cables, and peripheral devices. A loose or disconnected cable is a simple yet frequent source of problems.

Verifying Power Supply: Confirm that the system's power supply is functioning correctly. Check for any signs of damage or failure, such as strange noises from the PSU, burnt smells, or visible wear. Use a multimeter to verify that the power supply is delivering correct voltages to different components.

Step 3: Running Diagnostic Tests

Diagnostic tests can help identify failing components or confirm suspicions from earlier assessments.

Using BIOS/UEFI Tools: Most systems include BIOS or UEFI diagnostics that can test hardware components like RAM, hard drives, and sometimes CPUs. These tools are particularly useful for catching errors that don't manifest clearly in the operating system.

Third-party Software: For more thorough testing, third-party software tools can be invaluable. These programs often offer extensive testing capabilities beyond what built-in tools can provide, including stress tests and benchmarking to evaluate performance under load.

Step 4: Swapping Components

If diagnostic tests are inconclusive or indicate potential component failure, physically testing components can confirm the diagnosis.

Swapping with Known Good Components: Temporarily replacing suspected faulty hardware with components that are known to function can definitively indicate whether the original part was defective.

Testing in a Different System: If possible, test the suspected faulty component in a different compatible system. If the issue persists in a different system, the component is likely the problem.

Step 5: Monitoring System Behavior

After addressing potential hardware issues, observing the system's behavior ensures the solution is effective.

Stress Testing: Use tools to simulate high-load scenarios that may not occur during ordinary use. This can reveal problems that only appear under specific conditions.

Observation Period: Continue to monitor the system over an extended period to ensure that it operates without recurrence of the issue. Sometimes, problems believed to be resolved can reappear.

Step 6: Documenting and Reporting

Documenting the troubleshooting process and solutions applied is crucial for maintaining an effective IT environment.

Future Reference: Detailed records help diagnose future problems more quickly and prevent redundancy in troubleshooting efforts.

Knowledge Sharing: Documenting solutions helps disseminate knowledge among the team, improving the overall skill set and response time for future issues.

Understanding and implementing these expanded diagnostic steps equip IT professionals with a robust methodology for troubleshooting hardware issues. This detailed approach not only aids in quick resolution but also enhances reliability and efficiency in maintaining IT systems.

Error Identification Techniques

Effective troubleshooting in IT involves a keen understanding of system error codes, which are critical indicators of the health and functioning of computer hardware and software. These error codes are designed to help technicians quickly pinpoint and resolve problems, ensuring minimal downtime and maintaining system performance. This expanded section offers a deeper look at the types of error codes you may encounter, how to interpret them, and the most effective methods for resolving the issues they highlight.

Understanding System Error Codes

System error codes are generated when devices encounter issues that disrupt normal operations. They can come from various sources:

BIOS/UEFI Error Codes: These are the first codes that might be encountered during the boot process, even before the operating system starts. They can be displayed as a series of beeps (beep codes) or as numeric or text codes on the display screen (POST codes).

Operating System Error Codes: These are more specific and detailed, provided by the operating system when it encounters errors during operation. For example, Windows' Blue Screen of Death (BSOD) provides a stop code and sometimes a hexadecimal code, which can help identify and troubleshoot issues.

Types of Error Codes

Beep Codes: These are simple tones or a series of sounds emitted by the motherboard speaker. For instance, a single beep might indicate successful POST, while a sequence of beeps might indicate missing or faulty memory.

POST Codes: Displayed on the screen or a POST card, these codes can indicate at which stage the boot process failed, helping pinpoint whether the issue is with the memory, graphics card, or another component.

BSOD Error Codes: These are critical codes shown when Windows encounters a severe error that leads to a crash. The codes include a stop code, a hexadecimal error number, and sometimes an error message describing the fault.

Interpreting Error Codes

Consult Documentation: Every motherboard manufacturer provides a list of beep and POST codes unique to their hardware. The motherboard manual or manufacturer's website is a crucial resource for these, for operating system errors like BSODs, Microsoft and other operating systems offer detailed guides and troubleshooting documentation online.

Diagnostic Tools: For more comprehensive diagnostics, use tools integrated into the BIOS/UEFI or third-party applications to analyze system errors and logs. These tools often provide a more in-depth look at the error and can suggest corrective actions based on the codes.

Online Resources: Utilize online forums and databases specializing in error codes and troubleshooting. Websites like Tom's Hardware, TechNet, and others provide a community-based support framework where users can share solutions and advice on specific error codes.

Error Code Resolution Strategies

Hardware Replacement: If a beep or POST code indicates a hardware issue, such as a failure in memory or graphics card, testing with known good components can confirm the diagnosis. Replacing or reseating the component often resolves these errors.

Software Updates: For BSOD and other software-related errors, ensure that all system drivers and operating system patches are up to date. Software conflicts and outdated drivers are frequent sources of these errors.

System Configuration Changes: Sometimes, incorrect BIOS/UEFI settings can lead to system instability. Resetting to default settings or adjusting configuration options can often resolve these issues without the need for hardware changes.

Resolution Techniques

Effective troubleshooting not only involves diagnosing problems accurately but also applying the right techniques to resolve these issues efficiently. This section outlines practical resolution strategies for some of the most common hardware problems encountered in IT. By understanding these solutions, IT professionals can ensure that hardware operates reliably and continues to serve its purpose effectively.

Overheating Issues

Overheating can cause significant damage to computer components and lead to system instability or failure.
Resolution Strategies:

Enhance Cooling: Verify that all fans within the computer case are functioning correctly. Replace any non-working fans and consider adding additional fans or a better heat sink to improve air circulation.

Clean Dust Buildup: Dust accumulation can obstruct airflow and insulate heat. Regularly cleaning the internal components of the computer, especially fans and heat sinks, can significantly improve cooling efficiency.

Optimize Airflow: Reorganize cables and components to ensure unobstructed air movement within the case. Good cable management can often be overlooked but is vital for maintaining optimal airflow.

Memory Errors

Faulty or incompatible RAM can cause system crashes, data corruption, and frequent BSOD errors.
Resolution Strategies:

Reseat RAM: Remove and carefully reinsert the RAM sticks to ensure they are securely and correctly placed in their slots. This can often resolve intermittent issues caused by poor contact.

Test Memory: Use tools like MemTest86 to run comprehensive tests on the computer's RAM. This can help identify defective memory modules that need replacement.

Upgrade or Replace RAM: If memory issues persist or the system requires more memory to operate efficiently, consider upgrading the RAM or replacing old modules with new ones that meet the system's specifications.

Hard Drive Failures

Hard drive issues can manifest as slow performance, disappearing files, or a system that fails to boot.

Resolution Strategies:

Check for Connectivity Issues: Ensure that all cables connected to the hard drive are secure. Loose SATA or power cables can cause the drive to disconnect intermittently.

Run Diagnostic Software: Most hard drive manufacturers provide utilities to diagnose and repair problems with their products. These tools can often detect and fix issues without data loss.

Clone and Replace: If a hard drive is failing, it's crucial to clone it to a new drive immediately to prevent data loss. Once cloned, the old drive should be replaced to restore full functionality.

Graphics Card Problems

Issues with graphics cards can include artifacts appearing on the screen, crashes during graphics-heavy tasks, or drivers failing to load.

Resolution Strategies:

Update or Reinstall Drivers: Download and install the latest drivers from the card manufacturer's website. If issues persist, completely uninstalling and then reinstalling the graphics drivers can resolve driver conflicts.

Check for Overheating: Graphics cards can overheat due to intense use or inadequate cooling. Ensure the card's fans are clean and working, and consider improving case ventilation or adding supplemental cooling.

Re-seat the Card: Remove the graphics card and reinstall it to ensure it is firmly and correctly seated in the PCIe slot.

Test Your Knowledge (Chapter 3)

1. What is the main function of a motherboard?

A) Store data permanently

B) Supply power to the system

C) Connect all the components of a computer

D) Manage software applications

2. Which of the following is considered an input device?

A) Printer

B) Speaker

C) Keyboard

D) Monitor

3. Fill-in-the-Blank: The component responsible for processing all instructions in a computer is the _____.

A) Hard drive

B) RAM

C) CPU

D) GPU

4. Drag and Drop Activity: Place the following components in the order they are accessed when a computer boots up:

Components:

1. Hard Drive
2. CPU
3. RAM
4. BIOS

5. Which type of memory is volatile and requires power to maintain its information?

A) SSD

B) HDD

C) RAM

D) ROM

6. What is the purpose of a heat sink in a computer?

A) To provide extra storage

B) To enhance the speed of the processor

C) To cool down the processor

D) To convert AC to DC power

7. Which port is typically used to connect a printer to a computer?

A) HDMI

B) USB

C) Ethernet

D) DVI

8. Performance-Based Question: Configure a system unit by dragging the correct components into their respective slots on the motherboard.

Components:

1. RAM
2. Graphics Card
3. Sound Card

4. Network Card

9. What type of storage is considered permanent and non-volatile?

A) RAM

B) Cache

C) SSD

D) CPU Registers

10. Which component is directly responsible for generating visual output to a display?

A) Processor

B) Hard drive

C) Graphics card

D) Sound card

11. Fill-in-the-Blank: The _____ is used to connect the motherboard to the power supply.

A) SATA cable

B) USB connector

C) Power connector

D) HDMI cable

12. What is the role of the BIOS in a computer system?

A) It manages data flow between the operating system and attached devices

B) It stores the operating system

C) It is responsible for the initial booting of the computer

D) It upgrades the processor

13. Performance-Based Question: Identify the correct order of operations when installing a new hard drive.

Steps:

1. Mount the drive in the case
2. Connect the SATA cable
3. Format the drive
4. Partition the drive

14. Which RAM type is faster and used in performance-critical systems?

A) DDR3

B) DDR4

C) SDRAM

D) VRAM

15. What does a power supply unit (PSU) do in a computer?

A) Converts AC to DC power

B) Manages software installation

C) Provides connectivity to external networks

D) Enhances audio output quality

Please refer to the "Test Your Knowledge A+ (Answers)" chapter for the answers.

CHAPTER 4

Cloud Computing Concepts

Infrastructure as a Service (IaaS)

Delivers virtualized computing resources via the internet, enabling organizations to utilize virtualized infrastructure components such as storage, networking, and servers. This model eliminates the necessity for physical hardware investment. Examples include **Amazon Web Services (AWS) Elastic Compute Cloud (EC2) and Microsoft Azure Virtual Machines**, which provide scalable, on-demand resources to businesses. The main security concerns here involve ensuring the protection of the virtual machines from attacks, managing the security of the storage services, and configuring network security groups and firewalls correctly to avoid unauthorized access.

Security Considerations: Users are responsible for securing the operating systems, applications, and data running on top of the provided infrastructure. It is crucial to implement strong authentication and encryption mechanisms for data at rest and in transit. Regularly updating and patching software components, along with comprehensive monitoring and logging, are also essential to maintaining security.

Platform as a Service (PaaS)

On the other hand, removes the need for organizations to manage the underlying infrastructure, allowing them to focus on the deployment and management of applications. Services like **Google App Engine** or **Microsoft Azure App Services** provide a managed hosting environment where developers can build applications without worrying about hardware, storage, or network management. The security challenges in PaaS primarily revolve around application security, data security, and managing user access and permissions, ensuring that only authorized users can access and modify applications.

Security Considerations: While the service provider manages the infrastructure, users must secure the applications they deploy. This includes coding securely to prevent vulnerabilities such as SQL injection or cross-site scripting, ensuring proper configuration settings, and managing data access policies effectively.

Software As a Service (SaaS)

It is the most user-friendly model, offering complete software solutions on a subscription basis. Tools such as **Google Workspace** and **Microsoft Office 365** exemplify SaaS, enabling users to use software directly over the Internet without installation or maintenance. Security in SaaS is particularly challenging because the management of the software is entirely in the hands of the provider. Users must rely on contractual agreements for security and compliance, be vigilant about identity and access management, and protect the integrity and confidentiality of their data.

Security Considerations: Users have the least control in this model, so it's critical to understand the security measures the provider has in place. Ensuring the use of strong end-user security practices, such as secure passwords and two-factor authentication, and conducting regular security assessments of the services are vital practices.

Basic Virtualization Components

Understanding Hypervisors

A hypervisor, also known as a virtual machine monitor (VMM), is a crucial component in virtualization technology. It allows multiple operating systems to run concurrently on a single physical machine by abstracting the processor, memory, and other resources. This section provides a comprehensive overview of the types of hypervisors, their distinct roles, functionalities, and how they form the backbone of virtualization technology. By understanding hypervisors, IT professionals can better manage and implement virtual environments effectively, optimizing resource utilization and operational flexibility.

What is a Hypervisor?

A hypervisor is software, firmware, or hardware that creates and runs virtual machines (VMs). It sits between the hardware and the operating system, allowing multiple VMs to share a single hardware host. Each VM can run its own operating system and applications as if it were a separate physical device.

Types of Hypervisors

Hypervisors come in two primary types, each with distinct characteristics and uses:

Type 1 Hypervisors (Bare Metal): These hypervisors run directly on the host's hardware to control the hardware and to manage guest operating systems. For this reason, they are considered more efficient and secure than Type 2 hypervisors. Common examples include VMware ESXi, Microsoft Hyper-V, and Xen.

Type 2 Hypervisors (Hosted): These hypervisors run on a conventional operating system just as other computer programs do. A Type 2 hypervisor abstracts guest operating systems from the host operating system. VMware Workstation and Oracle VirtualBox are examples of Type 2 hypervisors.

Roles of Hypervisors in Virtualization

Resource Allocation: Hypervisors dynamically allocate hardware resources to VMs as needed. This includes managing and optimizing performance for CPU, memory, and storage among the different VMs to ensure that each has access to the resources it requires without interfering with others.

Isolation: One of the key roles of a hypervisor is to maintain isolation between VMs. This isolation ensures that processes running in one VM do not affect those running in another. Additionally, this helps in maintaining security across VMs, as one compromised VM does not lead to vulnerabilities in others.

Management and Automation: Hypervisors provide tools for managing virtual environments, making it easier to create, modify, monitor, and migrate VMs between host machines. Automation features include load balancing, disaster recovery management, and automated provisioning, which help streamline operations and improve reliability.

Benefits of Using Hypervisors

Improved Utilization of Resources: By allowing multiple VMs to run on a single server, hypervisors help in maximizing physical hardware utilization, reducing the need for physical machines.

Flexibility and Scalability: Virtual environments can be adjusted quickly and easily, providing businesses with the flexibility to scale resources up or down based on demand without significant downtime or cost.

Enhanced Security and Isolation: Despite sharing the same physical hardware, VMs are isolated from each other, which enhances security by ensuring that systems are not affected by the compromise of another.

Cost-Effective: Reduces the total cost of ownership by decreasing physical hardware needs, lowering energy consumption, and reducing the physical space required for server farms.

Practical Applications of Hypervisors

Server Virtualization: Multiple server instances on a single physical server.

Desktop Virtualization: Host virtual desktop environments that users can access remotely.

Software Development and Testing: Provide developers with the ability to create and test in different operating environments without the need for multiple physical devices.

Understanding hypervisors and their function within virtualization frameworks is essential for deploying efficient and secure IT environments. By leveraging the capabilities of hypervisors, organizations can enhance their IT operations' flexibility, efficiency, and scalability.

Managing Virtual Machines

Managing virtual machines (VMs) efficiently is a cornerstone of modern IT operations, particularly in environments leveraging virtualization for enhanced flexibility and resource utilization. This section offers detailed guidelines on creating, configuring, and maintaining VMs, ensuring that even beginners can understand and apply these principles effectively. By mastering VM management, IT professionals can optimize the operational aspects of their virtual environments, leading to improved performance and reduced overhead.

Creating Virtual Machines

The creation of a VM involves several key steps that configure the virtual environment to meet specific operational requirements.

Selecting a Hypervisor: First, choose a suitable hypervisor (Type 1 or Type 2, as previously discussed) based on the infrastructure requirements and the intended use of the VMs.

Allocating Resources: Define the amount of CPU, memory, and storage resources that each VM will be allocated. These should be based on the needs of the application or services that the VM will host.

Installing the Operating System: Install an operating system on the VM. This process is similar to installing an OS on a physical machine but is done through virtualization software.

Configuring Network Settings: Set up network configurations to ensure the VM can communicate with other VMs on the same host or across the network. This may include setting up virtual network interfaces and defining IP addressing.

Managing Virtual Machines

Once VMs are up and running, effective management involves regular monitoring and maintenance to ensure optimal performance and security.

Monitoring Performance: Regularly monitor the performance of VMs to ensure they are operating efficiently. Use tools provided by the hypervisor to track CPU usage, memory utilization, and disk activity.

Applying Security Measures: Just like physical machines, VMs are susceptible to security risks. Apply regular security updates and patches to the VM's operating system and applications. Implement security policies that govern access and use of the VMs.

Backup and Recovery: Implement a robust backup strategy for VMs. Regular backups ensure that you can quickly restore a VM to a previous state in case of software failure or data corruption.

Resource Scalability: Adjust resource allocations based on changing needs. Most modern hypervisors allow for dynamic resource management, enabling you to add or reduce resources without significant downtime.

Optimizing VM Performance

Optimizing VM performance involves fine-tuning various settings and being proactive in resource management.

Balancing Load: Distribute the workload evenly across VMs to prevent any single VM from becoming a bottleneck. This includes balancing CPU-intensive and memory-intensive applications across the virtual environment.

Updating Virtualization Software: Keep the virtualization software up-to-date to benefit from the latest features, security patches, and performance improvements.

Using Virtualization-Specific Hardware: Utilize hardware that is optimized for virtualization. Many modern CPUs offer features that enhance virtualization performance, such as Intel VT and AMD-V technologies.

Virtual Networks Configuration

Virtual networks are a pivotal component of virtualization, enabling isolated network environments within a single physical network infrastructure. This section discusses how to set up and manage virtual networks, providing a detailed, beginner-friendly guide that covers the essentials while ensuring the information is accessible and straightforward. By mastering the setup and management of virtual networks, IT professionals can enhance the efficiency and security of their virtualized environments.

Virtual networks allow multiple virtual machines (VMs) on the same physical machine to communicate as if they were connected to the same physical switch. They can also link VMs across different physical hosts, which is crucial for maintaining consistent network operations across a distributed environment.

Components of Virtual Networks:

Virtual Switches: Software-based switches that connect VMs on the same physical host.
Virtual Routers: Facilitate data routing between different virtual networks and between virtual and physical networks.
Virtual Network Interface Cards (vNICs): Assigned to each VM, these interface cards connect VMs to the virtual network.

Setting Up Virtual Networks

The setup process involves several key steps, each crucial for ensuring that the virtual network functions correctly and securely.
Define Network Layout: Plan the network architecture, including how VMs will be grouped, which resources they will access, and how they will connect to the internet or external networks.
Create Virtual Switches: Implement virtual switches within the hypervisor to connect VMs on the same host. Configure settings such as VLAN IDs for network isolation and QoS policies for traffic prioritization.
Configure Routing and Firewall Settings: Set up virtual routers to manage traffic between different subnets and virtual networks. Configure firewalls to protect and control the flow of traffic into and out of the virtual network.
Allocate IP Addresses: Decide whether to use static IP addresses or DHCP for assigning IP addresses to VMs. Setting up a DHCP server within the virtual environment can automate IP management.

Managing Virtual Networks

Effective management ensures that the virtual network remains operational, secure, and optimized for performance.
Monitor Traffic: Use network monitoring tools to track the flow of data and identify potential bottlenecks or security threats. Monitoring can help in optimizing traffic flows and ensuring compliance with network policies.
Maintain Security: Regularly update firewall rules and network security policies to guard against new vulnerabilities. Implement intrusion detection systems (IDS) and intrusion prevention systems (IPS) to enhance security measures.
Troubleshoot Connectivity Issues: Be prepared to diagnose and resolve issues such as IP conflicts, incorrect routing settings, or failures in network services.

Optimizing Virtual Network Performance

Segment Networks: Use network segmentation strategies such as VLANs to reduce congestion, enhance security, and improve network performance.

Balance Load: Implement load balancing solutions to distribute traffic evenly across network resources, preventing any single server or link from becoming a bottleneck.

Example Scenario: Setting Up a Virtual Network in a Corporate Environment

Setting up and managing virtual networks involves several key steps that ensure secure and efficient communication between virtual machines (VMs) and external networks. Here's a detailed, step-by-step example of how you might configure a basic virtual network using a Type 1 hypervisor, which is commonly used in enterprise environments for its direct access to hardware resources.

Step 1: Define the Network Layout

To create a virtual network that supports three departments (Sales, HR, Development) with separate subnetworks for security and performance optimization.

Action: Plan a network layout with three virtual LANs (VLANs) to isolate traffic from each department. Determine the number of VMs needed for each VLAN and their roles (servers, user desktops).

Step 2: Create Virtual Switches

Implement virtual switches to facilitate communication between VMs on the same physical host and across the network.

Action: Open the hypervisor's management console. Create three virtual switches, one for each VLAN.

Configure VLAN IDs (e.g., VLAN 10 for Sales, VLAN 20 for HR, VLAN 30 for Development) to enforce network segmentation at the data link layer.

Step 3: Configure Routing and Firewall Settings

Enable VMs from different VLANs to communicate securely and regulate access to external networks.

Action: Set up a virtual router to handle inter-VLAN routing, allowing controlled communication between the departments based on predefined policies.

Implement firewall rules for each VLAN to manage traffic flow and restrict unauthorized access. For example, block incoming traffic from the internet to HR and Development servers.

Step 4: Allocate IP Addresses

Efficiently manage IP addressing for all VMs within the network.

Action: Deploy a virtual DHCP server within each VLAN to automatically assign IP addresses to VMs. This simplifies network management and ensures proper IP address allocation.

Configure DHCP scopes for each VLAN, ensuring no IP address overlaps between VLANs.

Step 5: Monitoring Traffic

Maintain visibility into network traffic to optimize performance and enhance security.
Action: Install network monitoring tools on a dedicated VM to analyze traffic patterns, detect anomalies, and monitor network health. Set up alerts for unusual traffic spikes or unauthorized access attempts, enabling proactive management of potential issues.

Step 6: Maintain Security

Regularly update and manage security measures to protect network data.
Action: Regularly review and update firewall configurations to adapt to new security threats and organizational changes. Conduct periodic audits of network access logs and security settings to ensure compliance with corporate security policies.

Step 7: Troubleshoot Connectivity Issues

Quickly resolve any network issues to minimize downtime.
Action: Develop a troubleshooting guide that includes common issues such as IP conflicts, failed DHCP assignments, and connectivity problems. Train network administrators in using the hypervisor's diagnostic tools to identify and resolve network issues efficiently.

This example outlines a typical setup for a corporate virtual network using advanced virtualization tools and techniques. By following these steps, IT professionals can create a robust, scalable, and secure virtual network tailored to their organization's specific needs.

This methodical approach ensures operational efficiency and prepares the network for future expansion and integration with cloud services, which will be explored in the upcoming sections.

Resource Sharing and Virtual Machine Management

Allocation of Virtual Resources

Effective resource allocation is crucial in virtualized environments to ensure optimal performance and efficiency. This section provides a comprehensive guide on how to distribute resources such as CPU time, memory, and storage among virtual machines (VMs). It aims to equip IT professionals with the knowledge to manage resources wisely in a virtual environment, thereby enhancing the performance of VMs and ensuring that each can perform its intended functions without unnecessary resource contention.

Understanding Resource Allocation in Virtualization

Resource allocation in a virtualized environment involves assigning and managing the CPU, memory, storage, and network resources of the host machine among multiple VMs. This process is managed by the hypervisor, which acts as the mediator between the physical resources and the VMs.

CPU Allocation: The hypervisor schedules VM access to the CPU, ensuring that each VM gets the required processing time. This can be managed through settings that define the number of CPU cores assigned to each VM or the limit and reservation of CPU resources.

Memory Allocation: Memory allocation involves distributing the host's RAM among VMs. Techniques like ballooning, overcommitment, and swapping help manage memory in scenarios where the demand from VMs might exceed the available memory.

Storage Allocation: Involves distributing disk space to VMs from the physical storage pool. Storage can be allocated statically, where a fixed amount of disk space is assigned to a VM, or dynamically, where disk space grows as needed by the VM.

Network Bandwidth Allocation: Bandwidth must be managed to ensure that no single VM can monopolize network resources, affecting the performance of others.

Strategies for Effective Resource Allocation

Prioritization and Reservation: Set priorities for VMs that require more resources due to their critical nature. Reservations can be used to guarantee a minimum level of resource at all times, ensuring that these VMs function effectively even when the system is under load.

Resource Limits: Establish maximum resource usage limits for less critical VMs to prevent them from consuming excessive amounts of CPU, memory, or storage that could impact other VMs.

Load Balancing: Use load balancing techniques to distribute workloads evenly across VMs, maximizing the utilization of resources and enhancing overall system performance.

Monitoring and Adjusting: Continuously monitor resource usage and performance metrics. Adjust allocations based on trends and changing requirements to maintain balance and prevent bottlenecks.

Practical Application of Resource Allocation

Scenario-based Allocation: In a development environment, VMs might require different resources at various stages of the development cycle. For instance, more CPU and memory might be allocated during compilation processes, while less might be needed during the design phase.

Dynamic Resource Allocation: Implement tools and policies that allow for dynamic adjustment of resources based on real-time demand. This ensures that resources are available when needed without a constant manual intervention.

Challenges in Resource Allocation

Resource Contention: When multiple VMs compete for limited resources, it can lead to performance degradation. Effective monitoring and management policies are required to mitigate this.

Overcommitment: Allocating more virtual resources than the physical resources can support might lead to problems. While overcommitment can improve resource utilization, it must be carefully managed to avoid performance issues.

Having explored the allocation of virtual resources, the next section will delve into advanced management techniques for virtual environments. This includes automating resource allocation, scaling virtual resources, and using predictive analytics to foresee and respond to changes in resource demand. This progression from basic allocation to sophisticated management strategies is essential for IT professionals aiming to optimize virtual environments for maximum efficiency and effectiveness.

VM Health and Performance

Maintaining the health and performance of virtual machines (VMs) is essential to the efficiency of virtualized environments. This section explores best practices for VM management, aimed at helping IT professionals enhance the operation of their VM systems. By adhering to these guidelines, you can ensure that VMs remain robust, secure, and able to adapt to the needs of your business effectively.

Regular Updates and Patch Management

One of the cornerstones of VM maintenance is the regular application of software updates and patches. This practice is crucial not only for security but also for the functionality of VMs. Employing centralized management tools can streamline the patch deployment process, reducing errors and ensuring consistency. Planning updates during off-peak hours helps to minimize the impact on business operations, maintaining continuity and service availability.

Resource Allocation and Optimization

Effective management of resources is key to avoiding performance bottlenecks and ensuring that VMs function efficiently. Monitoring resource usage allows for real-time adjustments to allocations, ensuring resources are used judiciously and according to actual demand. Tools like VMware's Distributed Resource Scheduler can automate the process of resource balancing, helping to distribute workloads evenly across the host infrastructure.

Backup and Disaster Recovery

Implementing a reliable backup strategy is vital for data protection and quick recovery in case of system failures. Regular backups should be scheduled, and critical data should be stored in secure, offsite locations. It's also important to periodically test recovery procedures to ensure they are effective and can meet designated recovery objectives. While snapshots are useful for capturing the state of a VM at a specific point in time, they are not a substitute for full backups and should be used in conjunction with a comprehensive backup plan.

Security Practices

Securing VMs involves the same level of diligence as securing physical systems, especially since VMs often host critical applications and data. Robust firewall policies and intrusion detection systems should be employed both at the host and VM levels to protect against threats. Segregating sensitive workloads onto separate network segments can also reduce vulnerability and enhance security.

Performance Monitoring and Tuning

Continuous monitoring of VMs helps in identifying and addressing potential issues before they affect operations. Performance monitoring tools can track vital health indicators such as CPU usage, memory consumption, disk I/O, and network activity. Setting up alerts for abnormal activity enables prompt responses to issues, helping maintain system stability and performance. Adjustments to VM configurations may also be required to optimize them for current workloads, ensuring efficient use of resources.

Lifecycle Management

Managing the lifecycle of VMs ensures that resources are not wasted on unused or underutilized VMs. Automating the deployment and decommissioning of VMs helps maintain consistency and reduces the manual overhead involved in these processes. Keeping detailed documentation for each VM, including its purpose, configuration, and ownership, aids in effective lifecycle management and resource allocation.

Maintenance Strategies for Virtual Environments

Regular maintenance is essential for sustaining the performance, security, and reliability of virtual environments. This section outlines the critical maintenance tasks and checks that should be part of an ongoing strategy to manage virtual infrastructures. These practices not only help in preventing potential issues but also ensure that the virtual environment aligns with the evolving needs of the business.

Comprehensive Maintenance Tasks

Maintaining a virtual environment involves a variety of tasks, each designed to address specific aspects of the infrastructure:

Software Updates and Patch Management: Regularly updating hypervisor software and guest operating systems is critical. Updates fix security vulnerabilities and bugs, and enhance the overall functionality of the system. Establishing a routine schedule for updates minimizes disruption and ensures all components are current.

Hardware Checks: Even though the infrastructure is virtualized, physical hardware issues can still affect performance. Regular hardware inspections, including checking server health, storage redundancy, and network connectivity, help prevent hardware failures that could lead to significant downtime.

Performance Monitoring: Continuous monitoring of system performance is crucial. Use specialized tools to track resource utilization, load distribution, and potential bottlenecks. Monitoring tools can often predict issues before they become critical, allowing preemptive action.

Security Audits: Regular security assessments are necessary to ensure that the virtual environment adheres to best security practices. This includes checking for vulnerabilities within the VMs, enforcing strong authentication measures, and ensuring that all network communications are encrypted.

Backup and Disaster Recovery Procedures: Verify that backups are occurring as scheduled and test restore procedures to ensure they are effective. Regular testing of disaster recovery plans is essential to confirm that you can recover data and services promptly after an outage.

Resource Allocation Reviews: Periodically review and adjust resource allocations to ensure they meet the current demands of the applications running in the virtual environment. This dynamic adjustment helps in optimizing resource usage and costs.

Regular Checks for Virtual Environments

To keep the virtual infrastructure running smoothly, certain checks should be performed regularly:

Snapshot Management: While snapshots are useful for restoring VM states, they can accumulate and use significant storage space, potentially degrading performance. Regularly review and manage snapshots, deleting those that are no longer necessary.

VM Sprawl Control: Keep an eye on VM sprawl, where unused or unnecessary VMs consume valuable resources. Regular audits can help identify and decommission these VMs, freeing up resources for other needs.

Log Analysis: Regular review of system logs can provide insights into the health of the environment. Logs can indicate patterns that may lead to potential problems, allowing for proactive management.

Network Traffic Analysis: Analyze network traffic patterns to ensure optimal performance and to check for any unusual activity that might indicate a security issue.

By implementing these maintenance strategies, organizations can ensure that their virtual environments remain robust, secure, and capable of supporting business operations efficiently. Regular maintenance not only extends the lifespan of the infrastructure but also optimizes its performance and cost-effectiveness.

Test Your Knowledge (Chapter 4)

1. What is the primary benefit of IaaS in cloud computing?

A) It provides applications over the internet

B) It offers virtualized physical computing resources

C) It delivers development tools on the internet

D) It manages the network infrastructure

2. In a PaaS solution, what is the client NOT responsible for managing?

A) Applications

B) Hardware

C) Operating systems

D) Middleware

3. Which of the following is a characteristic of SaaS?

A) Customer manages the infrastructure

B) Vendor manages the infrastructure

C) Customer handles backups

D) Vendor provides raw storage

4. Drag and Drop Activity: Arrange the cloud computing models based on the increasing amount of management required by the client:

• Options: IaaS, PaaS, SaaS

5. Which layer of the cloud computing service model interfaces directly with the end-users' applications?

A) IaaS

B) PaaS

C) SaaS

D) None of the above

6. What does virtualization allow one physical server to do?

A) Run a single operating system

B) Function as multiple virtual servers

C) Serve more users than its hardware capabilities

D) Use less power

7. Which of the following is a type of hypervisor?

A) Type 1

B) Type 2

C) Both A and B

D) None of the above

8. Fill-in-the-Blank: _____ is the software that creates and runs virtual machines.

A) Hypervisor

B) Virtual manager

C) OS enhancer

D) Network switch

9. Performance-Based Question: Configure a virtual network setting by selecting the correct sequence of tasks:

• Steps: Assign IP addresses, Set subnet mask, Define gateway, Configure DNS

10. What is the main purpose of a virtual machine in a cloud environment?

A) To increase physical hardware costs

B) To reduce physical hardware utilization

C) To enhance software compatibility

D) To improve hardware efficiency

11. Which cloud computing model provides the most control over software environments?

A) IaaS

B) PaaS

C) SaaS

D) DaaS

12. Which virtualization product is an example of Type 1 hypervisor?

A) VMware Workstation

B) Microsoft Virtual PC

C) VMware ESXi

D) Oracle VirtualBox

13. What major benefit does VM snapshotting provide?

A) Increased storage usage

B) Ability to revert to a previous state

C) Enhanced network performance

D) Reduced memory usage

14. Drag and Drop Activity: Match the following terms with their correct descriptions in virtualization:

• Terms: VM, Hypervisor, Snapshot

• Descriptions: A) Takes a full copy of the VM at a specific point in time, B) Software layer that allows multiple OS to run on hardware, C) An isolated operating environment

15. Which is NOT typically considered a security feature of cloud computing environments?

A) Data encryption

B) Intrusion detection systems

C) Physical security

D) Application rollbacks

Please refer to the "Test Your Knowledge A+ (Answers)" chapter for the answers.

CHAPTER 5

Hardware and Network Troubleshooting

Systematic Troubleshooting Methods

Troubleshooting is both an art and a science, requiring not only technical knowledge but also systematic thinking and a methodical approach. In the context of hardware and network troubleshooting, having a structured process is crucial to identify, diagnose, and resolve issues efficiently. This section introduces fundamental systematic troubleshooting methods that are designed to guide IT professionals through the complex landscape of hardware and network problems.

Systematic troubleshooting involves a step-by-step approach that starts with the most general (and often simplest) solutions and gradually moves towards more specific diagnostics. This method ensures that common problems are quickly addressed without unnecessary effort in unlikely scenarios.

Identify the Problem: Clearly define the problem based on the symptoms observed. Gather as much information as possible from system logs, error messages, user reports, and any changes made to the system prior to the issue.

Establish a Theory of Probable Cause: List the possible reasons for the problem. Start with the simplest explanation—software malfunctions, loose connections—and work up to more complex issues like hardware failures or network bottlenecks.

Test the Theory to Determine Cause: Once you have hypothesized a probable cause, test to see if resolving it corrects the issue. This may involve swapping out hardware components, rebooting systems, or running diagnostic tests.

Establish a Plan of Action to Resolve the Problem and Implement the Solution: Develop a strategy to resolve the issue. This may involve repairing or replacing components, updating software, or reconfiguring network settings. Execute the plan methodically, documenting each step for future reference.

Verify Full System Functionality and, if Applicable, Implement Preventive Measures: After the issue has been resolved, verify that the system is fully operational. Run additional tests to ensure no other issues arise from the changes made. Implement measures to prevent future occurrences of the same problem.

Document Findings, Actions, and Outcomes: Keep detailed records of the problem, how it was diagnosed, the actions taken to resolve it, and the outcome. This documentation can help troubleshoot future issues and be used for training purposes.

Applying Systematic Troubleshooting to Specific Scenarios

Hardware Issues: For hardware problems, start by checking power supplies and cable connections. Test components individually in a controlled environment to isolate the faulty part. Use diagnostic software to run stress tests and monitor hardware health.

Network Issues: Begin with basic connectivity tests using tools like ping or traceroute. Check physical network components such as cables and routers. Review network configuration settings for errors and examine firewall logs for blocked connections.

The Role of Tools in Troubleshooting

Effective troubleshooting is supported by various tools that can simplify diagnostics and provide accurate readings of system health.

Hardware Tools: Multimeters, cable testers, and POST cards.

Software Tools: Diagnostic suites, network monitoring software, and built-in operating system utilities like Device Manager and Network and Sharing Center.

Having established a solid foundation in systematic troubleshooting methods, the next section will delve deeper into troubleshooting specific hardware issues, such as failures in power supplies, memory, and storage devices.

Common Scenarios and Solutions

Troubleshooting is an essential skill for any IT professional. This section focuses on providing practical solutions to some of the most common hardware and network issues that technicians encounter. Each scenario is accompanied by a straightforward explanation and step-by-step resolution guide, making the process accessible even for those new to the field.

Scenario 1: Computer Does Not Start

Symptoms: The computer does not power on when the power button is pressed.

Common Causes: Failed power supply, incorrect power connections, motherboard issues.

Solution Steps:

Check Power Supply: Ensure the power cord is securely connected to both the power supply and the outlet. If possible, test the power supply with a multimeter or swap it with a known working unit.

Inspect Motherboard Connections: Verify that all cables inside the computer, especially those connected to the motherboard, are secure. Look for any signs of damage on the motherboard.

Test with Minimal Setup: Disconnect all non-essential hardware (like external drives and additional RAM) and try to boot again. If the system boots, reconnect devices one at a time to identify the faulty component.

Scenario 2: Intermittent Internet Connectivity

Symptoms: The internet connection drops off periodically.
Common Causes: Router issues, signal interference, ISP problems.
Solution Steps:
Restart Router: Power off the router and modem, wait a minute, and then power them back on.
Check for Interference: Ensure the router is not near other electronic devices that could cause interference. Consider changing the Wi-Fi channel for less congestion.
Contact ISP: If issues persist, check if there are problems with the service provider or if maintenance is being conducted.

Scenario 3: Overheating PC

Symptoms: The computer shuts down unexpectedly, especially during resource-heavy tasks.
Common Causes: Dust buildup, failed fans, poor ventilation.
Solution Steps:
Clean Internal Components: Open the computer case and carefully clean out dust from fans, heat sinks, and other components.
Check Cooling System: Ensure all fans are operational. Replace any failed fans immediately.
Improve Airflow: Reorganize internal cables and ensure the case has adequate space for air circulation.

Scenario 4: Slow Network Performance

Symptoms: Network speed is consistently below expectations across multiple devices.
Common Causes: Bandwidth throttling, network congestion, outdated hardware.
Solution Steps:
Evaluate Network Usage: Check for any applications or devices consuming excessive bandwidth.
Upgrade Network Hardware: If the router or switches are outdated, consider upgrading to newer models that support higher speeds and better performance.
Optimize Configuration: Adjust your router's settings for optimal performance, including QoS settings to prioritize traffic.

Scenario 5: Printer Not Responding

Symptoms: The printer does not respond to print commands from the computer.
Common Causes: Connectivity issues, driver problems, printer errors.
Solution Steps:
Check Connections: Ensure the printer is properly connected to the network or directly to the computer.
Update or Reinstall Drivers: Download the latest drivers from the manufacturer's website or reinstall the current drivers.
Clear Print Queue: Sometimes, a stuck print job can cause issues. Clear the print queue and try printing again.

With a comprehensive understanding of the fundamental troubleshooting approaches for common hardware and network issues, we'll move into discussing best practices for ongoing hardware and network maintenance. This next section will guide you through essential maintenance strategies that prevent these issues from arising, ensuring systems remain operational and efficient

Best Practices for Maintenance

Care to Prevent Issues

Preventive maintenance is a cornerstone of effective IT management, crucial for maximizing the longevity and reliability of both hardware and network systems. By implementing routine checks and timely updates, IT professionals can preemptively address issues that might otherwise lead to costly downtime. This section outlines essential preventive maintenance techniques that foster robust IT operations, ensuring systems are not just reactive to issues but are maintained in a way that prevents them.

Preventive maintenance involves a series of regular examinations and actions that aim to prevent devices from failing. Keeping systems running smoothly and forestalling failures require both attention to detail and regular schedules.

Routine Inspections: Conducting regular inspections of physical hardware for signs of wear and potential failure, such as checking for overheating components, frayed cables, and accumulating dust within computer cases, which can impede airflow and cooling.

Software Assessments: Regular evaluations of software to ensure it operates efficiently, including updates, patches, and necessary upgrades that enhance functionality and security.

Hardware Maintenance Practices

Effective hardware maintenance combines visual inspections with the use of diagnostic tools and software to keep physical devices in optimal condition.

System Cleaning: Dust accumulation can significantly impact system performance and lead to overheating. Regular cleaning, using appropriate tools and techniques, is essential to maintain effective airflow and cooling.

Component Checks: Regular testing of critical components like hard drives, RAM, and power supplies with diagnostic software helps detect early signs of failure.

Update Firmware: Keeping firmware up-to-date can resolve potential hardware issues that impact performance and bring enhancements that extend the hardware's useful life.

Network Maintenance Strategies

Maintaining a network involves not only managing physical devices but also ensuring the software that manages these devices is optimized.

Network Performance Monitoring: Continuous monitoring of network performance using network management tools helps identify and mitigate network bottlenecks or failures before they affect users.

Security Updates: Applying the latest security patches to network devices such as routers, switches, and firewalls is critical in protecting against vulnerabilities that cyber threats could exploit.

Configuration Backups: Regularly backing up network configurations prevents prolonged downtime in the event of device failure, allowing quick restoration of previous settings.

Software and Operating System Updates

Keeping software up to date is as crucial as the maintenance of physical hardware, particularly from a security perspective.

Regular Updates: Automate software updates to ensure that all systems are protected against known vulnerabilities as soon as patches are available.

Virus and Malware Scans: Regular scans for malware and viruses are crucial in maintaining the integrity and security of IT systems.

System Optimizations: Periodic optimization of software settings to ensure systems operate efficiently under changing conditions and requirements.

Documenting Maintenance Activities

Documentation plays a critical role in preventive maintenance, providing a clear record of past activities and insights for future actions.

Maintenance Logs: Keep detailed logs of all preventive maintenance activities, noting what was done, by whom, and when. This documentation is vital for tracking recurring issues and verifying maintenance histories during troubleshooting.

Review and Plan: Regularly review maintenance logs to plan future maintenance activities, ensuring ongoing issues are addressed and systems are updated according to technological advancements.

Having established a comprehensive approach to preventive maintenance, we will next explore Software Update Strategies. This section will delve into the critical importance of keeping software and drivers up to date, a key component of maintenance that ensures hardware and network systems operate at peak efficiency and are protected against emerging security threats.

Software Update Strategies

In the fast-evolving world of information technology, keeping software and drivers up to date is not merely a best practice—it is essential for the security, functionality, and stability of both hardware and network systems. This section addresses the critical importance of regular software updates and provides a strategic approach to managing these updates effectively, ensuring that your IT infrastructure remains robust against operational challenges and security vulnerabilities.

Software updates play a crucial role in IT maintenance, addressing everything from minor bug fixes and performance enhancements to critical security patches that protect against exploitation by malware, ransomware, and other cyber threats. Staying updated is particularly vital in an era where security vulnerabilities can be exploited within hours of becoming publicly known.

Security Patches: These are often released in response to vulnerabilities that could be exploited to gain unauthorized access to systems. Regular updates close these security gaps, making it harder for attackers to penetrate defenses.

Performance Enhancements: Updates can optimize software by improving efficiency and compatibility with other systems, thereby enhancing overall system performance and user experience.

Feature Updates: Beyond security and performance, updates can also deliver new features and functionalities that enhance the capability of software and hardware devices.

Strategies for Effective Update Management

Maintaining up-to-date software across an organization's network can be challenging, especially in complex environments with diverse systems. The following strategies can simplify this process:

Automated Update Tools: Utilize tools that automatically check for, download, and install updates. This not only ensures that updates are applied promptly but also reduces the administrative burden on IT staff.

Patch Management Systems: Implement a patch management system to oversee all updates. These systems can help prioritize updates based on the criticality of the vulnerabilities they address and can manage the deployment of patches to ensure compatibility and minimize downtime.

Regular Scheduling: Establish a regular schedule for updates during off-peak hours to minimize impact on business operations. Ensure that all systems are backed up before applying updates to prevent data loss in case of a failed update or incompatibility issues.

Testing and Validation

Before widespread deployment, particularly for critical updates or in environments with customized systems, testing updates in a controlled setting is crucial.

Staging Environment: Test updates in a staging environment that mirrors the live environment to verify compatibility and functionality without risking the operational system.

Phased Rollout: Implement updates in phases, starting with the least critical systems. This approach allows IT teams to identify potential issues before they affect critical operations.

Documentation and Compliance

Maintaining detailed records of all updates is crucial for troubleshooting, compliance, and auditing purposes.

Update Logs: Keep logs of all updates, including details of the update, systems affected, and the implementation date.

Review and Audit: Regularly review and update policies and procedures to ensure they comply with industry standards and regulatory requirements.

Having established a comprehensive approach to software and driver updates, the next section will focus on Physical Cleaning and Care, detailing the techniques and practices essential for the physical upkeep of IT equipment.

Physical Cleaning and Care

Proper physical maintenance and cleaning of hardware components and peripherals are critical to the longevity and reliability of IT equipment. Dust accumulation, debris, and improper handling can lead to overheating, physical damage, and, ultimately, hardware failure. This section provides comprehensive guidelines on how to clean and care for hardware components and peripherals safely and effectively, helping IT professionals maintain optimal equipment performance and extend its usable life.

Importance of Regular Cleaning

Regular cleaning is essential to prevent dust and debris from clogging and overheating systems. Dust can insulate heat-producing components like CPUs and graphics cards, reducing their efficiency and lifespan. Moreover, clean equipment is less likely to malfunction and presents a more professional appearance in the workplace.

General Cleaning Tools:

Soft brushes or compressed air to remove dust from hard-to-reach areas. Microfiber cloths for wiping screens and surfaces without scratching. Isopropyl alcohol for cleaning contacts and removing grime from surfaces (ensure it is at least 70% concentration for effective sanitization).

Desktops and Laptops:

Power Down and Unplug: Ensure that the device is off and disconnected from any power source.

External Cleaning: Use compressed air to blow dust out of keyboards and ventilation ports. Wipe the exterior with a slightly damp microfiber cloth.

Internal Cleaning: Open the case in a clean, static-free environment. Gently use compressed air to remove dust from internal components, such as the motherboard, power supply unit, and cooling fans.

Printers and Scanners:

Remove Dust and Debris: Regularly open the device and remove paper dust and toner buildup. Use compressed air for hard-to-reach internal components.

Clean Scanning Glass: Use a lint-free cloth slightly dampened with glass cleaner to wipe down the scanning glass, ensuring no streaks or debris remain.

Network Devices:
Keep Cool and Dust-free: Ensure that devices like routers, switches, and modems are kept in cool, ventilated areas to prevent overheating.

Safety Precautions
Static Electricity: Use anti-static wristbands or mats when handling internal components to prevent static discharge, which can damage electronic parts.
Power Safety: Always ensure equipment is powered down and unplugged before attempting any cleaning. This prevents electrical shocks and damage to the components.
Chemical Safety: Use appropriate cleaning agents. Some chemicals can damage plastics or electronic components if used improperly.

Strategies for Preventive Maintenance

Preventive maintenance is a crucial aspect of ensuring the long-term health and efficiency of both hardware and network systems. While basic preventive measures like regular cleaning, software updates, and hardware checks are essential, there are more advanced strategies that can significantly minimize the risk of failures and extend the lifespan of your IT infrastructure. This section will delve into these advanced techniques, offering a comprehensive guide to proactive maintenance.

Predictive Maintenance Using Monitoring Tools

One of the most advanced strategies for preventive maintenance is the use of predictive maintenance tools. These tools monitor the health of hardware components in real-time and use data analytics to predict potential failures before they occur.

For instance, monitoring the temperature, voltage levels, and fan speeds of critical hardware components like CPUs, GPUs, and power supplies can help detect anomalies that might indicate impending hardware failure. By setting up alerts for when these metrics deviate from the norm, IT professionals can take proactive measures, such as replacing a failing component before it causes downtime.

In network environments, similar monitoring tools can track bandwidth usage, latency, and packet loss. These tools can predict network congestion or hardware failures, allowing for proactive adjustments to prevent disruptions.

Implementing Redundancy and Failover Systems
Redundancy is another critical aspect of advanced preventive maintenance. By implementing redundant systems, you ensure that if one component fails, another can immediately take over, minimizing downtime and preventing data loss.

For hardware, this might involve using redundant power supplies, hard drives in RAID configurations, or having backup servers on standby. For networks, implementing failover systems such as redundant links or alternate routing paths can ensure that network traffic continues to flow smoothly even if a primary link fails.

These systems require careful planning and regular testing to ensure they function as intended when needed. Regularly scheduled failover tests can help identify any issues in the redundancy setup and ensure that all systems are prepared for a potential failure.

Automated Maintenance Scripts

Automating routine maintenance tasks is an effective way to ensure consistency and reduce the burden on IT staff. Maintenance scripts can be scheduled to run at regular intervals to perform tasks such as clearing caches, defragmenting hard drives, or checking for software updates.

For networks, automated scripts can monitor and manage configurations, apply security patches, and even reconfigure network devices as needed. Automation not only saves time but also reduces the risk of human error, which can lead to security vulnerabilities or system misconfigurations.

These scripts should be carefully tested and regularly updated to accommodate new software and hardware changes. They should also be monitored to ensure they are performing their tasks correctly and efficiently.

Environmental Control and Monitoring

The physical environment in which hardware operates can significantly impact its longevity and performance. Advanced preventive maintenance includes monitoring and controlling environmental factors such as temperature, humidity, and dust levels.

Data centers, in particular, require precise environmental control. Installing sensors to monitor temperature and humidity levels can help prevent overheating and condensation, both of which can damage hardware components. Air filtration systems should be regularly maintained to prevent dust accumulation, which can clog fans and heat sinks, leading to overheating.

Regular inspections of the physical environment are also essential. This includes checking for leaks, ensuring that cables are properly managed to prevent tripping hazards, and verifying that all cooling systems are functioning correctly.

Proactive Hardware Replacement Cycles

Another advanced strategy for preventive maintenance is the implementation of proactive hardware replacement cycles. Instead of waiting for hardware to fail, which can lead to unexpected downtime, organizations can establish a schedule for replacing components before they reach the end of their expected lifespan.

This strategy requires tracking the age and usage of hardware components, as well as staying informed about manufacturer recommendations and technological advancements. By replacing hardware on a planned schedule, organizations can avoid the sudden costs and disruptions associated with emergency replacements.

Additionally, this approach allows for better budgeting and resource allocation, as hardware replacement can be planned for in advance rather than being an unplanned expense.

Comprehensive Documentation and Maintenance Logs

Keeping detailed records of all maintenance activities is essential for advanced preventive maintenance. Comprehensive documentation allows IT professionals to track the history of hardware and network components, identify patterns of failure, and refine maintenance strategies over time.

Maintenance logs should include information on all preventive tasks performed, the results of monitoring and diagnostic tests, and any repairs or replacements made. This documentation can be invaluable when troubleshooting recurring issues or when making decisions about hardware upgrades or replacements.

In addition to logs, having a well-documented maintenance plan that outlines all preventive tasks, schedules, and responsibilities ensures that nothing is overlooked. This plan should be regularly reviewed and updated to reflect any changes in technology or organizational needs.

Training and Continuous Improvement

Finally, advanced preventive maintenance requires a commitment to continuous improvement and training. IT staff should be regularly trained on the latest maintenance techniques, tools, and best practices. This ensures that they are equipped to handle new challenges and can effectively implement the strategies discussed in this section.

In addition to formal training, fostering a culture of continuous improvement is crucial. Encourage staff to identify areas where maintenance processes can be improved and to share their insights with the team. Regularly reviewing and refining maintenance practices ensures that they remain effective and up-to-date with the latest industry standards.

Automation Tools and Software

In the ever-evolving landscape of IT, the need for efficiency and precision in maintaining hardware and networks is paramount. Automation tools and software have emerged as vital assets in streamlining routine maintenance tasks, minimizing the likelihood of human error, and ensuring that systems remain in optimal condition. This section will explore various automation tools and software solutions available for automating routine maintenance tasks, enhancing efficiency and accuracy in maintaining systems.

Automation in IT maintenance refers to the use of software and tools to execute routine tasks with minimal human intervention. The primary goal is to increase efficiency, reduce errors, and free up IT personnel to focus on more complex issues that require human insight. Automation tools can be employed in various aspects of system maintenance, from software updates and patch management to performance monitoring and data backup.

Patch Management Tools:

These tools automatically apply software updates and security patches to operating systems and applications. Regular patching is crucial for maintaining security and performance, but manually applying patches across a network can be time-consuming and error-prone. Tools like Microsoft WSUS (Windows Server Update Services), SolarWinds Patch Manager, and ManageEngine Patch Manager Plus simplify this process by scheduling and deploying patches automatically.

Backup and Recovery Software:
Automating data backups is essential for protecting critical information and ensuring business continuity in the event of a disaster. Tools like Acronis Cyber Backup, Veeam Backup & Replication, and Commvault offer automated backup solutions that can be scheduled to run at regular intervals, reducing the risk of data loss. These tools also provide automated recovery options, allowing for swift restoration of systems and data.

Network Monitoring Tools:
Network monitoring tools like Nagios, PRTG Network Monitor, and SolarWinds Network Performance Monitor continuously track the health of network devices, servers, and applications. These tools automatically generate alerts when issues are detected, such as network congestion, server downtime, or security breaches, enabling IT staff to respond quickly. Automation in network monitoring also includes automated reports and performance analytics, helping to identify trends and potential issues before they escalate.

System Performance Optimization Tools:
To maintain peak system performance, tools like CCleaner for Windows, CleanMyMac for macOS, and BleachBit for Linux can automate the process of clearing temporary files, optimizing storage, and managing startup programs. These tools help ensure that systems run efficiently by removing unnecessary clutter that can slow down performance.

Security Automation Tools:
Security tools such as McAfee ePolicy Orchestrator, IBM QRadar, and Splunk automate the monitoring of security events, intrusion detection, and the enforcement of security policies. These tools can automatically quarantine infected files, block suspicious network traffic, and generate alerts for potential security threats, ensuring that systems are protected around the clock.

Task Scheduling Tools:
Task schedulers, such as the Windows Task Scheduler or Cron jobs in Unix-like systems, allow IT professionals to automate virtually any script or command-line task. For instance, routine maintenance tasks such as disk cleanup, defragmentation, and system scans can be scheduled to run during off-peak hours, ensuring that they do not interfere with business operations.

Implementing Automation Tools: Best Practices

Start with a Pilot Program:
Before fully integrating an automation tool into your IT infrastructure, it's wise to start with a pilot program. This allows you to test the tool's capabilities in a controlled environment, identify any potential issues, and fine-tune its configuration. Once you are confident that the tool functions as expected, you can gradually expand its use across the organization.

Prioritize Critical Tasks:
Focus on automating tasks that are repetitive, time-consuming, and critical to system performance or security. Prioritizing these tasks ensures that automation delivers the most significant impact in terms of efficiency and risk reduction.

Regularly Review and Update Automation Scripts: Automation scripts and configurations should not be set and forgotten. Regularly review and update them to accommodate changes in software, hardware, and organizational needs. This ensures that the automation remains effective and continues to align with your IT objectives.

Monitor Automated Tasks: Even though tasks are automated, it's crucial to monitor their execution to ensure they are completing successfully. Automated tasks should generate logs or reports that IT staff can review to verify that everything is functioning as intended.

Ensure Data Security and Compliance: When automating tasks that involve sensitive data or system changes, it is vital to ensure that the automation tools comply with your organization's security policies and regulatory requirements. Implementing access controls and encryption within automation tools can help protect against unauthorized access and data breaches.

Case Study: Automating Patch Management To illustrate the benefits of automation, let's consider a case study of a medium-sized organization that implemented automated patch management.

Scenario: The organization struggled with manually applying security patches across its network of over 200 devices, leading to inconsistencies and vulnerabilities. The IT team decided to implement SolarWinds Patch Manager to automate the process.

Implementation: The IT team configured the tool to automatically scan all devices for missing patches every Friday at 2 AM. Patches were then scheduled for deployment the following Sunday at 1 AM, outside of business hours. The tool was set to generate a report of successful and failed patch installations, which was automatically emailed to the IT manager every Monday morning.

Results: Within the first month, the organization saw a 90% reduction in the time spent on patch management. The consistency of patch deployment improved significantly, reducing the organization's exposure to security vulnerabilities. The automated reporting allowed the IT team to quickly identify and address any issues with patch installations, ensuring that all devices were up to date.

Future Trends in IT Automation

As technology continues to advance, so too will the capabilities of automation tools. Emerging trends include the integration of artificial intelligence (AI) and machine learning (ML) into automation platforms. These technologies can enhance predictive maintenance by analyzing historical data to identify patterns and predict potential failures with even greater accuracy. Additionally, AI-driven automation tools can optimize resource allocation, making real-time adjustments to system performance based on current usage patterns.

Another trend is the increasing use of cloud-based automation tools, which offer scalability, flexibility, and ease of management. These tools can manage both on-premises and cloud-based infrastructure, providing a unified approach to automation across hybrid environments.

Congratulations on completing the first part of this comprehensive guide to the CompTIA A+ certification! You have made significant progress in understanding the core concepts of mobile devices, networking, hardware, virtualization, and cloud computing, as well as mastering the essential practices for troubleshooting and maintenance.

As you move forward, I encourage you to take full advantage of the quizzes and practice questions provided throughout this guide. These are designed to reinforce the knowledge you've gained and prepare you thoroughly for the CompTIA A+ exam. Each quiz targets key curriculum areas, ensuring that you are well-practiced and confident in your abilities.

We have now completed Part I of our journey together and are ready to embark on Part II: CompTIA A+ 220-1102 (Core 2). This next part will dive deeper into operating systems, security measures, software troubleshooting, and operational procedures. It's designed to build on the foundation you've established here and expand your expertise into the practical and technical skills required in IT.

Again, congratulations on reaching this milestone. Keep up the great dedication and effort as we continue to explore the exciting world of IT and prepare for the next step in your certification process. Let's move forward with enthusiasm and a strong commitment to excellence in your learning journey!

Test Your Knowledge (Chapter 5)

1. What is the first step in systematic troubleshooting of hardware issues?
A) Replacing the faulty component
B) Identifying the problem
C) Contacting technical support
D) Installing new drivers

2. Which tool is commonly used to diagnose memory issues in a computer system?
A) MemTest86
B) chkdsk
C) ping
D) traceroute

3. When troubleshooting a network connectivity issue, which of the following commands would you use first to check for connectivity?
A) tracert
B) ipconfig
C) ping
D) nslookup

4. Drag and Drop the following steps in the correct order for troubleshooting a system that is not booting:
1. Check the power supply
2. Reset the BIOS
3. Check the boot order
4. Inspect the hard drive

A) 2, 1, 3, 4
B) 1, 3, 4, 2
C) 1, 2, 3, 4
D) 4, 3, 2, 1

5. What is a common cause of overheating in a desktop system?
A) Incorrect BIOS settings
B) Failing power supply
C) Dust buildup inside the system
D) Incorrect hard drive partitioning

6. What is the purpose of using a loopback plug in network troubleshooting?
A) To test the transmission of network data
B) To close the network connection
C) To diagnose issues with the NIC
D) To test the connectivity of the entire network

7. Fill-in-the-blank: The command _____ is used to repair bad sectors on a hard drive in Windows.
A) diskpart
B) chkdsk
C) format
D) defrag

8. Performance-Based Question: Configure a basic wired network. Arrange the following components in the correct order from the ISP to the user's computer:
Components:
1. Router
2. Firewall
3. Switch
4. PC

9. When a system fails to start and displays a series of beeps, what is the most likely issue?
A) Hard drive failure
B) RAM failure
C) Network card failure
D) Power supply failure

10. Which of the following commands would you use to trace the route packets take to a specific IP address?
A) ipconfig
B) tracert
C) ping
D) netstat

11. In a performance-based question, you are asked to resolve a system startup issue where the system displays a "Missing Operating System" error. What is the most likely solution?
A) Replace the power supply
B) Reinstall the operating system
C) Check the BIOS boot order
D) Replace the hard drive

12. Drag and Drop the following components to match their typical failure symptoms with their causes in a system:

1. RAM
2. Hard drive
3. Graphics card
4. Power supply

A) System crashes randomly

B) Display artifacts or no display

C) Continuous reboots

D) Blue screen errors

13. Which of the following tools is most useful when troubleshooting internet connectivity issues?

A) nslookup

B) ipconfig

C) ping

D) traceroute

14. Fill-in-the-blank: The _____ tool in Windows is used to defragment and optimize the file system for improved performance.

A) diskpart

B) disk cleanup

C) defrag

D) msconfig

15. When troubleshooting a network issue, you suspect a problem with the router. Which step should you perform first?

A) Restart the computer

B) Reset the router to factory settings

C) Power cycle the router

D) Replace the router

CompTIA A+ 220-1102 (Core 2)

CHAPTER 6

Operating Systems

Windows OS

Navigating the installation and configuration of Windows operating systems is a critical skill for IT professionals, essential for both personal computing and managing enterprise environments. This section provides a detailed, step-by-step guide on how to install and configure various Windows operating systems, ensuring you are well-equipped to handle one of the most commonly used platforms in the world.

Preparation for Installation

Before beginning the installation process, ensure that your system meets the minimum hardware requirements for the version of Windows you are installing. Common requirements include a compatible processor, sufficient RAM, adequate storage space, and a supported graphics solution.

Hardware Compatibility: Check the compatibility of your hardware with the Windows version you plan to install. This includes ensuring drivers are available for your hardware components.

Backup Important Data: Always back up important data before beginning the installation process to avoid loss of personal or critical business information.

Obtain Installation Media: You can download the installation media directly from Microsoft or use a physical disk or USB drive. Ensure that you have a valid product key if required.

Installation Process

The installation process for Windows can vary slightly depending on the version (such as Windows 10 or Windows 11), but the core steps generally include:

Boot from Installation Media: Insert your installation media and boot from it. You may need to enter your BIOS settings to set the boot order if your machine does not automatically boot from the media.

Begin Installation: Once booted, follow the on-screen prompts to begin the installation. You will choose your language, time, and keyboard preferences.

Enter Product Key: When prompted, enter your product key. For some versions, you can skip this step during installation and activate Windows later.

Select Installation Type: You can choose to upgrade an existing installation or perform a clean install. A clean install is recommended for the best performance.

Partition Your Hard Drive: Decide how you want to partition your hard drive. For most users, using the default partition setup is sufficient.

Format the Partition: Choose to format the partition where Windows will be installed. Be aware that formatting will erase all data on the partition.

Follow Installation Prompts: The installer will copy files and install features and updates. This process can take some time, depending on your system specifications.

Set Up User Accounts: Once Windows is installed, follow the prompts to set up user accounts, including setting up a username and password.

Configure Settings: Configure additional settings such as network connectivity, system security settings, and Windows Update preferences.

Post-Installation Configuration

After Windows is installed, further configuration may be necessary to optimize the operating system for your specific needs:

Install Drivers: Install all necessary drivers for your hardware, starting with chipset, video, and network drivers. Ensure they are the latest versions to avoid compatibility issues.

Install Updates: Run Windows Update to install the latest patches and security updates. This is critical to protect your system from vulnerabilities.

Install Essential Software: Install antivirus software and any essential applications you require for your daily operations.

Customize Settings: Customize your system settings according to your preferences, including power settings, display configurations, and accessibility options.

macOS

macOS is renowned for its intuitive design, robust performance, and seamless integration across Apple devices. Installing and configuring macOS requires an understanding of the unique aspects of Apple's hardware and software ecosystem. This section guides you through the process of installing macOS and setting up the system for optimal use, tailored to both new users and seasoned professionals looking to formalize their knowledge.

Preparing for Installation

Before installing macOS, ensure that your hardware is compatible. Apple provides clear guidelines on which models support different versions of macOS, so check these specifications on Apple's official website.

Check Compatibility: Ensure your Apple hardware is compatible with the version of macOS you plan to install.

Backup Data: Use Time Machine or another backup solution to secure your data before proceeding with the installation, as this will protect your files should anything go awry during the installation process.

Download macOS: macOS can be downloaded from the Mac App Store or via Apple's support website if you are reinstalling the OS on older hardware.

Installation Process

The macOS installation is a straightforward process, thanks to the macOS Utilities tool that guides users through the setup.

Boot Into Recovery Mode: Restart your Mac and hold down Command + R as it boots. This will take you to macOS Utilities, where you can choose to install macOS.

Disk Utility: Before installation, you can use Disk Utility to format or repair your hard drive if necessary. This is crucial if you're doing a clean installation.

Install macOS: Select 'Reinstall macOS' from the macOS Utilities menu. Follow the prompts to select your disk (typically the built-in drive) and begin the installation.

Setup Assistant: After installation, macOS boots into the Setup Assistant. Here, you'll configure basic settings like your region, network, and Apple ID.

Migration Assistant: If you're moving from another Mac or want to restore from a Time Machine backup, you can use Migration Assistant to transfer your data to the new installation.

Post-Installation Configuration

After installing macOS, customize your system to suit your preferences and needs, which enhances both functionality and security.

System Preferences: Navigate to System Preferences to adjust settings like display brightness, energy saver settings, and keyboard preferences.

Security Settings: Configure security settings, including firewall setup and FileVault for disk encryption to protect your data.

Software Updates: Check for software updates in the App Store to ensure all your applications and the system itself are up to date.

Install Essential Apps: Install any applications necessary for your work or personal use, such as office tools, creative software, or communication platforms.

Optimizing macOS

To get the most out of macOS, consider these additional steps:

Trackpad and Mouse: Customize gestures and mouse settings to enhance navigation efficiency.

iCloud Configuration: Set up iCloud to sync your documents, photos, and other data across all your Apple devices.

Accessibility Features: macOS offers a range of accessibility features which can be configured to meet specific needs, enhancing usability.

Now that you're familiar with the nuances of installing and configuring macOS, the next section will guide you through the diverse world of Linux. Understanding Linux will complete your skillset in managing major operating systems, making you a versatile and proficient IT professional ready to tackle a variety of computing environments.

Linux

Linux stands as a powerhouse in the operating system domain, renowned for its robustness, security, and flexibility. It caters to a wide array of users from beginners to seasoned IT professionals. This section provides an overview of popular Linux distributions (distros) and offers practical tips on choosing and installing the right one for your needs.

Linux is unique in that it comes in various distributions, each tailored for specific needs and preferences. Here are some of the most popular ones:

Ubuntu: Known for its user-friendliness and strong community support, Ubuntu is ideal for beginners transitioning from Windows or macOS.

Fedora: With cutting-edge features, Fedora is favored by developers who want the latest technologies in a relatively stable environment.

CentOS: A derivative of Red Hat Enterprise Linux, it offers a robust platform for servers and is highly valued in enterprise environments for its stability and long-term support.

Debian: Known for its stability and security, Debian is a great choice for servers and advanced users who require a reliable system.

Arch Linux: Suitable for experienced users, it allows you to build from the ground up, offering complete customization.

Choosing the Right Distribution

Selecting a Linux distro depends on several factors:

Purpose: Consider what the primary use of the system will be. Desktop users and beginners may prefer Ubuntu or Fedora, while system administrators might opt for CentOS or Debian.

Hardware Compatibility: Check the hardware compatibility for the distro, especially if you are using older or very specialized hardware.

Support and Community: Look for a distro with an active community and good documentation. Forums, wikis, and official documentation are invaluable resources.

Installation Tips

Installing Linux can be an enriching learning experience. Here are some tips to guide you through the installation process:

Prepare Installation Media: Most distros are available as ISO files which you can burn to a DVD or write to a USB drive to create bootable media.

Test Drive with a Live USB: Many distros allow you to boot from a live USB, letting you try the OS without installation.

Partition Your Hard Drive: If you plan to run Linux alongside another OS, partition your hard drive accordingly. Tools like GParted can help manage these partitions.

Follow Installation Instructions: Each distro comes with its own installation instructions. During installation, you'll typically need to set language options, time zones, and create user accounts.

Secure Your Installation: After installing, ensure your system is secure; this includes setting up a firewall, installing updates, and configuring user permissions.

Post-Installation Configuration

Once Linux is installed, configuring it to suit your needs is the next step:

Package Managers: Learn how to use your distro's package manager (APT for Debian/Ubuntu, YUM for Fedora, etc.) to install software.

GUI and Terminal: Familiarize yourself with the graphical user interface (GUI) and the command line terminal. Knowing basic terminal commands can enhance your Linux experience.

System Updates: Regularly check for and apply system updates to keep your system secure.

Configuration and Upgrades

System Settings Adjustments

Optimizing an operating system's performance involves a meticulous approach to adjusting a variety of settings. These adjustments affect the interaction between software and hardware, ultimately influencing the system's efficiency, responsiveness, and stability. This section delves deeper into the specific settings that can be fine-tuned across different operating systems such as Windows, macOS, and Linux, providing a detailed guide to enhance system performance for both beginners and experienced IT professionals.

System settings encompass a wide array of options that manage the core aspects of how an operating system functions and interacts with hardware and software applications. Adjusting these settings can significantly improve the operational efficiency of a system.

Performance Options: Most operating systems offer a balance between visual aesthetics and performance. For example, Windows users can adjust settings for the best performance by reducing animations and shadows, which can free up resources otherwise consumed by graphical effects.

Power Management: Effective power management is crucial, especially for portable devices. Settings like adjusting the screen brightness, setting aggressive sleep modes, and fine-tuning the processor's power state can extend battery life while maximizing performance.

Startup and Recovery: Managing which applications and services run at startup can dramatically reduce boot times and improve system responsiveness. Limiting the programs that start automatically conserves resources for essential tasks.

Performance Settings to Adjust

Virtual Memory Management: In Windows, adjusting the paging file size can be crucial for systems with limited RAM. Increasing the virtual memory can compensate for physical memory shortages, although SSDs should be used to host paging files when available due to their speed.

Resource Allocation: Using system tools to manage which processes can utilize the CPU and how much memory they can consume can prevent resource hogging by less important applications. This ensures that high-priority tasks receive the necessary resources.

Network Settings Configuration: Advanced settings such as adjusting the QoS (Quality of Service) can help prioritize essential network traffic, ensuring that critical applications receive the bandwidth they require for optimal performance.

Step-by-Step Guide to System Settings Adjustment

Accessing System Settings:

Windows: Navigate to 'Control Panel' > 'System and Security' > 'System' > 'Advanced system settings' > 'Settings' under the Performance section.
macOS: Use 'System Preferences' to adjust settings related to energy, display, and accessibility, which can impact system performance.
Linux: Depending on the distribution, graphical tools or terminal commands can be used to adjust system performance settings.

Configuring for Enhanced Performance:
Reduce or disable visual effects that are non-essential. Manage startup applications through system configuration utilities like 'msconfig' in Windows or 'Startup Applications' in Linux. Optimize power settings for performance, particularly setting aggressive CPU scaling policies when under load.

Evaluating the Impact of Changes:
After adjustments, monitor system metrics such as CPU usage, memory utilization, and startup times to gauge the impact. Employ benchmarking tools that provide quantitative data on system performance improvements.

Continuous Monitoring and Updating
Maintaining optimal performance requires ongoing monitoring using tools provided within the OS. Windows Performance Monitor, macOS Activity Monitor, and various Linux system monitoring applications offer real-time insights into system performance and help identify new areas for optimization.

Driver Updates and Management

Understanding the critical role of drivers within an operating system is paramount for any IT professional. Drivers are the software components that facilitate seamless communication between the operating system and the myriad of hardware devices. They are the foundational software that ensures your hardware performs at its peak and is fully compatible with the rest of the system. In this extensive section, we will explore why regular driver updates are essential, and how to manage these updates to maintain or enhance system stability, performance, and security.

Drivers act as translators between your system's hardware and software, allowing for smooth functionality and enabling your devices to perform complex tasks. Without proper drivers, the operating system might not recognize or properly interact with the hardware, leading to suboptimal performance or device malfunction.

Why Regular Driver Updates Are Crucial

Enhanced System Stability: Updated drivers resolve known bugs in previous versions that might cause system crashes or instability.
Optimized Hardware Performance: Manufacturers often release driver updates to improve the efficiency of hardware, offering better speed and output.

Security Enhancements: Updated drivers include patches for security vulnerabilities that could otherwise be exploited to compromise system integrity.

Strategies for Effective Driver Management

Identifying and Cataloging Current Drivers:
Utilize system information tools to audit existing drivers. In Windows, the Device Manager provides a detailed list of all installed hardware and corresponding driver information. In Linux, tools like lshw or lsmod can provide this information.

Regularly Checking for Driver Updates:

Automated Tools: Leverage tools like Windows Update which automatically scan for driver updates, or proprietary software from hardware manufacturers that notify users of available updates.
Manual Updates: For systems where drivers are not managed by the OS, visit the manufacturer's website to download the latest drivers. Ensure you are downloading from reputable sources to avoid malware.

Automating Driver Updates:
Set up automated updates where possible. This ensures drivers are consistently up-to-date without regular manual intervention. Consider using dedicated driver management software that can automate the detection and installation of drivers for multiple systems, particularly useful in an organizational context.

Backup and Recovery Plans:

Implement driver backup solutions before updating. This allows for a quick restoration should the new drivers compromise system functionality. Utilize Windows System Restore or similar features in other operating systems to set restore points before driver updates.

Testing and Performance Assessment

After updating drivers, conduct thorough testing to ensure they integrate well with the system and do not introduce new issues.
Use Diagnostic Software: Run diagnostic tests to ensure all components are communicating effectively.
Performance Monitoring: Monitor system performance logs post-update to check for any anomalies that could suggest issues with the new drivers.
Now that we have covered the vital aspects of driver management, the subsequent section, will guide you through the intricacies of upgrading operating systems.

OS Upgrades Process

Upgrading an operating system is a significant task that can greatly enhance system capabilities and security but requires careful planning and execution to avoid potential pitfalls. This section outlines the steps necessary to safely upgrade an operating system, covering preparation, execution, and post-upgrade activities across various platforms like Windows, macOS, and Linux.

Upgrades can bring enhanced features, improved user interfaces, better security measures, and performance enhancements. However, transitioning to a new version of an operating system must be handled with precision to ensure compatibility and minimize disruption to the user.

Preparation for Upgrade

Compatibility Check: Before proceeding with an upgrade, ensure that your hardware meets the new OS version's requirements. This includes processor speed, memory, storage space, and specific hardware drivers.

Data Backup: Always back up important data. Use cloud services, external drives, or whole system imaging to ensure you have a complete backup of your system before proceeding.

Review Software Compatibility: Some applications may not be compatible with the newer version of the OS. Check software compatibility and prepare updates or alternatives.

Create a Recovery Drive: This is crucial in case the upgrade fails and you need to revert to your old system. Most operating systems provide tools to create system recovery drives.

Executing the Upgrade

Close Applications: Before launching the upgrade, close all running applications to ensure there are no disruptions during the process.

Update Current OS: Ensure your current OS is fully updated to avoid issues during the transition.

Run the Upgrade Installer: Follow the instructions provided by the upgrade installer carefully. This usually involves downloading the OS upgrade from the official website or initiating it through the system's update utility.

Choose the Type of Installation: You may be prompted to choose between a clean install or an upgrade install. An upgrade install typically retains your files and some settings, whereas a clean install will provide a fresh version of the new OS.

Post-Upgrade Process

Check Device Functionality: Once the upgrade is complete, verify that all hardware components are working correctly. Check device manager for any unrecognized devices that might need new drivers.

Install Required Drivers: Install any drivers needed for your hardware to ensure optimal functionality.

Restore Data: If a clean install was performed, restore your data from the backup created prior to the upgrade.

Update Applications: Update or reinstall any essential applications to ensure they work correctly with the new OS.

Monitor System Performance: Keep an eye on system performance in the days following the upgrade. Look for any issues related to startup times, application performance, or system stability.

User Accounts and Permissions Setup

Effective management of user accounts and precise configuration of permissions are critical components of securing an operating system. By establishing structured access controls, organizations can safeguard sensitive information, ensure system integrity, and meet compliance requirements. This section expands on the process of creating user accounts and setting permissions across various operating systems, providing specific instructions and considerations for Windows, macOS, and Linux.

User account management is the backbone of internal security protocols, limiting access to sensitive data and system settings. Proper account settings help prevent data breaches and unauthorized system modifications, which are vital for maintaining operational security and regulatory compliance.

Steps for Creating User Accounts

Windows:
Access the Control Panel, navigate to 'User Accounts,' then select 'Manage Accounts' and click on 'Add a New User in PC Settings.' Opt for either a Microsoft connected account or a local account, depending on user requirements and network settings. Complete the form by providing the necessary user details and setting a strong password.

macOS:
Open 'System Preferences' and click on 'Users & Groups.' Authenticate by clicking the lock icon and entering the admin password. Press the plus (+) sign to create a new account, choosing from options such as Administrator, Standard, Managed with Parental Controls, or Sharing Only, depending on the user's role.

Linux:
Utilize the terminal window for creating a new user with the adduser command (e.g., sudo adduser username). Set a secure password when prompted and fill out any additional information necessary for the new user profile. Optionally customize further configurations by adding the user to specific groups with usermod commands for refined access control.

Setting and Managing Permissions

Permissions dictate what users can do within the system, affecting their ability to view, modify, or delete files and execute programs.

File and Directory Permissions:
Windows: Navigate to the properties of a file or folder, select the 'Security' tab, and modify permissions to define what actions different users can perform.
macOS and Linux: Use terminal commands such as *chmod* for changing permissions and *chown* for changing ownership, specifying detailed access levels with symbolic or numerical values.

Administrative Privileges:
Carefully assign administrative rights to limit who can make significant changes to system configurations. In Windows, manage this via 'User Accounts,' in macOS through 'Users & Groups,' and in Linux by adding users to the 'sudo' group.

Implementing Robust Account Policies

Password Policies: Implement stringent policies enforced through system settings, requiring passwords to meet criteria like minimum length, complexity, and expiration cycles.

Account Lockout Policies: Configure settings to lock user accounts after a series of failed login attempts to defend against brute-force attacks.

Advanced Practices for Enhanced Account Security

Role-Based Access Control (RBAC): Deploy RBAC to align user access rights with their job responsibilities, minimizing the risk of excessive privileges.

Audit and Review: Regularly review user accounts and permissions for anomalies or deviations from established policies, adjusting settings as necessary to address new security challenges.

Building upon solid user account and permission frameworks, the next critical area to address is network-level defenses, particularly through firewalls. In subsequent section, will explore effective strategies to configure and manage firewalls, thereby enhancing the security posture against external threats. This progression ensures a holistic approach to securing both the user environment and network infrastructure.

Configuring Firewalls and Security Protocols

In the realm of IT security, firewalls serve as the first line of defense, controlling incoming and outgoing network traffic based on predetermined security rules. This essential component helps protect operating systems from malicious attacks and unauthorized access. In this section, we will explore effective methods for configuring firewalls and other crucial security settings to ensure comprehensive protection across different operating systems—Windows, macOS, and Linux.

Firewalls can be hardware-based or software-based, each serving the same function but in different layers of the network. They examine network traffic and block or permit data packets based on a set of security rules.

Key Firewall Configuration Steps

Identifying Firewall Needs:
Determine the scope of protection needed based on the network configuration and potential threats. Assess which firewall type best suits your environment: software applications for individual systems or hardware-based solutions for network perimeters.

Setting Up Firewall Rules:
Define rules that specify which traffic to allow or deny based on criteria such as IP addresses, domain names, protocols, ports, and programs. Prioritize rules for effectiveness—more specific rules should come before general ones to ensure precise traffic management.

Testing Firewall Configuration:

Regularly test firewall configurations to prevent unauthorized access while allowing legitimate traffic.

Windows:

Access firewall settings through Control Panel > System and Security > Windows Defender Firewall. Customize inbound and outbound rules to control network traffic. This can include setting up rules for specific programs, system services, or protocols.

macOS:

Navigate to System Preferences > Security & Privacy > Firewall. Enable the firewall and configure settings for specific applications by selecting 'Firewall Options.'

Linux:

Use command-line tools such as iptables or graphical interfaces like *Gufw* (GUI for Uncomplicated Firewall) to set up and manage firewall rules.

Best Practices for Firewall Management

Regular Updates: Keep firewall software or firmware updated to protect against the latest threats.
Comprehensive Logging: Enable logging to monitor denied connections and other firewall activities. This data is crucial for identifying potential attacks or unauthorized access attempts.
Integration with Other Security Measures: Ensure that firewall policies are aligned with other security protocols, such as intrusion detection systems and antivirus software, for layered security.
Security Protocols to Enhance Firewall Efficiency

In addition to standard firewall configurations, implementing robust security protocols is essential for protecting data integrity and privacy.
Encryption Protocols: Use protocols like SSL/TLS for secure data transmission.
Authentication Protocols: Implement strong authentication methods such as two-factor authentication to enhance security for remote access.
Regular Security Audits: Conduct audits to review and improve firewall and security configurations.

OS	Access Path	Key Considerations
Windows	Control Panel > Windows Defender Firewall	Customize rules for applications, ports, and IP addresses
macOS	System Preferences > Security & Privacy > Firewall	Enable and manage application-specific settings
Linux	Terminal using *iptables* or *Gufw* for GUI	Set detailed rules based on IP, port, and protocol

With a solid understanding of firewall configuration and the integration of robust security protocols, we will next explore common software errors and effective strategies to address them. This ensures that users not only have secure access but also a stable and reliable system environment.

Troubleshooting Application Errors

Application errors can range from minor inconveniences to major system disruptions, affecting productivity and user experience. This section delves into common software errors encountered in operating systems like Windows, macOS, and Linux, providing a structured approach to diagnosing and resolving these issues. By understanding these errors and their solutions, IT professionals can ensure systems operate efficiently and reliably.

Application errors often manifest as error messages, crashes, or unresponsive programs. These issues can arise due to various reasons, including software bugs, system resource conflicts, corrupted files, or incompatible hardware.

Types of Common Application Errors:

Crash Errors: The application stops responding and closes unexpectedly.
Runtime Errors: Errors that occur while the application is running, often related to software bugs or issues with the program's environment.
Permission Errors: Errors due to inadequate user permissions that prevent an application from performing certain actions.
Installation Errors: Issues that occur during the installation of software due to corrupted files, insufficient permissions, or inadequate system resources.

Diagnostic Steps for Troubleshooting Application Errors

Error Identification: Read and analyze the error message carefully. It often contains clues about the error cause. Check the application logs and Windows Event Viewer or equivalent in macOS and Linux for detailed error reports.
Software and System Updates: Ensure that the application and the operating system are up-to-date. Developers regularly release patches and updates to fix known bugs.
Permission Verification: Verify that the user account has the necessary permissions to run the application. Adjust permissions if necessary.
Resource Availability Check: Check system resources (CPU, memory, disk space). Close other applications if resources are insufficient.
Reinstall the Application: Uninstall the application, ensuring that all components are removed. Reinstall to a freshly prepared environment.
Dependency Check: Ensure that all dependency applications or libraries are installed and correctly configured.

Advanced Troubleshooting Techniques

Safe Mode Operation: Run the application in safe mode (particularly useful in Windows) to determine if background applications are causing the conflict.
System Restore: If recent changes are suspected to have caused the errors, consider using system restore points to revert to a previous state.
Debugging Software: Use debugging tools to trace the application's operation and pinpoint where the failure occurs.

Error Type	Symptoms	Troubleshooting Steps
Crash Errors	Application closes unexpectedly	Check logs, update software, increase resources
Runtime Errors	Errors during operation, unexpected behavior	Update, debug, check dependencies
Permission Errors	Access denied messages	Adjust permissions, verify user roles
Installation Errors	Failure messages during installation	Reinstall, check disk space, run as administrator

Having addressed common application errors, we'll next explore troubleshooting methods for operating system boot issues. Understanding and resolving these startup problems is crucial as they can prevent a system from loading the OS, thus making it inoperable.

Managing OS Boot Issues

One of the most critical problems users may face with operating systems is boot issues. These problems can prevent a computer from starting up properly, leading to a range of symptoms from 'blue screen of death' (BSOD) in Windows to kernel panic in macOS and emergency mode in Linux. This section will detail common boot issues and step-by-step resolutions to help restore system functionality.

Boot issues can stem from various causes, including corrupted boot files, faulty hardware, incorrect BIOS settings, or damaged software. Identifying the root cause is the first step in troubleshooting these problems.

Common Boot Errors and Their Causes:

Missing Boot Loader: Often due to incorrect BIOS configuration or hard drive failure.
Corrupted System Files: Can occur after failed updates, malware attack, or abrupt shutdowns.
Hardware Failures: Such as a faulty motherboard, RAM, or power supply.

Step-by-Step Troubleshooting Methods

Initial Diagnosis:
Perform a hard reset and restart the computer to see if the issue resolves itself.
Check for any error messages or beep codes during startup, which can indicate specific hardware failures.
Boot in Safe Mode (Windows) or Recovery Mode (macOS and Linux):
Safe mode loads the OS with a minimal set of drivers and can help diagnose issues related to software or drivers.
Recovery mode provides tools to repair and restore your operating system.
Check BIOS/UEFI Settings:
Enter BIOS/UEFI settings during boot (using keys like F2, Del, or Esc) and ensure the boot order is correct and all hardware is recognized.
Repair Boot Files:
Windows: Use tools like Startup Repair from the Advanced options in the recovery environment.

macOS: Use Disk Utility from the Recovery Partition to repair permissions and check the disk.

Linux: Use boot-repair tools or manually reinstall the GRUB bootloader via a Live CD.

Run System Diagnostics:

Many systems have built-in diagnostic tools to check hardware integrity and functionality.

Restore System:

Use system restore points in Windows or Time Machine in macOS to revert the system to a previous state before issues began.

Reinstall the Operating System:

If other methods fail, a fresh installation may be necessary. Ensure data backup before proceeding.

Table of Systematic Boot Troubleshooting Steps:

Step	Action	Tools/Methods Used
Diagnostic	Perform initial checks for error codes and hardware beeps	BIOS/UEFI, System Beeps
Safe Mode/Recovery	Boot into safe or recovery mode to diagnose software issues	F8 or Shift+F8 (Windows), Command+R (macOS)
BIOS/UEFI Settings	Ensure correct boot sequence and hardware recognition	BIOS/UEFI Setup
Repair Boot Files	Repair or replace corrupted or missing boot files	Startup Repair, Disk Utility, GRUB Repair
Hardware Diagnostics	Run tests to check for hardware failures	Built-in diagnostics, Third-party tools
System Restore	Revert to a previous working state	System Restore (Windows), Time Machine (macOS)
Reinstall OS	Perform a clean installation if all else fails	Installation media for Windows, macOS, or Linux

Implementing System Recovery Techniques

In the dynamic world of IT, the ability to quickly and efficiently restore system functionality after a failure is crucial. This section delves into the various built-in recovery and backup features that Windows, macOS, and Linux offer, guiding users through the essential processes and best practices for system recovery. These techniques ensure that users can recover their operating systems and critical data with minimal downtime.

System recovery encompasses a range of techniques aimed at reverting a computer system to a previous, stable state following a crash, system failure, or malware attack. This includes utilizing built-in tools provided by operating systems that can handle everything from minor restore points to complete reinstalls.

System Restore Points (Windows and macOS):

Windows: Uses a feature called System Restore to revert system files, installed applications, Windows Registry, and system settings to a previous state.

macOS: Utilizes Time Machine to automatically back up your entire system, including system files, applications, accounts, preferences, email messages, photos, movies, and documents.

Snapshot and Rollback (Linux):

Many Linux distributions can use tools like Timeshift to take snapshots of the system state, including the system file and user data. These snapshots can be scheduled regularly and used to restore the system to a prior state after a crash.

Recovery Drives:

Windows: A recovery drive can be created to boot the system and restore Windows from a serious error.

macOS: Recovery Mode allows users to repair or reinstall macOS from the recovery partition.

Linux: Live CDs or USB drives can serve as recovery tools, allowing users to boot and repair Linux distributions without affecting system files.

Step-by-Step Guide to System Recovery

Creating and Managing Backup: Ensure regular backups of important data and system settings using system tools or third-party software. Automate backups to reduce the risk of data loss.

Using System Restore or Time Machine: Access System Restore in Windows through the Control Panel or by searching in the Start menu. On macOS, activate Time Machine by connecting an external storage device and following prompts to encrypt and configure backups.

Recovery Drive Creation and Use: For Windows, search for 'Create a recovery drive' and follow the prompts with a USB drive ready.

- For macOS, use Disk Utility in Recovery Mode to reinstall macOS or repair disks.
- For Linux, create a Live CD or USB using tools like UNetbootin or Rufus, ensuring it matches the installed Linux distribution for compatibility.

Restoration Process:

Follow on-screen instructions carefully during the restoration process to avoid further complications.

If possible, restore only essential files and settings to minimize the risk of reintroducing errors into the system.

Best Practices for Effective System Recovery

Regularly Update Backup and Recovery Tools: Keeping your software up to date ensures compatibility and efficiency in restoring your system.

Test Recovery Procedures: Periodically test your backup files and recovery processes to ensure they work correctly when needed.

Secure Backups: Use encryption and secure storage locations to protect your backups from unauthorized access.

With a robust system recovery strategy in place, the next step involves deepening our understanding of advanced security measures and system maintenance techniques.

Test Your Knowledge (Chapter 6)

1. Which of the following is the primary file system used by Windows operating systems?

A) FAT32

B) NTFS

C) EXT4

D) HFS+

2. What is the purpose of the Device Manager in Windows OS?

A) To view and configure hardware drivers

B) To manage installed software

C) To update Windows

D) To configure user accounts

3. During the installation of Windows OS, which partition style is required for booting from a drive larger than 2TB?

A) MBR

B) GPT

C) NTFS

D) FAT32

4. Arrange the steps in order for installing Windows OS on a new system:

    1. Boot from installation media

    2. Choose installation type

    3. Select partition

    4. Configure user settings

A) 1, 3, 4, 2

B) 1, 2, 3, 4

C) 2, 3, 4, 1

D) 1, 4, 2, 3

5. What is the primary difference between macOS and Windows in terms of file systems?

A) macOS uses NTFS, while Windows uses HFS+

B) macOS uses HFS+ or APFS, while Windows uses NTFS

C) macOS uses FAT32, while Windows uses EXT4

D) Both macOS and Windows use the same file system

6. What command in Windows OS would you use to display the directory structure of a drive?

A) dir

B) ls

C) cd

D) pwd

7. In macOS, which utility is used to manage disk partitions and format drives?

A) Disk Management

B) Disk Utility

C) Time Machine

D) Finder

8. Drag and drop activity: Match the operating systems with their corresponding boot loaders:

1. Windows
2. macOS
3. Linux

A) GRUB

B) Boot Camp

C) Windows Boot Manager

9. What does the "chmod" command in Linux do?

A) Change directory

B) Change permissions of a file

C) View running processes

D) List files in a directory

10. Fill-in-the-blank: The primary tool used in Windows to create system backups is called _____.

A) System Restore

B) Backup and Restore

C) File History

D) Task Manager

11. Which Windows feature allows users to manage user accounts and access permissions?

A) Control Panel

B) Task Manager

C) User Account Control (UAC)

D) Registry Editor

12. What tool is used in macOS to create backups and restore files?

A) File History

B) Time Machine

C) Backup and Restore

D) Command Prompt

13. Which Linux distribution is often considered the most beginner-friendly for new users?

A) Arch Linux

B) Debian

C) Ubuntu

D) Fedora

14. What is the purpose of the "sudo" command in Linux?

A) Display system processes

B) Execute commands with elevated permissions

C) Create a new file

D) Delete a directory

15. Performance-based question: Configure user accounts in Linux by assigning appropriate permissions using the "chmod" command. What is the correct syntax to give read, write, and execute permissions to the owner of the file "data.txt"?

A) chmod 744 data.txt

B) chmod 777 data.txt

C) chmod 755 data.txt

D) chmod 700 data.txt

Please refer to the "Test Your Knowledge A+ (Answers)" chapter for the answers.

CHAPTER 7

Physical Security Measures

Securing Devices with Physical Locks

In the realm of IT security, while much focus is placed on digital threats, physical security remains a critical foundation. Effective physical security measures prevent unauthorized access to physical IT assets such as servers, laptops, desktops, and network devices. This section explores various types of physical locks and their applications in securing these devices, providing a crucial layer of protection against theft or tampering.

Physical locks are the first line of defense in securing IT equipment. These locks can range from basic key locks to more advanced biometric and electronic systems, each offering different levels of security based on the environment and the sensitivity of the information stored.

Types of Physical Locks:

Cable Locks:
Widely used for laptops and portable devices. Comprises a cable made from steel and a lock that can be keyed or combination-based. The cable can be secured to a desk or a heavy stationary object, preventing the device from being moved.

Padlocks:
Suitable for securing server racks or storage units. Available in various sizes and security grades, with options for key or combination unlocking mechanisms.

Biometric Locks:
Use unique physical characteristics such as fingerprints or retina scans to allow access. Ideal for high-security areas where access needs to be restricted to specific individuals.

Electronic Keypad Locks:
Require a numeric code for access, eliminating the risk of lost keys but necessitating strict code confidentiality to maintain security. Often used in data centers and server rooms to secure rack cabinets.

Implementing Physical Locks in IT Environments

Choosing the right type of lock depends on several factors, including the asset's value, the potential threat, and the environment in which the device is located.

Risk Assessment:
Evaluate the security risks to determine the appropriate level of physical security measures. High-value devices in public areas may require more robust locking mechanisms compared to those in restricted or monitored spaces.

Installation and Maintenance:
Proper installation is crucial for the effectiveness of physical locks. Ensure that installations are performed by professionals, if possible. Regular maintenance and checks should be conducted to ensure that the locks remain in good working condition and have not been tampered with.

Integration with Other Security Measures:
Physical locks should be part of a comprehensive security plan that includes surveillance, alarm systems, and cybersecurity measures. Coordinating physical security with IT security teams ensures all aspects of asset protection are covered.

Best Practices for Physical Security Locks

Keep an Inventory of Keys and Access Codes:
Manage who has access to keys and codes, and keep a log of check-outs and returns.

Regularly Update Access Codes:
Change codes periodically and following any security breach or personnel changes.

Combine Physical Locks with Other Security Measures:
Use CCTV, security personnel, and intrusion detection systems to complement physical locks for enhanced security.

Secure Access Control Points

In any secure environment, controlling access to sensitive areas is paramount to safeguarding both physical and digital assets. Secure access control points are crucial in preventing unauthorized entry and ensuring that only authorized personnel have access to restricted areas. This section explores the various methods and technologies used to control physical access, offering a robust framework for security professionals. Access control points are locations at which users are granted or denied access to specific areas through the use of mechanical, electronic, or biometric systems. These points are critical in environments such as server rooms, data centers, and offices where sensitive information and valuable equipment are stored.

Types of Access Control Systems:

Mechanical Locks: Traditional locks and keys. Simple, cost-effective but limited in security features and tracking capabilities.

Electronic Access Systems: Use electronic keys, PIN codes, or magnetic cards. Allow for better tracking and can be easily reconfigured as needed.

Biometric Systems: Utilize fingerprints, facial recognition, or retinal scans. Offer high security and ensure that only authorized personnel can access certain areas.

RFID and NFC Systems: Employ radio-frequency identification or near-field communication for access. Common in corporate environments for seamless access control.

Implementing Effective Access Control Strategies

To effectively manage and secure access points, several strategies and components need to be considered:

Layered Security:
Combine different types of access control systems to create layers of security. For example, use a card swipe to enter a building and a biometric scan to access a server room.

Centralized Management System:
Use access control software to monitor entry points, manage permissions, and log access attempts. Ensure the system includes alerts for unauthorized access attempts.

Regular Audits and Updates:
Conduct regular audits to ensure all access points are functioning correctly and security protocols are being followed. Update access rights based on personnel changes and evolving security requirements.

Integration with Other Security Systems:
Combine access control with other security systems such as CCTV cameras and alarms for comprehensive coverage. Integration enhances the ability to monitor and respond to incidents in real-time.

Table: Access Control Technologies and Their Applications

Technology Type	Description	Common Applications
Mechanical Locks	Traditional key and lock systems	Low-security internal doors
Electronic Access	Access cards, keypads	Main building entrances, IT rooms
Biometric Systems	Fingerprint, facial recognition	High-security areas, data centers
RFID/NFC	Wireless access using tags or cards	Corporate offices, restricted warehouses

Securing Wired and Wireless Networks

Network Encryption Techniques

In today's digital age, securing data as it travels across networks is paramount to maintaining privacy and integrity. Network encryption plays a crucial role in protecting data from interception and unauthorized access during transmission. This section explains the essential encryption techniques and protocols used to secure both wired and wireless networks, ensuring that data remains confidential and secure from source to destination.

Network encryption involves encoding data sent over networks so that only authorized parties can read it. This process utilizes algorithms to transform readable data into a secure format that can only be deciphered with the correct decryption key.

Key Encryption Protocols and Their Applications:

Secure Sockets Layer (SSL) and Transport Layer Security (TLS):
Protocols for securing communications between web browsers and servers. They ensure secure browsing, data transfers, and confidentiality.
Applications: Web browsing, email, and any service requiring data to be securely exchanged over a network.

Wi-Fi Protected Access (WPA2/WPA3):
Security protocols and security certification programs developed by the Wi-Fi Alliance to secure wireless computer networks.
WPA3: Enhances Wi-Fi security with features like robust password protection and 256-bit encryption strength.
Applications: Wireless networking in homes and businesses to prevent unauthorized access and ensure data privacy.

Internet Protocol Security (IPsec):
A suite of protocols for securing Internet Protocol (IP) communications by authenticating and encrypting each IP packet in a data stream.
Applications: VPNs (Virtual Private Networks), secure remote access, and network-to-network communications.

Secure Shell (SSH):
A cryptographic network protocol for operating network services securely over an unsecured network.
Applications: Secure remote login from one computer to another, secure file transfer, and remote command execution.

Implementing Network Encryption: A Step-by-Step Guide

Assess the Network Environment:
Determine the types of data transmitted over the network and identify potential risks and compliance requirements.

Choose Suitable Encryption Protocols:
Based on the assessment, select appropriate encryption protocols that match the security level required for your network.

Deploy Encryption Technologies:
Implement tools and software that support the chosen encryption protocols. For instance, install and configure SSL/TLS for a website or set up WPA3 for a Wi-Fi network.

Regularly Update and Patch:
Keep encryption technologies up-to-date with the latest security patches and updates to protect against vulnerabilities.

Monitor and Audit:
Continuously monitor the encrypted traffic for anomalies and perform regular audits to ensure encryption standards are maintained.

Table: Comparison of Network Encryption Protocols

Protocol	Description	Strengths	Applications
SSL/TLS	Secures HTTP connections	Strong privacy and data integrity	Web transactions, email
WPA3	Latest wireless security standard	Improved encryption and user privacy	Wi-Fi networks
IPsec	Secures IP communications	Versatile and highly secure	VPNs, network-to-network links
SSH	Encrypts remote commands	Prevents interception of data	Remote server management

Authentication Protocols

Authentication protocols play a vital role in network security by verifying the identity of users and devices before granting access to network resources. This section outlines various authentication methods used in both wired and wireless networks, explaining how they enhance security by ensuring that only authorized entities can access sensitive data.

Authentication is a security process that verifies the credentials provided by a user or device against an authoritative database. If the credentials match, access is granted. Effective authentication protocols protect against unauthorized access and potential breaches, forming the backbone of secure network communication.

Key Authentication Protocols and Their Applications:

Password-Based Authentication:
The most common form of authentication involves users entering a secret password to gain access.
Strengths: Simple to implement and use.
Weaknesses: Vulnerable to brute force attacks and phishing.

Two-Factor Authentication (2FA):
Combines two different factors: something you know (a password) and something you have (a mobile device or security token).
Strengths: Provides an additional layer of security, making unauthorized access more difficult.
Applications: Online banking, email services, and any application requiring enhanced security.

Public Key Infrastructure (PKI):
Uses a pair of public and private cryptographic keys to authenticate users.
Strengths: Extremely secure, as the private key is never transmitted over the network.
Applications: SSL/TLS for secure websites, secure email, and signing software.

Biometric Authentication:
Uses unique physical characteristics of the user to verify identity, such as fingerprints, facial recognition, or iris scans.
Strengths: Hard to forge, provides high security.
Applications: Mobile device security, access to secure facilities, and high-security applications.

RADIUS and TACACS:
Network protocols that manage authentication, authorization, and accounting for users who connect and use a network service.
RADIUS (Remote Authentication Dial-In User Service): Used for network access or IP mobility.
TACACS (Terminal Access Controller Access-Control System): Often used for device management security on networks.

Implementing Authentication Protocols

To effectively implement these protocols, organizations must:
Assess Security Requirements: Evaluate the sensitivity of the data and the potential risks to determine the appropriate authentication methods.
Deploy and Configure Authentication Systems: Set up infrastructure for chosen authentication methods, such as servers for RADIUS or biometric scanners for biometric verification.
Educate Users: Provide training on the importance of security and how to use the new authentication methods effectively.
Regularly Update and Maintain: Keep authentication systems updated to protect against vulnerabilities and ensure they are functioning correctly.

Table: Overview of Authentication Protocols

Protocol	Description	Applications	Strengths
Password-Based	Uses secret passwords for access	General access across platforms	Easy to implement and use
Two-Factor	Combines two different authentication factors	Enhanced security for sensitive accounts	Adds a layer of security
PKI	Utilizes a pair of cryptographic keys	Secure communications and document signing	High security, privacy ensured
Biometric	Uses physical characteristics	Access to devices and secure areas	Hard to replicate, very secure
RADIUS/TACACS	Network protocols for access management	Network access and device management	Centralized management, secure

Secure Network Configuration

Creating a secure network is critical to protecting sensitive data, ensuring privacy, and maintaining the integrity of IT systems. This section delves into the fundamental practices necessary to configure both wired and wireless networks securely, ensuring they are resilient against cyber threats and unauthorized access.

Secure network configuration involves a combination of strategic planning, implementation of advanced technologies, and continuous management to safeguard against potential security threats.

Effective network security not only prevents unauthorized access but also ensures that the network can withstand and recover from attacks swiftly.

Best Practices for Secure Network Setup

Implement Strong Authentication and Encryption:
Protect data transmissions by implementing state-of-the-art encryption protocols. For wireless networks, Wi-Fi Protected Access 3 (WPA3) offers robust encryption that secures wireless traffic. For websites and web services, HTTPS ensures secure communication over the internet.

Enhance security measures by employing multi-factor authentication (MFA), which requires users to provide two or more verification factors to gain access to the network, significantly increasing security.

Network Segmentation:
Segregate the network into smaller, manageable segments that can contain security breaches within isolated environments. This strategy limits the spread of malicious activities and simplifies the management of security policies. Virtual LANs (VLANs) and network firewalls play crucial roles in directing and controlling the traffic that flows between these segments.

Keep Firmware and Software Up-to-Date:

Regularly update all network devices, including routers, switches, and firewalls, with the latest security patches and firmware updates. This proactive approach addresses vulnerabilities and strengthens network defenses.

Disable Unused Ports and Services:

Minimize potential entry points for attackers by disabling any network ports and services that are not in active use. Keeping the network footprint as small as possible reduces exposure to attacks.

Deploy Intrusion Detection and Prevention Systems:

Install intrusion detection systems (IDS) to monitor network traffic for suspicious activity and potential threats. Complement this with intrusion prevention systems (IPS) that actively block detected threats based on predefined security rules.

Firewall Configuration:

Configure firewalls to meticulously govern both inbound and outbound traffic. Establish strict rules that align with the organization's security policies to effectively manage and control network access.

Network Monitoring and Auditing:

Continuously monitor network traffic using advanced network monitoring tools. This oversight helps to promptly identify and respond to unusual activities or security breaches. Regular audits of network activity logs further enhance security by enabling retrospective analyses that can identify potential security loopholes.

Incident Response Planning:

Develop a comprehensive incident response plan that details actions to be taken in the event of a security breach. This plan should include procedures for quickly isolating affected systems, eradicating threats, and restoring normal operations while minimizing impact on the business.

Implementations in Wired and Wireless Networks

The realm of network security is in constant flux, driven by evolving technologies and escalating threats. Modern network environments leverage a combination of advanced hardware and sophisticated software to protect data and ensure secure communication channels. This section delves into the latest technologies and methods employed in securing wired and wireless networks, highlighting how these innovations fortify network defenses and enhance operational security.

Encryption remains a cornerstone of network security, vital for protecting data as it traverses networks. Recent advancements have seen the development and adoption of more robust encryption standards:

PA3 for Wireless Networks:
As the successor to WPA2, Wi-Fi Protected Access 3 (WPA3) introduces stronger cryptographic protocols to wireless networks. It enhances privacy in open networks through individualized data encryption and robust protection against brute-force attacks by implementing Simultaneous Authentication of Equals (SAE).

Quantum Cryptography:
While still in the experimental stage, quantum cryptography promises to revolutionize network security by using the principles of quantum mechanics to encrypt data. This technology offers potential immunity against the computational power of quantum computers, which could otherwise break traditional encryption algorithms.

Intrusion Detection and Prevention Systems (IDPS)

Modern IDPS are more adept at detecting and responding to threats due to their integration of AI and machine learning technologies. These systems analyze network traffic in real-time to identify patterns indicative of malicious activities and can automatically respond to threats without human intervention.

AI-Enhanced Detection:
By learning normal network behavior, AI-enhanced IDPS can detect anomalies that may signify a security breach, such as unusual traffic flows or uncharacteristically large data transfers, with greater accuracy.

Automated Response Mechanisms:
Some advanced systems can not only detect but also respond to threats autonomously. For instance, they can isolate infected segments of the network, block suspicious IP addresses, or terminate malicious processes automatically.

Secure Access Service Edge (SASE)

SASE is an emerging framework that combines network and security functions with WAN capabilities to support dynamic secure access. It is particularly beneficial for organizations with geographically dispersed locations and remote workforces, as it provides:

Simplified WAN Management:
SASE converges networking and security into a single, cloud-delivered service model, simplifying the management of wide-area networks and reducing complexity.

Enhanced Security Posture:
By integrating services such as SD-WAN, secure web gateways, and cloud access security brokers (CASB), SASE enhances security posture by applying consistent security policies across all access points.

Zero Trust Architecture

The Zero Trust model is a strategic initiative that helps prevent successful data breaches by eliminating the concept of trust from an organization's network architecture. Rooted in the principle of "never trust, always verify," Zero Trust is designed to protect modern digital environments by leveraging network segmentation, preventing lateral movement, providing Layer 7 threat prevention, and simplifying granular user-access control.

Micro-segmentation:
This technique divides security perimeters into small zones to maintain separate access for separate parts of the network. If a breach occurs, micro-segmentation limits potential lateral exploration of networks by attackers.

Least Privilege Access Control:
In Zero Trust, access policies are enforced on a need-to-know basis, which means users are granted access only to the resources they need to perform their duties.

Next-Generation Firewalls (NGFW)

NGFWs go beyond traditional firewall capabilities by integrating additional functionalities such as encrypted traffic inspection, intrusion prevention systems, and the ability to identify and block sophisticated attacks. They are smarter, more flexible, and more comprehensive in their threat detection capabilities, making them a critical component in modern network security strategies.

Deep Packet Inspection:
NGFWs use deep packet inspection (DPI) to look beyond basic header information in packets. By examining the data within the packet, NGFWs can detect, categorize, and stop packets with malicious data before they reach their destination.

Application Awareness:
These firewalls are application-aware, providing insights into which applications are running on the network, who is using them, and the associated security risks. This visibility allows for more controlled and secure management of application usage across an enterprise.

Authentication Methods: OAuth, SAML, and OpenID Connect

In the contemporary digital landscape, securing data and services against unauthorized access is paramount. Authentication plays a crucial role in this security, with methods such as OAuth, SAML (Security Assertion Markup Language), and OpenID Connect leading the charge. This section offers an in-depth analysis of these protocols, detailing their mechanisms, advantages, applications, and how they differ from each other to better inform your security strategy.

OAuth (Open Authorization)
OAuth is an open standard for access delegation commonly used as a way for Internet users to grant websites or applications access to their information on other websites but without giving them the passwords. It acts as an intermediary on behalf of the end user by providing a token to the server, an identifier combined with a secret key.

Key Features and Use Cases:
- **Token-based Authentication:** OAuth uses access tokens rather than credentials to access their data.
- **Delegated Authorization:** Perfect for situations where you need to grant limited access to your server on behalf of a user.
- **Wide Adoption:** Commonly used by major tech companies such as Google, Facebook, and Microsoft for third-party services.

SAML (Security Assertion Markup Language)

SAML is an XML-based framework that allows identity providers (IdPs) to pass authorization credentials to service providers (SPs). What makes SAML unique is its feature of allowing secure web domains to exchange user authentication and authorization data.

Key Features and Use Cases:
- **Single Sign-On (SSO):** Enables SSO to allow users to log in once and access a variety of systems without re-authenticating.
- **Data Security and Integrity:** Utilizes XML encryption and signing to secure data in transit.
- **Interoperability:** Supports cross-domain communication, making it suitable for enterprise-level businesses where numerous applications and systems are in use.

OpenID Connect

OpenID Connect builds on top of OAuth 2.0, allowing clients to verify the identity of the end-user based on the authentication performed by an authorization server, as well as to obtain basic profile information about the end-user in an interoperable and REST-like manner.

Key Features and Use Cases:
- **Identity Layer:** Adds an identity layer on top of OAuth 2.0, providing a standardized protocol for identity verification.
- **JSON Web Tokens (JWT):** Employs JWT for the ID token, providing a compact token format.
- **Mobile Applications:** Extensively used for mobile apps where application clients need to verify the identity of users and retrieve their profile information.

Comparative Analysis

Feature	OAuth	SAML	OpenID Connect
Main Use	Access delegation	Single Sign-On for enterprise	Identity verification
Token Format	Access tokens	XML-based assertions	JSON Web Tokens (JWT)
Deployment	Common in consumer apps	Predominantly used in enterprises	Preferred for mobile and web apps
Complexity	Moderate	High	Moderate
Data Security	Secure token handling	XML encryption and signing	Encryption and signing of JWT
Interoperability	High with multiple services	High within enterprise settings	High across various platforms

In summary, choosing the right authentication protocol hinges on the specific requirements of your security architecture, the nature of the client applications, and the environment in which they operate. OAuth provides broad support for access management across many services, SAML is best suited for enterprise applications requiring high levels of security and complex identity management across systems, and OpenID Connect offers a more streamlined and flexible approach particularly useful in mobile and modern applications. By understanding the distinctions and strengths of each, organizations can better protect their digital assets and user data.

Latest Cryptographic Standards

In the realm of digital security, cryptography stands as the cornerstone of protecting data and ensuring privacy. As threats evolve, so too do the cryptographic standards designed to thwart them. This section explores the latest cryptographic standards and their practical applications in today's security landscape, providing readers with an understanding of how these standards can be deployed to enhance security measures across various platforms.

Cryptographic standards are protocols and algorithms that provide the foundation for securing digital communications and data. They are crucial for authentication, confidentiality, data integrity, and non-repudiation. These standards are continually updated to address new security challenges and to leverage advances in technology.

Latest Cryptographic Standards

Advanced Encryption Standard (AES): AES remains one of the most widely used algorithms for secure data encryption. It is employed in various security protocols, including SSL/TLS for Internet security and WPA2 for securing Wi-Fi networks.

RSA-OAEP (Optimal Asymmetric Encryption Padding): An enhancement of the original RSA algorithm, RSA-OAEP offers improved security by adding padding to the data before encryption, making it more resistant to attacks such as those exploiting the data's predictability.

Elliptic Curve Cryptography (ECC): ECC offers stronger security with smaller key sizes, reducing processing power and bandwidth requirements. It is particularly effective for use in mobile devices and smart cards where computational resources are limited.

SHA-3 (Secure Hash Algorithm 3): As the latest member of the Secure Hash Algorithm family, SHA-3 enhances the robustness of its predecessors by providing resistance to the same vulnerabilities found in SHA-1 and SHA-2.

TLS 1.3: The latest version of the Transport Layer Security protocol introduces streamlined connections, enhanced privacy, and improved performance. TLS 1.3 eliminates outdated cryptographic features and reduces the potential for misconfigurations.

Real-World Applications of Cryptographic Standards

Financial Transactions: Banks and financial institutions leverage these cryptographic standards to secure online transactions and protect against fraud. AES and ECC are extensively used to encrypt transaction data.

IoT Security: As the Internet of Things (IoT) expands, ensuring the security of connected devices is paramount. ECC is commonly used in IoT devices for its efficiency in environments with limited resources.

Secure Communications: Applications like WhatsApp and Signal use end-to-end encryption protocols based on these standards to ensure that only the communicating users can read the messages.

Cloud Security: Cloud service providers implement these cryptographic standards to secure data at rest and in transit, assuring clients that their data is protected from unauthorized access.

E-Government Services: Government portals and services utilize TLS 1.3 to secure communications between citizens and government servers, ensuring that sensitive information such as social security numbers and tax details are transmitted securely.

Implementing Logical Security Concepts

Effective Password Management

In the realm of network security, passwords stand as the first line of defense, protecting sensitive data from unauthorized access. The strength and management of these passwords are paramount to ensuring that this line of defense holds firm against potential security breaches. This section outlines robust strategies for crafting and maintaining secure passwords, thereby enhancing the overall security posture of an organization.

Passwords act as gatekeepers to vast stores of information and access points within networks. The creation, handling, and storage of these passwords are therefore critical components of a security strategy, requiring careful attention and stringent controls to prevent unwanted access.

Creating Strong Passwords

To create a strong password, consider the following guidelines, which combine complexity and memorability:

Length and Complexity: Opt for passwords that are at least 12-16 characters long and include a mix of uppercase and lowercase letters, numbers, and special symbols. The greater the complexity and length, the harder the password is to crack.

Avoid Common Pitfalls: Steer clear of common passwords such as "password," "123456," or "qwerty." These are easily guessable and often the first targets during brute force attacks.

Use Passphrases: Construct passphrases that are easy to remember but hard for others to guess. For example, a phrase like "Time flies over us but leaves its shadow behind" could be transformed into "Tfoubl!tsb_1821", incorporating symbols and numbers to increase complexity.

Managing Passwords Effectively

Effective password management is crucial for maintaining the security integrity of an organization. Implement the following practices to ensure that passwords provide the intended level of security:

Regular Updates: Encourage or mandate regular password changes, ideally every 90 days, to mitigate the risks of long-term exposure from possibly compromised credentials.

Unique Passwords for Different Accounts: Avoid using the same password across multiple platforms or accounts. This practice helps contain the damage to a single account if a password is compromised.

Employ Password Managers: Utilize reliable password managers to generate, retrieve, and store complex passwords. These tools help in managing a plethora of strong passwords without the risk of forgetting them.

Educate and Train: Regularly conduct training sessions to educate employees about the importance of password security, the methods of creating strong passwords, and the best practices for managing them securely.

Advanced Tips for Password Security

To further bolster password security, consider integrating the following advanced measures:

Two-Factor Authentication (2FA): Implement 2FA wherever possible to add an additional layer of security. This method requires a second form of identification, which significantly reduces the risk of unauthorized access.

Audit and Compliance Checks: Regularly perform audits to check the strength and compliance of passwords within the organization. Use tools that can analyze password strength and enforce compliance with security policies.

Incident Response for Breached Passwords: Develop and implement a clear incident response strategy for situations where password breaches occur. This should include immediate password resets and potentially broader security assessments to prevent further intrusions.

While effective password management forms a critical barrier against unauthorized access, evolving security challenges demand more sophisticated measures. The next section explores how the implementation of two-factor authentication for enhanced security.

Two-factor Authentication

Two-factor Authentication (2FA) represents a critical enhancement in security protocols, significantly bolstering defenses against unauthorized access. By requiring two distinct forms of identification before granting access, 2FA minimizes the risk associated with compromised passwords and enhances the overall security posture of an organization. This section delves into the benefits and practical implementation of 2FA, providing a comprehensive guide to adopting this essential security measure. Two-factor Authentication adds an extra layer of security by using two different types of identification:

Something You Know: This could be a password, PIN, or another piece of information that only the user knows.

Something You Have: This is often a physical device, such as a smartphone app that generates a time-sensitive code, a security token, or a smart card.

By combining these two factors, the security of user accounts and sensitive data is significantly enhanced, as both elements would need to be compromised for an unauthorized access to occur.

Benefits of Two-factor Authentication

Enhanced Security: The primary benefit of 2FA is the significant increase in account security. Even if a password is stolen or hacked, unauthorized access is unlikely without the second factor.

Reduced Fraud and Data Theft: By adding an extra layer of security, 2FA helps reduce the risk of fraud and data breaches, protecting both user data and organizational resources.

Increased Trust: Organizations that implement 2FA are often viewed as more secure, increasing trust among customers, clients, and partners.

Regulatory Compliance: Many industries have regulations that either recommend or require 2FA to ensure better protection of sensitive information.

Implementing Two-factor Authentication

The implementation of 2FA involves several critical steps that ensure both effectiveness and user compliance:

Choose the Right 2FA Method: Select a 2FA method that best suits the organization's needs and is convenient for users. Common methods include SMS codes, authentication apps, and hardware tokens.

Educate and Train Users: Proper training and education are crucial for ensuring that all users understand how to use 2FA and why it's important. This reduces resistance and increases adoption rates.

Integrate with Existing Security: Seamlessly integrate 2FA with existing security measures without compromising user experience or system integrity.

Regular Testing and Updates: Regularly test the 2FA setup to ensure it works correctly and update it as needed to deal with new security threats or software updates.

Challenges and Considerations

While 2FA provides substantial security benefits, it is not without challenges:

User Inconvenience: Some users may find 2FA methods cumbersome, especially if they require additional hardware or frequent access.

Dependency on Physical Devices: Methods that rely on hardware tokens or mobile phones can face issues if the device is lost, stolen, or malfunctions.

Technical Complexity: Setting up and maintaining 2FA systems can be technically challenging and may require additional resources.

As technology evolves, so do the methods attackers use to breach systems. While 2FA is an effective security measure, it is part of a broader strategy that includes physical security, cybersecurity, and operational protocols.

Recent Advancements in Multi-Factor Authentication Technologies

In the ever-evolving landscape of cybersecurity, Multi-Factor Authentication (MFA) continues to be a critical defense mechanism against unauthorized access and data breaches. MFA, which requires users to provide two or more verification factors to gain access to a resource, has seen significant technological advancements aimed at enhancing security without compromising user convenience. This section explores the latest developments in MFA technologies, detailing how they integrate into modern security infrastructures to provide robust protection against increasingly sophisticated threats.

Multi-factor authentication has expanded beyond the traditional knowledge, possession, and inherence factors to include more dynamic and adaptive methods. These advancements address the growing need for stronger security in personal and enterprise environments due to the rise in remote work and mobile access.

Latest Developments in MFA

Biometric Authentication Improvements: Modern MFA systems increasingly leverage biometric factors, such as facial recognition, fingerprint scans, and voice recognition, which offer a high level of security due to their uniqueness to each individual. Enhanced algorithms and sensors have improved the accuracy and speed of biometric verification, reducing false rejections and enhancing user experience.

Behavioral Biometrics: This new frontier in authentication technology analyzes patterns in user behavior such as keystroke dynamics, mouse movements, and even walking patterns. By continuously authenticating users based on their behavior, systems can detect anomalies that may indicate unauthorized access attempts, providing a seamless yet secure user experience.

Location-Based Authentication: Integrating location as a factor in MFA, where access is granted or denied based on the geographic location of the user, has seen increased adoption. This method utilizes GPS and IP address data to create geofencing protocols that enhance security for remote access scenarios.

Time-Based Restrictions: Coupling MFA with time-based controls offers an additional layer of security, limiting access to sensitive systems and data to specific times of the day or specific durations, minimizing the window of opportunity for attackers.

Adaptive Authentication: This approach uses a risk-based analysis to determine the level of authentication required. Factors such as the user's location, device security status, network security level, and time of access request are considered to dynamically adjust the authentication requirements, providing stronger security for higher-risk scenarios.

Real-World Applications of Advanced MFA

Financial Services: Banks and financial institutions employ advanced MFA to secure transactions and protect customer data, integrating biometrics and behavioral analytics to detect and prevent fraud.

Healthcare: In healthcare settings, where data sensitivity is paramount, advanced MFA methods are used to ensure that only authorized personnel can access patient records, particularly when accessing records remotely.

Government Services: Government agencies implement robust MFA protocols to protect critical infrastructure and sensitive data from cyber threats, often using a combination of biometric data and adaptive authentication techniques.

Education Sector: With the rise of digital learning platforms, educational institutions are adopting MFA to secure access to student and faculty accounts, safeguarding personal information and academic integrity.

Malware and Virus Mitigation Techniques

Antivirus Software Utilization

In the digital landscape, where threats evolve rapidly, antivirus software remains a fundamental tool in the cybersecurity arsenal. Effective use of antivirus software not only prevents the infiltration of malware but also plays a crucial role in the ongoing battle against emerging threats. This section explores how to select and optimally use antivirus software to safeguard information systems from malware and viruses.

Antivirus software serves as the first line of defense against malicious software that can compromise system integrity and security. It scans, detects, and removes viruses before they can inflict damage. Beyond just protecting against viruses, modern antivirus solutions are designed to combat a wide range of threats, including worms, spyware, adware, ransomware, and more.

Criteria for Choosing Antivirus Software

Selecting the right antivirus software involves considering several factors to ensure comprehensive protection:

Detection Rate:
Opt for software with a high detection rate, which indicates its effectiveness in identifying and neutralizing threats. Reputable industry tests and reviews can provide insights into the detection capabilities of various antivirus programs.

System Impact:

Evaluate the software's impact on system performance. The best antivirus programs provide robust protection without significantly slowing down the computer or network.

Feature Set:

Assess the features offered by the antivirus software. Look for functionalities beyond basic virus scanning, such as phishing protection, firewall integration, behavior-based detection, and system optimization tools.

User Interface and Usability:

Choose software that offers a user-friendly interface and easy-to-navigate controls. This ensures that all users, regardless of technical proficiency, can effectively manage their security settings.

Support and Documentation:

Ensure that there is adequate support available, including customer service, online resources, and comprehensive user manuals. Good support can be crucial in resolving issues that arise during the software's use.

Effective Usage of Antivirus Software

To maximize the benefits of antivirus software, it is essential to use it properly:

Regular Updates:

Keep the antivirus software up to date to ensure it can protect against the latest threats. Most antivirus programs offer automatic update features; ensure these are activated.

Real-time Protection:

Enable real-time protection, which allows the software to continuously scan and monitor the system for threats as they occur, providing immediate defense against malware.

Scheduled Scans:

Set up scheduled scans to regularly check the system for viruses and other malware. These scans can be set to run during off-peak hours to minimize their impact on system performance.

Safe Browsing Practices:

Combine the use of antivirus software with safe browsing habits. Avoid downloading files from unknown or untrusted sources, and be cautious with email attachments and links.

Backup and Recovery:

Use antivirus software in conjunction with a robust backup system. Regular backups can restore data during a malware attack, reducing potential losses.

Integrating Antivirus Solutions in a Comprehensive Security Strategy

While antivirus software is indispensable, it is just one part of a comprehensive security strategy. Integrating antivirus defenses with other security measures such as firewalls, two-factor authentication, and encryption creates a multi-layered defense system that significantly enhances overall security.

The focus will shift from traditional antivirus solutions to comprehensive anti-malware strategies as we move forward. The following section will explore advanced methods and tools designed to detect and neutralize a broader spectrum of malicious software, providing a deeper layer of security for increasingly complex threats. This progression ensures that the security measures are robust, adaptive, and capable of handling current and emerging digital threats.

Anti-Malware Tools and Techniques

In the digital age, the threat landscape is continually evolving, making robust anti-malware strategies a cornerstone of any comprehensive cybersecurity plan. Malware, which encompasses a variety of malicious software designed to harm or exploit any programmable device, network, or service, continues to pose significant challenges to cybersecurity professionals. This section elaborates on advanced tools and methods to effectively combat these threats, ensuring the integrity and security of IT environments.

Understanding the various forms of malware, including viruses, worms, trojans, ransomware, and spyware, is foundational to developing effective mitigation strategies. Each type has unique characteristics and behaviors that dictate the necessary defensive measures. For instance, ransomware encrypts a user's data and demands payment for the decryption key, while spyware covertly gathers user information without their knowledge. Recognizing these patterns helps in tailoring specific anti-malware defenses.

Anti-Malware Tools

Comprehensive Antivirus Solutions:
Modern antivirus programs do more than scan for known viruses; they provide holistic protection against a range of malware by employing real-time detection, heuristic analysis to catch previously unknown threats, and automatic updates to stay abreast of the latest malware definitions.

Endpoint Protection Suites:
These are advanced platforms combining several security technologies to protect endpoints such as desktops, laptops, and mobile devices from malware, offering features like firewall protection, application control, and data encryption.

Network Firewalls:
Firewalls control the incoming and outgoing network traffic based on security rules, forming a barrier against cyber threats trying to access the network through the internet.

Intrusion Detection and Prevention Systems (IDPS):
These tools not only detect malicious activities on the network but also take preventive actions to stop the threat from spreading or causing damage.

Strategic Implementation of Anti-Malware Techniques

To ensure effective malware mitigation, a strategic approach encompassing various layers of defense is essential:

Proactive Software Management:
Regularly updating and patching software to close security gaps that could be exploited by malware. This includes operating systems, applications, and all types of software used within the organization.

Routine Security Assessments:
Conducting thorough scans of the IT environment to identify vulnerabilities and ensure that all systems are adequately protected against known threats.

User Education and Awareness:
Training users to recognize suspicious emails, links, and online behavior that may lead to malware infections. Empowering users to be the first line of defense can significantly reduce the risk of malware entering the system.

Isolation of Infected Systems:
Implementing protocols to quickly isolate devices suspected of being compromised to prevent the spread of malware to interconnected systems.

Robust Backup Solutions:
Maintaining regular backups of critical data and ensuring they are stored securely. In the event of a malware attack, particularly ransomware, the ability to restore data from backups is invaluable.

Integrating Anti-Malware Tactics into Broader Security Policies

To effectively combat malware, these tools and strategies must be seamlessly integrated into the broader organizational security policies. This integration should encompass setting up regular updates, mandating comprehensive security audits, and establishing clear communication channels for reporting potential security breaches.

Advancing from foundational anti-malware measures to specific browsing safety protocols, the forthcoming section, will outline essential tactics for navigating the web securely. This progression ensures not only individual device safety but also the protection of the broader network environment, fortifying defenses against increasingly sophisticated cyber threats.

Safe Browsing Practices

The internet, while an indispensable resource, presents a myriad of security risks that can compromise personal and organizational safety. This section details essential safe browsing practices that can significantly mitigate the risk of malicious attacks. By understanding and implementing these strategies, users can protect their data and maintain privacy across various online platforms.

Safe browsing extends beyond the basic security measures of installing antivirus software. It encompasses a set of practices designed to minimize exposure to harmful content and prevent unauthorized access to your data:

Update and Patch Regularly:
Ensure that your browser and any plug-ins are always up-to-date with the latest security patches. Developers frequently update software to patch vulnerabilities that could be exploited by attackers.

Use Secure Connections:
Always look for a secure connection (HTTPS) when visiting websites. HTTPS ensures that the data sent and received is encrypted, providing a secure barrier against eavesdropping and content tampering.

Enable Privacy Settings:

Adjust the privacy settings on your browser to limit tracking and data sharing. Consider using privacy-focused browsers or extensions that block trackers and intrusive ads.

Be Cautious with Downloads:

Avoid downloading files from unknown or untrusted sources. Malware can be disguised as legitimate software, leading to severe security breaches.

Beware of Phishing Attacks:

Stay vigilant about phishing techniques. Phishing emails or messages often mimic legitimate sources to steal personal information. Always verify the authenticity of requests for personal information.

Advanced Browsing Security Techniques

To further enhance your online security posture, consider the following advanced techniques:

Use a Virtual Private Network (VPN):

A VPN encrypts your internet traffic, hiding your browsing activity from potential eavesdroppers on the same network. This is particularly important when using public Wi-Fi networks.

Employ Content Blockers:

Use ad blockers and script blockers to prevent malicious scripts and ads from running on your browser. Many malware infections stem from malicious ads or compromised websites.

Securely Manage Passwords:

Utilize a reputable password manager to generate and store complex passwords. Password managers can help you maintain a unique password for each site, significantly reducing the risk of credential compromise.

Educate on Social Engineering Tactics:

Regular training on recognizing social engineering attacks can empower users to make safer decisions online, particularly in recognizing suspicious emails, links, and web requests.

Implementing and Maintaining Safe Browsing Habits

Creating a culture of security-first browsing within an organization involves:

Regular Training Sessions:

Conducting ongoing education and training sessions to keep all users informed about the latest browsing safety tips and cyber threats.

Policy Development and Enforcement:

Developing and strictly enforcing a comprehensive internet usage policy that includes guidelines for safe browsing practices.

Monitoring and Reporting:

Implementing tools and procedures to monitor network traffic and quickly identify potential threats. Encourage users to report suspicious activities immediately.

Test Your Knowledge (Chapter 7)

1. **Which type of physical lock is typically used to prevent theft of laptops in public places?**
   A) Combination lock
   B) Kensington lock
   C) Deadbolt lock
   D) Padlock

2. **Which of the following is a common method used to control physical access to data centers?**
   A) RFID badges
   B) CCTV cameras
   C) Firewalls
   D) Antivirus software

3. **Which type of surveillance system allows for real-time monitoring of multiple areas within a facility?**
   A) Keycard system
   B) Biometric scanner
   C) CCTV
   D) Alarm system

4. **Which is NOT an example of a secure access control method?**
   A) Smart card
   B) Username and password
   C) Unencrypted guest Wi-Fi access
   D) Biometric scanning

5. **Which of the following can help protect sensitive areas from unauthorized access?**
   A) Proximity cards
   B) Software firewalls
   C) USB encryption
   D) Wireless networks

6. **Which of the following technologies is most commonly used to manage user authentication in a secure facility?**
   A) Multi-factor authentication
   B) Dynamic IP addresses
   C) VPN tunneling
   D) Public key encryption

7. **What is the primary purpose of a biometric access control system?**
   A) To monitor internet activity
   B) To control access using unique physical traits
   C) To provide cloud storage for sensitive data
   D) To enhance firewall capabilities

8. **Arrange the following security measures in the correct sequence for accessing a secured server room:**
   1. Enter building and pass through biometric scanner
   2. Swipe proximity badge at the data center entrance
   3. Use a physical key to enter the server room
   4. Swipe RFID keycard at the main entrance

9. **Which type of authentication method is based on a user's fingerprint, facial recognition, or retina scan?**
   A) Two-factor authentication

B) Password management

C) Biometric authentication

D) Smart card

10. **Which of the following is an advantage of using CCTV in physical security?**

    A) Preventing unauthorized access

    B) Storing sensitive information

    C) Real-time surveillance and deterrence

    D) Managing network security

11. **Which of the following represents a form of logical access control?**

    A) Password

    B) Door lock

    C) Security camera

    D) Key fob

12. **Fill in the blank: The primary purpose of _____ is to ensure only authorized personnel can physically access sensitive areas.**

    A) VPN

    B) Physical access controls

    C) Email encryption

    D) Firewall

13. **Which of the following is considered a multi-factor authentication method?**

    A) Username and password

    B) Fingerprint and smart card

    C) Email address and password

    D) CAPTCHA

14. **Which method provides the highest level of security for physical access to a data center?**

    A) Password-protected doors

    B) Multi-factor authentication with biometric and smart card access

    C) Firewall with guest access

    D) Simple key entry

15. **Performance-Based Question: Configure the correct access control by dragging the following methods into the appropriate security category (physical or logical):**

    Methods:
    - Password
    - Biometric scanner
    - CCTV
    - Keycard

Please refer to the "Test Your Knowledge A+ (Answers)" chapter for the answers.

CHAPTER 8

Software Troubleshooting

Using Crash Logs for Diagnosis

Crash logs are vital tools in diagnosing and understanding the reasons behind software malfunctions and system crashes. They provide a detailed record of what the system was doing at the time of the crash, making them indispensable for troubleshooting issues efficiently. This section will guide you through interpreting crash logs to identify and resolve problems effectively.

Crash logs, often generated automatically by operating systems upon encountering a failure, contain data about the software or system state at the moment of the crash. This information typically includes the date and time of the incident, the processes running, and the specific error codes involved. By analyzing these logs, technicians can trace the root cause of a problem without needing to replicate the user's actions at the time of the crash.

Steps to Effectively Use Crash Logs for Troubleshooting

Locating Crash Logs: On Windows systems, crash logs can be accessed through the Event Viewer. On macOS, you can find them using the Console app. For Linux, system logs are typically located in /var/log.

Reading the Logs: Focus on the timestamp, the error message, and the modules or drivers involved. Key details often include Exception Codes on Windows or Traceback errors on Linux.

Identifying Patterns: Look for recurring patterns in the logs if multiple crashes have occurred. Commonalities in error codes or affected modules can point to systemic issues with specific software or hardware components.

Researching Error Codes and Messages: Use the specific error codes and messages to search for solutions online. Manufacturers' forums, tech support sites, and IT communities are invaluable resources for finding others who have resolved similar issues.

Using Logs to Guide Repairs: Apply the insights gained from the logs to implement fixes—whether updating drivers, patching software, or changing configuration settings.

Best Practices for Maintaining and Analyzing Crash Logs

Regular Monitoring: Set up regular reviews of system logs to catch issues before they lead to crashes.

Automated Analysis Tools: Utilize tools that can automate the analysis of crash logs to quickly identify common issues and solutions.

Training: Ensure IT staff are trained in the latest diagnostic techniques and understand how to interpret and act on the information contained within crash logs.

Incorporating Log Analysis into Troubleshooting Protocols

Effective troubleshooting protocols include proactive log analysis to prevent issues from recurring. Integrating log analysis into regular maintenance schedules ensures that systems remain stable and can prevent downtime. **Documentation:** Maintain records of the crashes and their analyses to aid in future troubleshooting and to provide a basis for improving system stability.

Example: How to Read and Use Crash Logs to Troubleshoot

Let's walk through a practical example of using crash logs to troubleshoot an application crash on a Windows system, using a structured approach with each step detailed in a table format. This method provides a clear and organized way to navigate through the troubleshooting process.

Step 1: Accessing the Crash Logs

Action	Description
Open Event Viewer	Press Windows + R, type eventvwr.msc, and press Enter.
Navigate to Logs	Click on "Windows Logs", then select "Application".
Filter for Errors	Click on "Filter Current Log", check "Error" under "Event level".

Step 2: Identifying the Relevant Log Entries

Action	Description
Locate Errors	Look for error entries related to "ExampleApp" around the time of the crash.
Examine Details	Double-click on entries to view detailed information about the crash.

Example Error Log Entry Details

Log Information	Details
Application Name	ExampleApp.exe
Version	1.2.3.4
Module Name	ExampleModule.dll
Module Version	1.0.0.1
Exception Code	0xc0000005 (Access Violation)
Fault Offset	0x0001a2b3
Process ID	0x1234
Application Path	C:\Program Files\ExampleApp\ExampleApp.exe
Module Path	C:\Program Files\ExampleApp\ExampleModule.dll
Report ID	12345678-1234-5678-1234-56789abcdefg

Step 3: Analyzing the Crash Log Details

Action	Description
Exception Analysis	The code 0xc0000005 indicates an access violation, suggesting a read or write to protected memory.
Faulting Module	Identifies "ExampleModule.dll" as the problematic component causing the crash.

Step 4: Research and Solution

Action	Description
Online Research	Search for the exception code and module name for known fixes.
Check for Updates	Visit the official support page for any patches or updates.
Reinstall Module	If necessary, reinstall the module or application to fix corrupt files.

Step 5: Testing the Fix

Action	Description
Restart Application	After applying the fix, restart the application to ensure the issue is resolved.
Monitor Performance	Keep an eye on the application's performance to ensure no recurrence of the issue.

Documentation

Action	Description
Record Steps	Document each step from accessing logs to applying fixes for future reference.

This table-driven approach clarifies each step of the troubleshooting process and ensures that each action is methodically planned and executed, thereby increasing the effectiveness of the troubleshooting efforts.

System Restore and Recovery Options

Navigating through system failures and malfunctions requires a solid understanding of system restore and recovery options. This section explores various techniques and tools that IT professionals can utilize to efficiently restore operating systems to a fully functional state after disruptions such as malware attacks, system failures, or corrupt installations.

System restoration involves reverting a device's operating system to a previous state where it was functioning optimally, without errors. This is crucial for mitigating issues that cause system instability or data loss.

Techniques for System Restoration

System Restore Points:

Creation and Management: It is best practice to create system restore points before implementing significant system changes or updates. This proactive step ensures that there is a recent, reliable restore point to revert to if new changes cause issues.

Restoration Process: Most modern operating systems, like Windows and macOS, incorporate a system restore feature that allows users to select a restore point and revert the system settings, installed applications, and drivers to that particular snapshot without affecting personal files.

System Image Backups:

Creating System Images: System images are comprehensive backups that include a copy of all system files, settings, programs, and files at the time of the backup. Regularly scheduled system image creation is recommended as it provides a recovery option that is far more encompassing than basic restore points.

Restoration from Image: In the event of severe system corruption or hard drive failure, restoring from a system image can return the entire system to the state captured in the image, which includes the operating system, installed applications, system settings, and all user data.

Recovery Partitions:

Accessing Recovery Partition: Many computers come with a factory-installed recovery partition by the manufacturer, which can be used to reset the system to factory settings—a useful feature when dealing with pervasive system issues.

Using Recovery Drives: Creating a recovery drive that includes system repair and recovery tools is essential for situations where the system cannot boot. This drive can facilitate a startup repair, a complete restore, or provide access to a command prompt for advanced recovery operations.

Tools for System Recovery

Windows Recovery Environment (WinRE): This toolset is crucial for Windows systems, offering options like system restore, command prompt access, system image recovery, and startup repair.

macOS Recovery: macOS users can utilize the macOS Recovery to reinstall the operating system, access utilities to repair or erase disks, and restore from a Time Machine backup when the system is unresponsive.

Linux Bootable Media: For Linux systems, creating a live USB stick that can boot the system independently of the hard drive allows users to repair or reinstall the OS without risking data loss on the main system drive.

Best Practices for System Recovery

Regular Backups: Engage in a routine that includes frequent backups of important data and system settings to external drives or cloud storage.

Testing Backup Integrity: Periodically test backups to confirm that they are not only complete but also effective when needed. This practice ensures that in the case of system failure, the recovery process will proceed smoothly.

Documentation: Maintain thorough documentation of system configurations, backup schedules, and specific recovery processes. This documentation can be invaluable during critical recovery operations and for training purposes.

Armed with the knowledge and skills to restore systems effectively, we can now turn our focus toward addressing more nuanced software issues that may emerge even after a successful recovery. In the next section we'll delve into sophisticated diagnostic strategies and the latest troubleshooting tools, which enhance our ability to diagnose and resolve complex software problems efficiently, ensuring robust and reliable IT system maintenance.

Problem-solving Techniques and Tools

Employing Software Diagnostic Tools

Software diagnostics are an integral part of maintaining the health and efficiency of computer systems. These tools help troubleshoot issues that affect software operation, from minor glitches to system-wide failures. This section provides an in-depth look at various diagnostic tools that are indispensable for IT professionals when dealing with software-related problems.

Understanding and utilizing the right diagnostic tools can significantly enhance the ability to quickly and effectively identify and resolve software issues. Here are key tools that every technician should be familiar with:

Built-in Operating System Tools:

Windows:
Event Viewer: Tracks information in several types of event logs including Application, Security, and System logs, helping to pinpoint causes of software crashes or system events.
Resource Monitor and Task Manager: Offer real-time monitoring of system resources like CPU, memory usage, disk activity, and network traffic.

macOS:
Console: Access system logs to monitor application behavior and system processes.
Activity Monitor: Similar to Task Manager in Windows, it provides a detailed overview of resource usage including CPU, memory, energy, disk, and network usage.

Linux:
System Log Files (var/log): Various logs like syslog, kern.log, and others provide detailed reports on different aspects of the system.
top/Htop: Command-line tools that offer real-time views of the system processes and resource usage.

Third-party Diagnostic Utilities:

Wireshark: An advanced network protocol analyzer tool that captures and displays data traveling back and forth on a network in real-time, invaluable for diagnosing network-related software issues.

Sysinternals Suite (Windows): A suite of tools to manage, troubleshoot, and diagnose your Windows systems and applications.

OnyX (macOS): A multifunction utility for macOS that allows you to verify the startup disk and the structure of its system files, run miscellaneous maintenance and cleaning tasks, configure parameters in the Finder, Dock, Safari, and some Apple applications.

Remote Diagnostic Tools:

Remote Desktop: Allows technicians to view and control a computer from a remote location, enabling troubleshooting without being physically near the device.

SSH (Secure Shell): Used primarily on Linux and macOS, it provides a secure way to access remote computers over an unsecured network.

Best Practices for Using Diagnostic Tools

Regular Monitoring: Employ these tools not only for troubleshooting but also for regular monitoring of system health to preempt potential issues.

Detailed Documentation: Always document the diagnostic processes and findings to ensure that troubleshooting steps are repeatable and informative.

Security Considerations: Ensure that any diagnostic tool used complies with your organization's security policies, especially tools that handle data over the network.

Techniques for Remote Troubleshooting

In today's interconnected world, the ability to troubleshoot systems remotely is an invaluable skill for IT professionals. Remote troubleshooting allows technicians to provide support without being physically present, which is crucial for managing distributed networks and supporting remote users. This section delves into effective methods and tools for remote troubleshooting, ensuring IT professionals are equipped to handle issues from anywhere at any time. Remote troubleshooting involves diagnosing and resolving issues over a network. This capability is essential for supporting remote work environments, managing servers in data centers, and providing customer support efficiently.

Core Techniques and Tools for Effective Remote Troubleshooting

Remote Desktop Tools:

Microsoft Remote Desktop: Allows secure connection to a remote computer using the Remote Desktop Protocol (RDP) to manage and troubleshoot Windows devices.

TeamViewer: A versatile tool that provides remote access and support over the internet, allowing you to manage computers, provide updates, and troubleshoot issues across different platforms.

VNC (Virtual Network Computing): Enables remote access to computer screens, providing the ability to interact with a remote system as if seated directly in front of it.

Command Line Tools:

SSH (Secure Shell): Vital for securely accessing remote machines, particularly servers. SSH allows command-line based management for Unix-like systems, including Linux and macOS, and can also be used on Windows.

PowerShell Remoting: Utilizes Windows PowerShell to execute scripts and commands on remote systems, ideal for automation and batch troubleshooting tasks.

Remote Monitoring and Management Software (RMM):

SolarWinds RMM: Offers comprehensive monitoring and management capabilities that allow IT professionals to keep track of system health, perform remote updates, and troubleshoot issues.

ConnectWise Automate: Provides tools for proactive monitoring, management, and automation of IT tasks on remote computers, enhancing operational efficiency.

Web-Based Management Platforms:

Google Remote Desktop: A simple, web-based solution that allows access to your computers from another computer or mobile device, ideal for quick support tasks and monitoring.

Cloud-based IT Management Platforms: Tools like Microsoft Intune and VMware Workspace ONE provide centralized cloud platforms to manage and troubleshoot devices remotely, applying policies, pushing updates, and ensuring compliance across devices.

Best Practices for Remote Troubleshooting

Establish Clear Communication: Always maintain open lines of communication with the remote user to understand the problem fully and guide them through diagnostic steps if needed.

Maintain Security Standards: Ensure all remote sessions are conducted over secure channels and that both the client and host machines have adequate security measures like VPNs and updated antivirus software.

Documentation and Reporting: Keep detailed records of all remote troubleshooting activities, including the tools used, the diagnostics performed, the findings, and the outcome of the troubleshooting session.

Test Your Knowledge (Chapter 8)

1. Which of the following is the first step in troubleshooting a software issue?

A) Restart the system

B) Identify the problem

C) Reinstall the operating system

D) Contact customer support

2. What tool would you use to check for system errors and diagnose hardware issues in Windows?

A) Task Manager

B) Event Viewer

C) Control Panel

D) Device Manager

3. Fill-in-the-Blank: To troubleshoot issues with the system boot process, the command _____ can be used to fix boot records.

A) chkdsk

B) bootrec

C) msconfig

D) ipconfig

4. Drag-and-drop activity: Arrange the following steps in the correct order for diagnosing a software issue:

1. Identify the problem
2. Establish a theory of probable cause
3. Test the theory
4. Document findings

5. What does the "Safe Mode" boot option primarily do?

A) Reinstall the operating system

B) Disable all network drivers

C) Boot with minimal drivers and services

D) Perform a complete system format

6. Which command can be used to trace the route data takes from your computer to a specified destination on the network?

A) ping

B) ipconfig

C) tracert

D) nslookup

7. When would you use the "System Restore" tool?

A) To remove viruses from the computer

B) To recover lost files

C) To restore the system to an earlier state after installing faulty software

D) To uninstall the operating system

8. Which tool is used to configure which programs start when Windows boots?

A) Task Manager

B) Device Manager

C) System Configuration (msconfig)

D) Disk Management

9. Drag-and-drop activity: Match the following troubleshooting tools with their correct descriptions:

1. Task Manager
2. Device Manager
3. Disk Cleanup

    Descriptions:

    A) Used to manage startup programs

    B) Used to delete temporary files

    C) Used to monitor active processes

10. What is the purpose of using the "Safe Mode with Networking" option in troubleshooting?

A) To troubleshoot networking problems with minimal drivers

B) To disable all networking connections

C) To reinstall network drivers

D) To run Windows without any networking capabilities

11. Which of the following can be used to check for corrupt system files in Windows?

A) sfc /scannow

B) chkdsk /r

C) ipconfig /flushdns

D) nslookup

12. Performance-Based Question: You need to restore a system to its previous state after a failed update. What steps would you take using the "System Restore" tool?

A) Choose the "System Restore" option in the recovery menu, select the most recent restore point, and confirm the restoration process.

13. Which of the following is not a step in the problem-solving methodology?

A) Establish a plan of action

B) Verify full system functionality

C) Implement preventive measures

D) Replace the CPU

14. What is the primary purpose of using "Event Viewer" in troubleshooting?

A) To manage system files

B) To view and troubleshoot system, security, and application logs

C) To uninstall programs

D) To configure network settings

15. Which command-line tool is used to manage and partition disks in Windows?

A) diskpart

B) format

C) ipconfig

D) netstat

Please refer to the "Test Your Knowledge A+ (Answers)" chapter for the answers.

CHAPTER 9

Operational Procedures

Electrostatic Discharge (ESD) Precautions

Electrostatic Discharge (ESD) is a common and potentially damaging occurrence in the handling of electronic components. ESD can cause immediate, latent, or catastrophic damage to electronic devices, which might not be immediately evident but can significantly shorten the lifespan of the equipment. This section outlines effective measures and best practices to mitigate ESD risks when working with or around sensitive electronic equipment.

ESD occurs when an electrical charge is suddenly transferred from one object to another. In the context of computer hardware, this can happen when a person or a tool comes into contact with electronic components, potentially causing damage or destruction to sensitive parts such as CPUs, RAM, and motherboards.

Comprehensive Measures to Prevent ESD Damage

ESD-Safe Workstations:
ESD Mats: Utilize ESD mats that are grounded. These mats have a conductive layer that dissipates static charges, thereby protecting sensitive equipment.
ESD Wrist Straps: Wear an antistatic wrist strap that is properly grounded to equalize the body's electrical charge with that of the equipment or ESD mat. This prevents a charge from building up and discharging onto sensitive components.

Handling and Storage Protocols:
Component Handling: Always handle electronic components by the edges. Avoid touching pin connectors, chips, or circuitry to minimize the risk of static charge transfer.
Antistatic Bags: Store and transport electronic components (especially sensitive ones like memory modules and expansion cards) in antistatic bags. These bags are designed to protect the contents from ESD damage.

Environment Controls:
Humidity Levels: Maintain an environment with a relative humidity level of 40-60% to reduce the likelihood of static buildup, as dry air increases static charge.
Flooring Materials: Use antistatic flooring or mats in areas where electronic components are handled or assembled to prevent the accumulation of static electricity.

ESD Training and Awareness:
Regular Training: Conduct regular training sessions for all personnel who handle or are in proximity to sensitive electronic components to ensure they understand and apply ESD prevention measures.
ESD Signs: Post clear signage reminding staff of the need for static precautions in critical areas.

Best Practices for Incorporating ESD Precautions
Tool Use: Ensure that all tools used in and around sensitive electronic devices are ESD-safe. Tools should either be made of antistatic materials or have handles that are ESD safe.
Equipment Testing: Regularly test ESD equipment like wrist straps and mats to ensure they are functioning correctly and provide the necessary protection.
Documentation and Policies: Develop and enforce a comprehensive ESD control policy, which includes procedures for handling, storage, and disposal of ESD-sensitive equipment.

By adopting these ESD precautions, IT professionals can significantly mitigate the risks associated with electrostatic discharge, ensuring the longevity and reliability of electronic components.

Proper Disposal of Electronic Waste

Electronic waste (e-waste) is a growing environmental concern globally. It encompasses a variety of discarded electronic and electrical equipment that is no longer usable or desirable. Proper disposal of e-waste is crucial not only to avoid environmental damage but also to recover valuable materials and prevent potential health risks from hazardous substances. This section provides a comprehensive guide on best practices for responsibly disposing of electronic waste, aligning with environmental regulations and promoting sustainability.

Electronic waste includes items such as computers, printers, televisions, mobile phones, and batteries, all of which contain substances that can be harmful if not managed properly. These include heavy metals like lead, mercury, and cadmium, along with other toxic chemicals.

Best Practices for Electronic Waste Disposal

Recycle: Always look for certified e-waste recycling options in your area. These facilities ensure that all parts of discarded electronics are handled responsibly, with harmful components disposed of correctly and valuable materials like gold, silver, and copper recovered.
Manufacturer Take-Back Programs: Many electronic manufacturers offer take-back or recycling programs for their products, which ensure that the e-waste is handled in compliance with the environmental standards they adhere to.
Donating: Functional electronics can be donated to schools, non-profit organizations, and low-income families, extending their life cycle and reducing waste.
Refurbishment: Many organizations specialize in refurbishing old electronics for reuse. This process often includes upgrading older systems to meet current software requirements and fixing any physical damage.

Responsible Disposal:

Local Regulations: Follow local and national regulations regarding e-waste disposal. Many regions have specific rules about how and where to dispose of electronics safely.

Certified Disposal Services: Utilize services that have certification under recognized standards like the Responsible Recycling (R2) Standard or e-Stewards, which adhere to strict environmental and health safety measures.

Awareness and Education:

Educational Programs: Implement educational programs within your organization or community to raise awareness about the importance of e-waste recycling and proper disposal methods.

Employee Training: Train employees on the correct procedures for handling and disposing of electronic items, especially those that are part of regular business operations.

Documenting and Monitoring Disposal Practices

Documentation: Keep thorough records of how e-waste is managed, including receipts from recycling centers or documentation from donation programs. This helps in compliance with environmental policies and can be useful for corporate social responsibility reporting.

Audit and Review: Regularly review and audit disposal practices to ensure compliance with the latest environmental laws and to discover new ways to improve e-waste management strategies.

Proper disposal of electronic waste is a crucial part of maintaining environmental sustainability and ensuring that hazardous materials do not end up causing soil, water, or air pollution. By following these best practices, businesses and individuals can contribute to a healthier planet and a more sustainable future.

Professional Communication

Developing Effective Communication Skills

Effective communication is essential in the IT sector, not just for exchanging information but for ensuring that this information is understood and acted upon effectively. This chapter explores how IT professionals can enhance their communication skills to improve interactions with colleagues and clients, thereby fostering better workplace relationships and project outcomes.

At its core, effective communication is about conveying messages in a way that they are fully understood by others. This involves grasping the emotions and intentions behind the information as much as the information itself. An effective communicator is adept at listening, speaking clearly, and adjusting their message to suit their audience.

Techniques for Enhancing Communication Skills

Active listening is fundamental. This means being fully present during conversations—maintaining eye contact, nodding in agreement, and avoiding interruptions while others speak. It also means asking clarifying questions and paraphrasing what others say to confirm understanding.

When it comes to conveying your own messages, clarity and conciseness are key. Use straightforward language that your audience can easily understand, and supplement your words with visual aids like diagrams or charts to clarify more complex information. Whether you're addressing a fellow tech expert or a non-technical stakeholder, the goal is to make your communication as accessible as possible.

Adapting to your audience is another critical skill. This involves tailoring your communication style to fit the cultural and professional backgrounds of your audience. For instance, interactions with colleagues from different cultural backgrounds may require a sensitive approach to communication styles and preferences.

Feedback is a two-way street in effective communication. Regularly seeking and offering feedback helps refine your approach to communication. When providing feedback, focus on the message and how it is delivered rather than on the person. This constructive approach helps maintain a positive atmosphere and encourages continuous improvement.

Utilizing Technological Tools

In today's digital world, technology plays a crucial role in communication. Emails, instant messaging apps, and project management software are invaluable for tracking discussions and decisions. Virtual meetings have their own set of rules—understanding and respecting these can greatly enhance communication efficiency.

Documenting Communication Efforts

Keeping detailed records of significant communications is not just good practice—it's essential for accountability. Whether it's logging client interactions or documenting project meetings, these records ensure that everyone involved has a clear reference point and that nothing important is overlooked.

By mastering these communication techniques, IT professionals can ensure that their interactions are clear and effective and conducive to a collaborative work environment.

Best Practices for Customer Service

Providing outstanding customer service is a cornerstone in the IT field, as professionals often directly interact with users experiencing technological difficulties. The key to successful customer service lies not just in resolving these issues but in fostering relationships that build trust and promote a positive image of the IT department or the company. Effective customer service in IT revolves around several pivotal skills and practices. First and foremost is the ability to listen actively and with empathy. When a customer presents an issue, the immediate response should be to listen attentively, showing understanding and acknowledging their frustration, which helps in de-escalating tensions and making the customer feel heard and respected.

Equally important is technical competence. IT professionals must possess a thorough understanding of the technical details of their products and services. This expertise allows them to address problems efficiently and provides the foundation for explaining solutions in a manner that is accessible to non-technical users.

Efficiency in handling problems is also critical. Customers appreciate quick responses, and being proactive in communicating the steps being taken to solve their problems can significantly enhance satisfaction. Following up with customers after an issue has been resolved ensures the solution was effective and continues to foster goodwill.

Professionalism must be maintained at all times, regardless of the stress or complexity of the situation. Treating customers with respect and courtesy is non-negotiable; simple acts of politeness and expressions of thanks can leave lasting positive impressions.

Finally, problem-solving skills are vital. IT professionals should be prepared to think creatively to solve complex issues and make informed decisions about when to escalate a problem or try an alternative solution path.

Deepening Customer Relationships Through Structured Interactions

Every interaction with a customer is an opportunity to deepen the relationship. This starts with the initial contact, where a clear understanding of the problem is established, and extends to the follow-up, ensuring the resolution has held and the customer remains satisfied. Each step should be documented thoroughly. This not only helps in future troubleshooting but also aids in personal and organizational learning.

Customer feedback is a valuable asset. Encouraging customers to share their experiences provides insights that can drive improvements in service delivery. By implementing changes based on this feedback, IT professionals can make meaningful improvements to their service strategies.

Mastering these customer service principles will enhance your capability as an IT professional and increase customer satisfaction and loyalty.

Logical Troubleshooting Techniques

Logical troubleshooting is a systematic approach essential for diagnosing and resolving issues effectively in the IT field. This methodical process involves several stages, each designed to gradually narrow down the potential causes until the root problem is uncovered. This section provides an in-depth exploration of logical troubleshooting tailored for IT professionals aiming to enhance their problem-solving prowess.

At its core, logical troubleshooting in IT follows a structured methodology that divides the problem-solving process into distinct, manageable stages. Each stage is geared towards achieving specific goals, ensuring a comprehensive evaluation of the issue without overlooking any details.

The process begins by identifying the problem through an initial assessment, where you gather information directly from users experiencing the issue. Understanding what the problem is, when it started, and under what conditions it occurs forms the foundation for the troubleshooting process. Following this, you'll need to ask detailed questions to clarify the symptoms and understand the sequence of actions leading to the problem. This step is critical as it helps to define the scope and specific nature of the issue at hand.

Once the problem is clearly defined, the next step involves establishing a theory of probable cause. You'll list all possible causes that could explain the symptoms observed and then prioritize these causes based on their likelihood, informed by both the user's input and your technical expertise.

Testing the theory to determine the actual cause is your next move. Start by examining the most likely causes through practical tests, which may involve inspecting hardware connections, reviewing software settings, or analyzing system logs. If the initial tests don't resolve the issue, you'll need to methodically test each subsequent possible cause until the actual problem is identified.

Developing a plan of action to resolve the problem follows. The plan should be practical, cost-effective, and minimally disruptive to the user. After planning, you'll implement the solution, taking care to mitigate any potential risks that could exacerbate the issue.

Verification of full system functionality and the implementation of preventive measures is crucial once the issue is resolved. This involves performing comprehensive system checks to ensure the problem has been fully resolved and implementing measures to prevent future occurrences, such as updating software or enhancing security protocols.

Documenting the entire process is also vital. Detailed records of what was tested, findings, actions taken, and the outcome are invaluable for future reference and for improving the troubleshooting process over time.

To refine your troubleshooting skills, it is advisable to participate in ongoing training and stay abreast of new technological developments and problem-solving techniques. Regular practice of these techniques will build your confidence and efficiency in handling IT issues.

Management and Documentation

The Importance of Documentation

In IT support and management, documentation is the backbone of operational integrity and efficiency. This chapter delves into documentation's critical role in maintaining system reliability and coherence across various IT practices. We'll explore the multifaceted benefits of meticulous documentation and provide a comprehensive guide on mastering the art of documenting IT environments effectively.

Why is Documentation Crucial?

Foundation for Consistency and Continuity:
Comprehensive documentation is a blueprint for operations, ensuring that every task, from routine maintenance to complex deployments, follows a consistent approach. This consistency is crucial for maintaining quality standards and ensuring that operations can continue smoothly in the face of staff changes or other disruptions.

Enabler of Knowledge Sharing and Training: In dynamic IT environments, where staff turnover and technological upgrades are common, documentation is a critical knowledge repository. It allows for the efficient onboarding of new staff and serves as a training resource, thereby minimizing knowledge gaps and enhancing team capability.

Audit and Compliance Readiness: Many industries are governed by regulatory requirements that mandate the maintenance of detailed records of IT processes and data security measures. Effective documentation ensures that organizations are always prepared for audits and compliance checks, avoiding potential legal and financial penalties.

Optimization of Troubleshooting and Recovery: In crisis scenarios, such as system outages or security breaches, having detailed documentation can drastically reduce downtime. It provides clear guidelines and protocols for recovery, essential for quick and effective response to issues.
Implementing a robust documentation strategy requires a thoughtful approach that includes several key practices:

Identification of Documentation Needs: Start by identifying what elements of your IT environment need documentation. This typically includes hardware configurations, software processes, network setups, security protocols, and troubleshooting guides.

Selection of Tools and Formats: Choose documentation tools and formats that enhance readability and accessibility. Options may include digital wikis, cloud-based collaboration tools, or specialized documentation software that offers features like version control and access logs.

Standardization of Documentation Procedures: Develop and implement a standardized documentation protocol across all departments. Utilize templates to maintain uniformity in document formats, terminology and update procedures. This standardization helps reduce confusion and enhance the usability of documents.

Accessibility and Security Measures: Documentation should be readily accessible to authorized personnel but secured against unauthorized access. To safeguard sensitive information, implement robust security measures such as encryption, password protection, and access controls.

Regular Updates and Reviews: IT environments are continually evolving, making regular updates to documentation essential. Establish routines for periodic review and updates to documentation to ensure it reflects the current state of the IT environment.

Training and Culture Building: Cultivate a culture that values documentation through regular training sessions and incentives. Encourage team members to contribute to and maintain documentation as part of their regular workflow.

Effective documentation enhances operational efficiency and should be viewed as a strategic asset rather than just a procedural task. It supports compliance and strengthens organizational knowledge. By embracing these documentation practices, IT professionals can ensure that their operations are resilient, compliant, and optimized for continuous improvement.

Tools and Software Solutions

In the rapidly evolving IT landscape, effective change management is critical to maintaining stability and security. This section examines a variety of tools and software solutions that support change management processes, helping organizations manage transitions smoothly and maintain continuity of operations. These tools play a pivotal role in tracking changes, assessing their impacts, and ensuring that all modifications are documented thoroughly and auditable.

Change management tools are designed to help organizations plan, implement, and monitor changes in their IT environments. These tools facilitate a structured approach to handling changes and can significantly reduce the risks associated with changes to software, hardware, networks, and data.

Key Features of Effective Change Management Software

Automation Capabilities: Automation streamlines the change process, reducing manual errors and speeding up response times. Automated tools can schedule and execute changes during off-peak hours, ensuring minimal disruption to services.

Integration with IT Service Management (ITSM): Integrating change management tools with ITSM solutions ensures that changes are aligned with broader service management processes. This integration helps maintain service quality and compliance with established IT standards.

Real-time Monitoring and Alerts: Effective tools provide real-time monitoring of the IT environment, alerting administrators to unauthorized changes or potential issues arising from a change. This immediate feedback allows for quick corrective actions.

Rollback Features: To safeguard against potential disruptions, the best tools include capabilities to revert systems to their pre-change state. This is crucial for mitigating the impact of changes that do not go as planned.

Comprehensive Reporting: Detailed reports are essential for evaluating the success of changes and for auditing purposes. These reports should provide insights into what changes were made, who made them, and any associated impacts on the system.

Popular Change Management Tools

ServiceNow: This platform offers a robust change management module that integrates seamlessly with other service management processes. It provides tools for risk assessment, impact analysis, and automated change workflows.

Atlassian Jira: While primarily known for project management, Jira also offers features for change management, especially useful in software development settings. It allows for tracking changes through customizable workflows and dashboards.

IBM Change Management: IBM's solution offers extensive tools for automating and managing changes across complex IT environments. It includes capabilities for planning, tracking, and executing changes, with strong emphasis on security and compliance.

Microsoft Azure DevOps: This suite includes tools for version control, testing, release management, and automation, making it suitable for managing changes in cloud environments and software development projects.

GitLab: Combining source code management with CI/CD (continuous integration/continuous delivery), GitLab facilitates comprehensive management of the lifecycle of software development changes.

Using Documentation Tools Effectively

In the previous section, we explored the pivotal role of effective documentation in ensuring operational consistency and compliance within IT environments. Now, we will dive into the practical aspects of documentation by examining the tools and techniques that can optimize the creation, maintenance, and utilization of these essential resources.

Choosing the right tools for documentation is critical as it directly affects the efficiency and effectiveness of the documentation process. Here's an overview of some widely used documentation tools and their applications:

Wiki Systems:

Confluence, MediaWiki
Wikis are ideal for collaborative environments because they allow multiple users to create, edit, and update documentation in real-time. They are particularly useful for maintaining comprehensive operational manuals, project documentation, and IT inventories.

Document Management Systems (DMS):

Microsoft SharePoint, Google Workspace
These systems offer robust features for storing, indexing, and securing documents. DMS solutions are excellent for handling large volumes of documentation, providing advanced search capabilities, version control, and access controls.

Note-taking Applications:

Evernote, Microsoft OneNote: For quicker, more flexible documentation, note-taking apps are invaluable. They are perfect for jotting down troubleshooting steps, meeting notes, or quick references and can sync across multiple devices for on-the-go access.

Diagramming Tools:

Microsoft Visio, LucidChart: Diagramming tools are essential for creating network diagrams, architectural diagrams, and other visual aids that help in understanding complex systems and workflows.

Integrated Development Environments (IDEs):

Visual Studio Code, JetBrains IntelliJ IDEA: For software development teams, IDEs with integrated documentation features enable developers to maintain code and its documentation simultaneously, ensuring consistency and reducing discrepancies.

To maximize the benefits of these tools, consider the following best practices:

Integration and Automation: Whenever possible, integrate documentation tools with other systems such as ticketing systems, network monitoring tools, and project management platforms. Automation of documentation tasks, such as auto-generating reports or logs, can significantly reduce manual overhead and improve accuracy.

Regular Training and Updates: Conduct regular training sessions for all team members on how to use documentation tools effectively. Keep the team updated on any new features or updates to the tools to ensure they are utilized to their full potential.

Access and Permissions Management: Implement strict access controls and permissions to ensure that sensitive information is secured and only accessible to authorized personnel. This is crucial not only for security but also for maintaining the integrity of the documentation.

Regular Reviews and Audits: Schedule regular reviews and audits of the documentation to ensure it remains accurate, relevant, and compliant with any regulatory standards. This practice helps in identifying any gaps or outdated information that could potentially lead to operational risks.

Feedback Mechanism: Establish a feedback mechanism that allows users to report errors, suggest improvements, or update documentation. This participatory approach not only improves the quality of the documentation but also encourages a culture of continuous improvement.

By leveraging the right tools and adhering to best practices, organizations can ensure that their documentation processes are not just a compliance requirement, but a cornerstone of operational excellence. Effective documentation is dynamic, and with the right tools, it becomes a powerful asset that enhances decision-making, supports training, and boosts productivity across all levels of the organization.

Use documentation tools effectively

Documentation is the backbone of effective IT management, providing crucial information that supports system maintenance, troubleshooting, and compliance. Tools like Confluence and SharePoint are at the forefront of facilitating robust documentation practices. This section explores how these tools can be leveraged to optimize workflows and manage information effectively in IT environments.

Confluence, developed by Atlassian, is a content collaboration tool that allows teams to create, share, and collaborate on projects in a centralized space. It is particularly popular among software development teams for its seamless integration with Jira and other Atlassian products.

SharePoint, developed by Microsoft, is a document management and storage system that is highly integrated with Microsoft Office. It is used for creating websites and allows to store, organize, and access information from any device.

Key Features of Confluence and SharePoint

Content Management: Both tools provide powerful content management capabilities, allowing teams to create, store, and manage documents in a centralized location. Confluence offers a user-friendly interface with easy navigation and page hierarchy management, while SharePoint provides extensive tools for document libraries, list management, and site organization.

Collaboration: Confluence and SharePoint excel in collaborative features. Confluence's real-time editing and comment functions make it ideal for teams to work together on documents and projects. SharePoint's integration with Microsoft Teams and email facilitates broader collaboration across an organization.

Integration and Customization: Confluence integrates well with software development tools, especially those from Atlassian's suite, enhancing its utility in agile projects. SharePoint can be customized extensively with workflows, forms, and custom apps created using PowerApps and Power Automate, aligning it closely with business processes.

Access Control: Both tools provide robust access control mechanisms. Confluence allows for detailed permission settings at the space, page, and even section levels. SharePoint offers detailed security settings that can align with an organization's compliance and governance policies.

Searchability: Effective search tools are vital in documentation tools. Confluence provides a quick search feature that lets users find content easily across all documents. SharePoint's search capabilities are powered by Microsoft Search, which supports complex queries and integration with AI to enhance findability.

Best Practices for Using Confluence and SharePoint

Structured Organization: Create a logical structure for your documentation from the outset to avoid information silos. Utilize the hierarchical capabilities of Confluence and the site and library structures in SharePoint to organize content.

Regular Updates: Keep all documentation up to date with regular reviews and updates. This ensures that the information remains relevant and useful for all stakeholders.

Comprehensive Training: Provide training for all users on how to use Confluence and SharePoint effectively. Understanding the features and best practices can greatly enhance the productivity of teams.

Integration with Other Tools: Maximize the effectiveness of Confluence and SharePoint by integrating them with other tools used by your organization. This could include project management software, CRM systems, and more.

Use Templates: Both Confluence and SharePoint offer templates for various types of content, such as meeting notes, project plans, and technical documentation. Utilizing these templates can speed up the documentation process and ensure consistency across documents.

Confluence and SharePoint are powerful tools for managing documentation in IT environments. By leveraging these tools effectively, organizations can ensure that their documentation practices enhance information sharing, collaboration, and compliance.

Emerging Standards in IT Documentation

In the rapidly evolving landscape of information technology, the standards and methodologies for documentation are continuously adapting to meet new challenges and leverage cutting-edge technologies. This section delves into the emerging trends and standards that are shaping the future of IT documentation, highlighting how these advancements can be utilized to enhance documentation practices.

New Trends in IT Documentation

Automation in Documentation: Automation tools are becoming increasingly integral in the creation and maintenance of IT documentation. Tools that automatically generate documentation from code, such as Swagger for APIs or tools like Doxygen for software development, reduce manual efforts and ensure accuracy and consistency.

Interactive Documentation: Traditional static documentation is giving way to interactive platforms where users can experiment and learn in a controlled environment. Interactive tutorials, embedded code snippets that can be edited and run, and dynamically generated diagrams are examples that enhance user engagement and understanding.

Integration with Development and Operations: The rise of DevOps has influenced documentation practices significantly. Documentation is now integrated into the development lifecycle, with updates being part of continuous integration/continuous deployment (CI/CD) pipelines. This integration ensures that documentation is continuously updated with each version of the product.

Emerging Standards

Markdown and Lightweight Markup: Markdown has become a de facto standard for creating quick and easy-to-understand documentation. Its simplicity and portability make it ideal for a wide range of documentation needs, from README files to comprehensive user manuals.

Documentation as Code: Treating documentation like code—storing it in version control systems, reviewing it through pull requests, and applying the same quality standards as to software—enhances maintainability and traceability. This approach is being adopted widely, especially in environments that emphasize automation and DevOps practices.

Accessibility Standards: With an increasing focus on inclusivity, documentation is also adapting to meet accessibility standards. This includes creating content that is accessible to people with disabilities, ensuring compatibility with screen readers, using inclusive language, and following guidelines such as the Web Content Accessibility Guidelines (WCAG).

Methodologies Influencing IT Documentation

Single Source of Truth (SSoT): This methodology emphasizes having one source of accurate and current information that is disseminated across multiple formats and platforms. This approach minimizes inconsistencies and duplication of content.

Docs as a User Experience (UX): Viewing documentation through the lens of user experience design, focusing on the user's journey through the documentation. This involves user feedback loops, usability testing for documentation, and iterative improvements based on user interactions.

Agile Documentation: In agile environments, documentation is created incrementally, just like software. This means documentation is developed sprint by sprint, evolving as the product evolves, which keeps the documentation relevant and timely.

Emerging trends and standards in IT documentation are geared towards making documentation more integrated, interactive, and inclusive. By adopting these new standards, IT professionals can ensure their documentation practices are robust, efficient, and ready for the future's challenges. As documentation continues to evolve, staying abreast of these trends will be crucial for maintaining effective and efficient IT operations.

Test Your Knowledge (Chapter 9)

1. What does ESD stand for in relation to hardware safety?

A) Electrical Safety Device

B) Electrostatic Discharge

C) Electromagnetic Shielding Device

D) Environmental Safety Detection

2. Which tool is essential for preventing ESD when handling internal hardware components?

A) Rubber gloves

B) Antistatic wrist strap

C) Insulated pliers

D) Safety goggles

3. Which of the following environmental conditions is most likely to increase the risk of ESD?

A) High humidity

B) Low humidity

C) High temperature

D) Low temperature

4. Which of the following best describes a key method to prevent damage from ESD?

A) Wearing rubber-soled shoes

B) Touching the computer's power supply

C) Working on an insulated mat

D) Grounding yourself with a metal object before touching components

5. Which of the following materials is most effective in minimizing ESD?

A) Metal

B) Plastic

C) Cotton

D) Rubber

6. What is the purpose of an antistatic mat in a workspace?

A) To prevent overheating

B) To protect the workspace from scratches

C) To prevent static electricity from damaging components

D) To keep tools organized

7. What should you always do before removing a component from a computer system to prevent ESD damage?

A) Power off the system

B) Ground yourself

C) Wear rubber gloves

D) Hold the power button for 10 seconds

8. What are the common symptoms of ESD damage in computer components?

A) Visible sparks and burns on the component

B) Component overheating

C) Intermittent failure or complete failure without visual damage

D) A strong burning smell

9. Which component is most vulnerable to ESD damage?

A) Hard disk drive

B) Power supply unit

C) RAM

D) Keyboard

10. In what type of environment is ESD most likely to occur?

A) A humid, warm room

B) A dry, cold room

C) A room with poor ventilation

D) A room with excessive moisture

11. What should you do immediately if you suspect ESD damage during hardware installation?

A) Turn off the computer and remove all power sources

B) Restart the computer to check if the problem persists

C) Contact technical support

D) Use a software diagnostic tool

12. Drag-and-drop activity: Match the following environmental hazards with their respective effects.

Hazards:

1. Excessive dust
2. ESD
3. High humidity

Effects:

A) Causes short circuits

B) Damages sensitive electronic components

C) Leads to overheating of components

13. Which of the following is an example of proper disposal of electronic waste?

A) Throwing it in the regular trash

B) Burning the components

C) Recycling the e-waste at a certified facility

D) Storing it indefinitely

14. Why is it important to properly dispose of electronic waste?

A) To prevent data loss

B) To comply with international shipping laws

C) To prevent environmental contamination

D) To maximize the resale value

15. What should you do before donating or recycling old electronic devices?

A) Ensure the device is powered off

B) Remove all personal data from the device

C) Perform a hardware diagnostic

D) Install a new operating system

Please refer to the "Test Your Knowledge A+ (Answers)" chapter for the answers. (Next page)

Test Your Knowledge A+ (Answers)

Test Your Knowledge (Chapter 1)

1. C) Larger screen size

2. B) SSD

3. C) Contactless payment

4. Smartphone: Android   **Tablet:** iOS

5. B) NFC

6. A) SIM card

7. B) Gyroscope

8. B) Larger screen

9. B) NFC

10. SD card

11. B) OLED

12. B) Orientation detection

13. A) Navigation

14. B) Bluetooth

15. C) Physical keyboard

Test Your Knowledge (Chapter 2)

1. B) A network spread across a city

2. C) DHCP

3. Order: 2, 1, 3, 4

4. C) PAN

5. B) Connect multiple devices on a network providing communication between them

6. Correct placement: Modem connected to the WAN port of the Router, the Router's LAN port connected to the Switch, and PCs connected to the Switch.

7. A) 192.168.1.1

8. C) ping

9. Definitions matched:

1. B) Divides network into subnetworks

2. C) Device that routes traffic from a local network to other networks

3. A) Translates domain names to IP addresses

10. D) Ethernet

11. netstat

12. B) Virtual Private Network; used to establish a secure connection over the internet

13. B) Layer 3

14. Uses matched:

1. B) Tests connectivity in network cables

2. C) Attaches connectors to Ethernet cables

3. A) Measures electrical current

15. D) To block unauthorized access

Test Your Knowledge (Chapter 3)

1. C) Connect all the components of a computer

2. C) Keyboard

3. C) CPU

4. Order: 4, 2, 3, 1

5. C) RAM

6. C) To cool down the processor

7. B) USB

8. Correct slots:

- RAM in RAM slot
- Graphics Card in PCIe x16 slot
- Sound Card in PCIe x1 slot
- Network Card in PCIe slot

9. C) SSD

10. C) Graphics card

11. C) Power connector

12. C) It is responsible for the initial booting of the computer

13. Correct order:

- 1, 2, 4, 3

14. B) DDR4

15. A) Converts AC to DC power

Test Your Knowledge (Chapter 4)

1. **B)** It offers virtualized physical computing resources

2. **B)** Hardware

3. **B)** Vendor manages the infrastructure

4. **Correct Order:** SaaS, PaaS, IaaS (from least to most management required by the client)

5. **C)** SaaS

6. **B)** Function as multiple virtual servers

7. **C)** Both A and B

8. **A)** Hypervisor

9. **Correct Sequence:** Assign IP addresses, Set subnet mask, Define gateway, Configure DNS

10. **D)** To improve hardware efficiency

11. **A)** IaaS

12. **C)** VMware ESXi

13. **B)** Ability to revert to a previous state

14. **Correct Matches:**

- A) Snapshot

- B) Hypervisor
- C) VM
15. **D)** Application rollbacks

Test Your Knowledge (Chapter 5)

1. B) Identifying the problem
2. A) MemTest86
3. C) ping
4. Order: 1, 3, 4, 2
5. C) Dust buildup inside the system
6. C) To diagnose issues with the NIC
7. B) chkdsk
8. Order: 1, 2, 3, 4
9. B) RAM failure
10. B) tracert
11. C) Check the BIOS boot order
12. A) System crashes randomly (RAM)
    B) Display artifacts or no display (Graphics card)
    C) Continuous reboots (Power supply)
    D) Blue screen errors (Hard drive)
13. C) ping
14. C) defrag
15. C) Power cycle the router

Test Your Knowledge (Chapter 6)

1. **B)** NTFS
2. **A)** To view and configure hardware drivers
3. **B)** GPT
4. Order: 1, 2, 3, 4
5. **B)** macOS uses HFS+ or APFS, while Windows uses NTFS
6. **A)** dir
7. **B)** Disk Utility
8. 1: **C)** Windows Boot Manager
   2: **B)** Boot Camp
   3: **A)** GRUB
9. **B)** Change permissions of a file
10. **B)** Backup and Restore
11. **C)** User Account Control (UAC)
12. **B)** Time Machine
13. **C)** Ubuntu
14. **B)** Execute commands with elevated permissions
15. **D)** chmod 700 data.txt

Test Your Knowledge (Chapter 7)

1. B) Kensington lock

2. A) RFID badges

3. C) CCTV

4. C) Unencrypted guest Wi-Fi access

5. A) Proximity cards

6. A) Multi-factor authentication

7. B) To control access using unique physical traits

8. A) 4,1, 2, 3

9. C) Biometric authentication

10. C) Real-time surveillance and deterrence

11. A) Password

12. B) Physical access controls

13. B) Fingerprint and smart card

14. B) Multi-factor authentication with biometric and smart card access

15. Physical: Biometric scanner, Keycard, CCTV

   Logical: Password

Test Your Knowledge (Chapter 8)

1. B) Identify the problem

2. B) Event Viewer

3. B) bootrec

4. Order: 1, 2, 3, 4

5. C) Boot with minimal drivers and services

6. C) tracert

7. C) To restore the system to an earlier state after installing faulty software

8. C) System Configuration (msconfig)

9. 1. A, 2. C, 3. B

10. A) To troubleshoot networking problems with minimal drivers

11. A) sfc /scannow

12. A) Choose the "System Restore" option in the recovery menu, select the most recent restore point, and confirm the restoration process.

13. D) Replace the CPU

14. B) To view and troubleshoot system, security, and application logs

15. A) diskpart

Test Your Knowledge (Chapter 9)

1. B) Electrostatic Discharge

2. B) Antistatic wrist strap

3. B) Low humidity

4. D) Grounding yourself with a metal object before touching components

5. D) Rubber

6. C) To prevent static electricity from damaging components

7. B) Ground yourself

8. C) Intermittent failure or complete failure without visual damage

9. C) RAM

10. B) A dry, cold room

11. A) Turn off the computer and remove all power sources
12. Order: 2, B; 1, C; 3, A
13. C) Recycling the e-waste at a certified facility
14. C) To prevent environmental contamination
15. B) Remove all personal data from the device

Congratulations on reaching the end of this comprehensive journey through the **CompTIA A+ 220-1101 (Core 1) and 220-1102 (Core 2)** material! I want to thank you for your dedication and persistence in completing this guide. Your commitment to learning and mastering the content is truly commendable, and it brings you one step closer to becoming a certified IT professional.

As you prepare for your exam, remember that practice is key to success. We've included additional quizzes and exam tests in the bonus section of this book, designed to further challenge and sharpen your skills. I encourage you to take full advantage of these resources to solidify your knowledge and boost your confidence before the big day.

Once again, congratulations on your progress so far, and best of luck with your exam and your future endeavors in the world of IT! You're well on your way to an exciting and rewarding career. Be sure to visit the bonus section and put your knowledge to the test!

BONUS

Scan the QR code to claim your exclusive bonus and access to Audiobooks, Quizzes, Mock exams and more to enhance your knowledge.

I want to express my gratitude for your selection of my book.

Your review on Amazon would be invaluable and greatly appreciated.

Thank you.

CompTIA Security + SYO-701

CHAPTER 1

Fundamental Concepts

Key Principles and Terminology

Welcome to the foundational layer of your cybersecurity education—the fundamental information security concepts and terminology. This section is designed to equip you with the essential principles and the language used in the field, setting a solid groundwork for more advanced topics covered later in this book.

CIA Triad

The triad often summarizes the core principles of information security: Confidentiality, Integrity, and Availability (CIA). Each element of this triad is a foundational goal for security practices and protocols within any organization.

Confidentiality: Ensures that information is accessible only to those authorized. It is about protecting personal privacy and proprietary information. Data encryption and rigorous access controls are employed to uphold confidentiality.

Integrity: Maintaining the consistency, accuracy, and trustworthiness of data over its entire lifecycle. Data must not be altered in transit, and steps must be taken to ensure that data cannot be altered by unauthorized people (for example, using file permissions and user access controls). Techniques such as data checksums and digital signatures help ensure integrity.

Availability: Ensures that information is available and accessible to authorized users when needed. Measures such as redundant hardware, failover clustering, robust disaster recovery plans, and network bandwidth help maintain availability.

Essential Terminology

To effectively communicate in the cybersecurity field, understanding the terminology is crucial. Here are some fundamental terms that every cybersecurity professional should know:

Threat: A potential cause of an unwanted impact on a system or organization. A threat could be intentional, like malware or an attacker trying to gain unauthorized access, or accidental, such as a user mistakenly deleting critical data.

Vulnerability: A flaw or weakness in a system's design, implementation, operation, or management that could be exploited to violate the system's security policy. Vulnerabilities, if not corrected, can allow threats to compromise the system's security.

Risk is the potential for an asset's loss, damage, or destruction due to a threat exploiting a vulnerability. It is essentially the intersection of assets, threats, and vulnerabilities.

Mitigation: Actions taken to reduce the damage caused by a security incident or to decrease the chance of a threat exploiting a vulnerability in the system.

Encryption: The process of encoding data to prevent unauthorized access. It is one of the primary tools used to protect the confidentiality and integrity of data.

Authentication: The process of verifying a person's or device's identity, often as a prerequisite to granting access to resources in an IT system.

Cybersecurity: Defending computers, servers, mobile devices, electronic systems, networks, and data from malicious attacks.

The real power of understanding these principles and terms comes from applying them. Whether you are designing a new security policy for your organization, performing a risk assessment, or setting up network defenses, these foundational concepts guide your decision-making process.

For instance, when assessing a new software solution, you would consider:

- How does the software ensure data confidentiality?
- What measures are in place to maintain data integrity?
- Are there mechanisms to ensure the software is available when authorized users need it?

This framework helps evaluate security postures and communicates effectively with stakeholders about potential risks and proposed or implemented security measures.

The Evolution of Cybersecurity Threats

Delving into the history of cybersecurity threats provides crucial insights into the evolution of security measures, illustrating the arms race between cybersecurity professionals and threat actors. This historical exploration showcases the increasing sophistication of attacks and the innovative defense mechanisms developed in response.

The Early Days: Viruses and Worms

The origins of computer viruses trace back to the early 1970s with the Creeper virus, which targeted DEC PDP-10 computers. This experimental self-replicating program created the first antivirus software prototype, Reaper, designed to delete Creeper. The proliferation of personal computers in the 1980s marked a significant increase in malware diversity. The Brain virus, emerging in 1986, is considered the first for MS-DOS systems, illustrating the shift towards more personal and widespread computing threats.

By the late 1990s, the digital world witnessed the rapid spread of the Melissa virus and the ILOVEYOU worm. These early forms of malware demonstrated the potential for significant damage, disrupting large networks and signaling a clear need for robust security protocols.

The Internet Age: Exploits and Network Attacks

As internet connectivity became mainstream in the 1990s, cyber threats evolved with the technology. The SQL Slammer worm 2003 exploited vulnerabilities in Microsoft SQL Server, causing widespread outages and highlighting the importance of network security. This period also saw the rise of distributed denial-of-service (DDoS) attacks, which overwhelmed websites with traffic to force them offline, showcasing the need for greater network resilience and advanced monitoring capabilities.

The Modern Era: Advanced Persistent Threats and Ransomware

The landscape of cybersecurity has become increasingly complex with the advent of advanced persistent threats (APTs) and ransomware. APTs represent sophisticated, targeted attacks often launched by nation-states aimed at long-term espionage or sabotage. Conversely, ransomware attacks, such as WannaCry and NotPetya, have shown how malicious actors can lock critical data and demand ransom, causing extensive economic and operational disruptions.

Each wave of cyber threats has spurred developments in cybersecurity, from simple antivirus solutions to complex frameworks designed to mitigate diverse and sophisticated attacks. Understanding the evolution of these threats helps professionals anticipate and prepare for future challenges, ensuring that defensive measures evolve in parallel with emerging threats.

The Value of Security+ Certification

Benefits for Your Career

Advancing Your Career with CompTIA Security+

CompTIA Security+ is not just a certification but a career accelerator in the ever-growing field of cybersecurity. Recognized globally, Security+ validates your skills in tackling fundamental security issues and equips you with the necessary tools to manage and mitigate security threats effectively. This certification is renowned for its comprehensive approach to foundational security principles that are crucial across a vast array of IT roles.

Industry Recognition and Credibility

CompTIA Security+ holds a prestigious place in the IT world, endorsed by industry leaders and maintained by continuous updates to align with the latest in technology and security practices. As a Security+ certified professional, you gain an edge in the job market, showcasing your expertise to potential employers who recognize the rigorous training and knowledge that the certification entails. This acknowledgment opens doors to career opportunities that might otherwise be inaccessible, setting you apart in the competitive tech landscape.

Job Opportunities

The cybersecurity job market is burgeoning, with an ever-increasing demand for skilled professionals safeguarding sensitive information and infrastructures. Industries spanning finance, healthcare, government, and beyond are in dire need of experts who can navigate the complexities of information security. Holding a Security+ certification signifies to employers that you possess a robust understanding of security concepts and practices, making you a prime candidate for roles such as systems administrator, security consultant, or network engineer.

Salary Advantages

One of the tangible benefits of earning your Security+ certification is the potential for higher earnings. Certified professionals typically enjoy better salary prospects compared to their non-certified peers, reflecting the premium that employers place on validated skills and knowledge. Security+ acts as a lever in salary negotiations, providing you with the confidence and backing to advocate for a salary that matches your certified expertise.

Foundation for Further Specializations

Starting with Security+, you lay the groundwork for deeper specializations in the cybersecurity field. This certification is a stepping stone towards more advanced credentials, which can propel your career into specialized areas such as threat intelligence, penetration testing, or cybersecurity leadership roles. Pursuing further education and certifications expands your skill set and enhances your career trajectory, opening up new avenues for professional growth.

Professional Development and Lifelong Learning

The dynamic nature of cybersecurity demands ongoing education and adaptation. Security+ certification is just the beginning of a lifelong journey in professional development, where continuous learning is not optional but essential. Engaging with the latest security trends, technologies, and threats through the CompTIA Continuing Education program ensures that your skills remain sharp and relevant, preparing you for whatever new challenges the digital world may throw your way. CompTIA Security+ certification is a powerful tool in your professional arsenal, enhancing your career prospects, salary potential, and growth opportunities in the cybersecurity field.

Overview of the Job Market in Cybersecurity

Navigating the Cybersecurity Job Landscape

The cybersecurity job market is experiencing a dynamic expansion, propelled by the increasing importance of digital security in all sectors. This growth is not just a temporary spike but a sustained trend, reflecting the ongoing need for businesses and governments to bolster their defenses against cyber threats. Understanding this job market can provide insights into how a Security+ certification positions you within this evolving landscape.

Demand for Cybersecurity Professionals

There's an undeniable surge in demand for skilled cybersecurity professionals. Studies and market analysis consistently highlight cybersecurity as one of the fastest-growing job sectors globally. The ubiquitous nature of digital transformation drives this demand—every industry, from healthcare to finance, from retail to government, requires robust cybersecurity measures to protect sensitive data and maintain customer trust.

As businesses increase their reliance on digital technologies, they also expand their vulnerability to cyber attacks, fueling the need for cybersecurity expertise. This trend is not limited to large corporations; small and medium-sized enterprises are equally at risk and are actively seeking cybersecurity professionals.

Impact of Emerging Technologies on Cybersecurity Jobs

Emerging technologies such as artificial intelligence (AI), the Internet of Things (IoT), and blockchain are creating new opportunities and challenges in the cybersecurity field. Each of these technologies introduces unique vulnerabilities and new areas for cybersecurity experts to address. For instance:

AI and Machine Learning are being used to enhance security protocols and pose new risks, such as AI-powered cyber attacks.

IoT devices proliferating in both home and industrial settings expand the attack surface that security professionals must defend.

Blockchain technology enhances security in transactions and requires new strategies to mitigate risks in decentralized networks.

Professionals with a grounding in these areas, especially those who can bridge the gap between advanced IT skills and practical cybersecurity applications, are particularly valuable.

Career Pathways and Roles

The career paths in cybersecurity are varied, ranging from technical positions like network security engineers and cybersecurity analysts to governance roles such as compliance officers and risk managers. The Security+ certification is often the stepping stone into these careers, providing the foundational skills necessary to advance to more specialized positions. Here are a few roles that typically require or benefit from a Security+ certification:

- **Cybersecurity Analyst**: Protects systems by identifying and solving potential and actual security problems.
- **Security Specialist**: Focuses on specific security solutions or areas of cybersecurity.
- **Network Administrator**: Manages network operations with a strong focus on security.
- **Security Consultant**: Provides expert advice to organizations on how to protect their information and services.

The Role of Certifications in Advancing Careers

Certifications like CompTIA Security+ play a critical role in the cybersecurity job market. They validate the skills and knowledge of professionals, helping them not only to enter the field but also to advance to higher-level positions. Certifications are often used by employers as a benchmark to assess the qualifications of potential hires and are frequently listed as job requirements in postings.

The cybersecurity job market offers tremendous opportunities for those equipped with the necessary skills and certifications. As you navigate through this book and towards obtaining your Security+ certification, consider how each topic and skill set might align with these market demands and your personal career goals. With the right preparation and credentials, you can position yourself advantageously within this dynamic and rewarding field.

CHAPTER 2
Basic Security Principles

Access Control and Identity Management

Access control and identity management are pivotal in crafting robust security frameworks within organizations. These systems ensure that only authenticated and authorized users can access specific resources, protecting against unauthorized access and potential security breaches. Let's delve deeper into these critical components of cybersecurity.

Access control is a fundamental security mechanism that restricts users' access to resources within an organization. It is designed to ensure that users can only access the information and resources necessary for their job functions. This is crucial for maintaining operational security and protecting sensitive information.

Access control systems are composed of two main functions:

- **Authentication**: Verifying the identity of a user, typically through credentials like usernames and passwords, biometric scans, security tokens, or a combination of these methods.
- **Authorization**: The process that takes place after authentication, determining whether the user should be allowed to access the resource they have requested.

Access Control Models

Each access control model serves distinct security needs and aligns with specific organizational protocols:

Discretionary Access Control (DAC): In this model, resource owners have the authority to decide who can access specific resources. DAC is flexible, allowing owners to delegate control based on their discretion, which is beneficial in environments that require frequent changes in access permissions.

Mandatory Access Control (MAC): Used predominantly in high-security environments like military or government institutions, MAC enforces strict policies that govern access rights. These policies are configured by administrators and enforced by the system, preventing users from changing permissions.

Role-Based Access Control (RBAC): This model assigns permissions to roles rather than individuals. Users are granted roles based on their responsibilities, which simplifies management and ensures that users only have access to resources necessary for their duties. RBAC supports the principle of least privilege and is widely used in both commercial and organizational settings.

Attribute-Based Access Control (ABAC): ABAC uses policies that evaluate attributes (or characteristics), rather than roles, to make access decisions. These attributes can be related to the user, the resource being accessed, or the relevant operational context. This model offers high granularity and flexibility, adapting to complex and dynamic environments like cloud computing.

Identity Management Systems

Identity management is crucial for ensuring that each entity within a system can be uniquely authenticated and authorized. Enhanced components include:

User Provisioning: This involves managing the life cycle of user identities in systems from creation to deletion. Automated provisioning tools can help streamline this process, ensuring that access rights are granted according to current policies and roles.

Password Management: Modern systems provide self-service capabilities for users to manage their passwords securely, reducing administrative overhead and enhancing security by encouraging users to change passwords regularly.

Directory Services: These are critical for managing user attributes and supporting authentication and authorization services across different applications. Advanced directory services support standards like LDAP and SAML, providing a unified approach to access management across numerous platforms.

Single Sign-On (SSO): SSO enhances user experience by allowing a single authentication process to access multiple applications. This reduces password fatigue and minimizes the chances of phishing attacks.

Best Practices for Access Control and Identity Management

1. Least Privilege Principle:
- **Definition**: This principle involves granting users only the permissions they need to perform their assigned tasks, no more and no less.
- **Application**: This can be implemented through role-based access control (RBAC) systems, where roles are defined according to job competencies and organizational structures. Regular updates and reviews ensure that access rights remain aligned with changes in job roles.

2. Regular Audits and Reviews:
- **Purpose**: To ensure that all access rights are correct and authorized and to verify that outdated permissions are revoked.
- **Method**: Use automated tools to track and manage access permissions. Schedule periodic audits, which can be quarterly or bi-annually, to review and adjust permissions as necessary.

3. Strong Authentication Measures:
- **Multifactor Authentication (MFA)**: Requires users to present two or more verification factors to gain access to a resource, combining something they know, something they have, or something they are.
- **Biometric Verification**: Implements biological input factors, such as fingerprint or facial recognition, to add a layer of security that is difficult to replicate.

Benefits: Enhances security by adding layers that an attacker must bypass, significantly reducing the risk of unauthorized access.

4. Education and Awareness:

- **Training Programs**: Develop comprehensive training programs to educate employees about the importance of security practices. This should include training on secure password management, recognizing phishing attempts, and the proper handling of sensitive information.
- **Continuous Learning**: Keep staff updated on the latest security threats and countermeasures. Regularly refresh training content to reflect the most current risks and technologies.

5. Implementation of Access Management Tools:
- **Single Sign-On (SSO)**: Allows users to log in once and gain access to multiple systems without being prompted to log in again at each of them.
- **Identity as a Service (IDaaS)**: Uses cloud services to manage identities more flexibly and scalably, often incorporating advanced security measures inherent in cloud-based solutions.

6. Secure Protocol Enforcement:
- **Protocol Security**: Ensure that only secure protocols are used within an organization. For example, replace HTTP with HTTPS, utilize SFTP instead of FTP, and employ SSH instead of Telnet.
- **Monitoring and Compliance**: Regular monitoring of protocol usage to ensure compliance with organizational security policies and external regulations.

Robust access control and identity management are pillars of effective cybersecurity frameworks. They protect sensitive information and optimize user access, balancing security with efficiency. As technology evolves, so should the strategies to effectively manage access and identity to counter emerging threats. These foundational elements are crucial as we delve deeper into specific network security measures in subsequent sections.

Data Protection Fundamentals

Data protection is a critical pillar of cybersecurity in the digital era. It ensures data safety, privacy, and integrity across various platforms and technologies. As organizations increasingly rely on digital information, implementing effective data protection strategies becomes paramount. This section explores the comprehensive methodologies and technologies that safeguard data against unauthorized access and corruption.

Principles of Data Protection

Effective data protection requires adherence to several principles that underpin security strategies:

- **Data Minimization**: Limiting processed data to what is strictly necessary minimizes risk exposure and simplifies management.
- **Access Limitation**: Access controls are crucial, ensuring that only authorized users can view or manipulate data.
- **Encryption**: Protecting data at rest, in transit, and in use through robust encryption methodologies secures data across different states.
- **Regular Audits**: Systematic audits help in maintaining compliance and security standards by identifying vulnerabilities and ensuring continuous improvement in security protocols.

Data Protection Techniques

To further enhance data security, organizations employ several advanced techniques:

- **Data Masking**: This method obscures specific data within a database to ensure that sensitive information is shielded from unauthorized access while still allowing non-sensitive data manipulation.
- **Tokenization**: Replacing sensitive data with unique identification symbols that retain essential information about the data without compromising its security.
- **Data Erasure**: Ensuring that data is irreversibly destroyed when it is no longer necessary or when required by law.
- **Redundancy**: Implementing duplication of critical data across different data storage systems to safeguard against data loss.

Impact of Data Protection on Compliance

Navigating the complex landscape of data protection regulations is vital for legal compliance and maintaining consumer trust:

- **General Data Protection Regulation (GDPR)**: Sets stringent guidelines for data handling and grants significant rights to individuals regarding their personal data in the European Union.
- **Health Insurance Portability and Accountability Act (HIPAA)**: Regulates the privacy and security of health information in the U.S., dictating how personal health information should be protected.
- **California Consumer Privacy Act (CCPA)**: This empowers California residents to have more control over the personal information collected by businesses.

These regulations not only mandate how data should be handled but also emphasize the importance of implementing comprehensive data protection strategies to mitigate risks and penalties associated with non-compliance.

Robust data protection is indispensable in today's digital landscape. It requires a multifaceted approach involving technical solutions, organizational policies, and compliance with international regulations. As this chapter unfolds, we will delve deeper into specific data protection technologies and their applications in securing enterprise and personal data. Understanding these fundamentals is crucial for any cybersecurity professional aiming to safeguard data against the evolving threats of the digital age.

Security Policies and Best Practices

Developing and Implementing Security Policies

Developing and implementing effective security policies are fundamental tasks for securing an organization's assets and data. Security policies provide a structured framework that dictates the organization's behavior regarding information security. These policies are essential for establishing a secure organizational environment and a proactive security posture.

Key Steps in Developing Security Policies

1. Identifying the Scope and Purpose:
Before drafting any policies, it is crucial to determine their scope. This includes identifying the assets that need protection, the risks those assets face, and the objectives the policy seeks to achieve. For example, policies may aim to protect customer data, ensure the integrity of financial information, or maintain operational uptime.

2. Conducting a Risk Assessment:
A comprehensive risk assessment helps to identify potential security threats and vulnerabilities. This step is vital for understanding which areas the security policies need to address. The risk assessment should consider internal and external threats, ranging from data breaches and system failures to cyberattacks and natural disasters.

3. Involvement of Stakeholders:
Engaging stakeholders from various departments, such as IT, legal, human resources, and operations—is crucial in developing effective policies. This collaboration ensures that the policies are comprehensive and practical, addressing the needs and concerns of different parts of the organization.

4. Drafting the Policy:
Write clear, concise, and actionable policy statements. Policies should be easily understandable to ensure all employees can comply. They should include roles and responsibilities, usage standards, security protocols, and consequences for violations.

5. Review and Approval:
Once drafted, the policy should be reviewed and refined with the help of legal teams, management, and IT security experts. This step ensures the policy is compliant with legal requirements and meets industry standards.

Implementing Security Policies

1. Communication and Training:
Effective implementation starts with communication. All employees should be made aware of the new policies through comprehensive training sessions. These sessions should educate employees on the importance of the policies, their role in maintaining security, and the specifics of the policies.

2. Enforcement:

Policies should be enforceable. This involves integrating them with the organization's culture and technological systems. Automated systems can help enforce policies, such as requiring strong passwords or limiting access to sensitive information.

3. Monitoring and Compliance:

Regular monitoring of the policy's efficacy is essential. Audits and reviews help determine if the guidelines are being followed and are effective. Non-compliance issues need to be addressed promptly to maintain security integrity.

4. Continuous Improvement:

Security policies should not be static; they must evolve with new security trends, business practices, and technologies. Regular updates to the policies ensure they remain relevant and effective in mitigating new threats.

Developing and implementing security policies requires careful planning, stakeholder engagement, and continuous improvement. These policies form the backbone of an organization's security infrastructure, guiding employees in maintaining the security and integrity of operational processes. By adhering to these guidelines, organizations can protect themselves against various security threats and maintain compliance with regulatory requirements.

Case Studies on Best Practices

Exploring real-world case studies is an effective way to understand how best practices in security policies are applied and the impact they can have on protecting an organization's assets. These case studies not only highlight successful strategies but also emphasize lessons learned from security challenges.

Case Study 1: Healthcare Industry - Protecting Patient Data

Context:

A leading healthcare provider operating multiple facilities across the United States faced significant challenges in protecting patient information while complying with stringent regulations set forth by the Health Insurance Portability and Accountability Act (HIPAA). The organization managed extensive records that included sensitive health data crucial to patient care and confidentiality.

Challenge:

The healthcare provider encountered repeated data breaches, primarily due to sophisticated phishing attacks aimed at employees and outdated access control systems that failed to adequately restrict sensitive data access. These breaches not only risked patient trust but also placed the organization at risk of non-compliance with HIPAA, potentially resulting in hefty fines and legal repercussions.

Solution:

To address these issues, the organization undertook a comprehensive overhaul of its cybersecurity measures:

Employee Training:

o   Implemented an ongoing cybersecurity training program focused on identifying and responding to phishing attempts.

o   Simulated phishing exercises were regularly conducted to test employee awareness and response strategies.

Enhanced Access Controls:

o   Transitioned to a role-based access control (RBAC) system to ensure that access to sensitive information was strictly based on the minimum necessary rule.

o   Introduced advanced user authentication processes, including multi-factor authentication (MFA), particularly for accessing patient records and administrative portals.

Regular Audits and Risk Assessments:

o   Engaged third-party cybersecurity firms to conduct thorough audits of their systems and processes.

o   Developed a schedule for regular internal reviews and updates to their security policies and procedures to adapt to new cybersecurity trends and potential threats.

Incident Response Plan:

o   Established a robust incident response framework that included immediate containment and mitigation procedures, followed by detailed forensic analysis to prevent future breaches.

o   Regular drills and role-playing scenarios were introduced to ensure the incident response team could act swiftly and effectively.

Outcome:

Implementing these strategic measures led to a substantial decrease in successful phishing attacks and unauthorized data access incidents. The healthcare provider not only achieved compliance with HIPAA regulations but also restored patient confidence in their ability to safeguard personal health information (PHI). Moreover, the regular audits and adaptive security strategies positioned the organization to respond proactively to evolving cybersecurity challenges.

Reflection:

This case study illustrates the critical importance of comprehensive training, stringent access controls, and adaptive risk management strategies in protecting sensitive health data. By prioritizing employee education and robust technical safeguards, healthcare providers can significantly enhance their defense against the increasingly sophisticated landscape of cyber threats.

Case Study 2: Financial Services - Securing Transactions

Context: A multinational bank faced significant cybersecurity challenges, particularly in securing online banking transactions against sophisticated cyber threats. As financial institutions are prime targets for cyber-attacks, the bank needed a robust strategy to protect client assets and maintain trust.

Challenge: The bank struggled with vulnerabilities in its digital platforms, making it susceptible to man-in-the-middle (MITM) attacks, where attackers could intercept and manipulate financial transactions. There was also a growing concern about identity theft and unauthorized access to customer accounts.

Solution: To fortify its defenses, the bank implemented a comprehensive security overhaul with the following key components:

- **End-to-end Encryption:** All data transmitted between customers and the bank was encrypted using advanced encryption standards. This step ensured that any data intercepted during transmission would remain indecipherable to unauthorized parties.
- **Multi-Factor Authentication (MFA):** The bank introduced MFA for all online and mobile banking activities. Customers were required to authenticate their identities through at least two different methods: something they know (password or PIN), something they have (a smartphone app or hardware token), and something they are (biometric verification like fingerprint or facial recognition).
- **Real-Time Transaction Monitoring:** The bank has developed capabilities for the real-time monitoring of transactions for unusual patterns that might indicate fraud. Using sophisticated algorithms and machine learning, the system could alert security teams about anomalies such as high-value transactions, unusual login times, or foreign access attempts.
- **Customer Education Programs:** Recognizing that customer behavior is a critical factor in security, the bank launched extensive education campaigns. These programs focused on safe online banking practices, recognizing phishing attempts, and the importance of securing personal devices.
- **Upgraded Infrastructure:** The bank upgraded its cybersecurity infrastructure with state-of-the-art firewalls, intrusion detection systems (IDS), and secure gateways. This not only strengthened the perimeter defense but also improved the internal safeguards against potential insider threats.

Outcome: These strategic implementations significantly enhanced the security of financial transactions. The encryption of data protected against data breaches, while MFA reduced the risk of unauthorized account access. Real-time monitoring allowed the bank to quickly respond to potential security threats, minimizing the risk of financial loss. The customer education programs helped reduce the incidence of security breaches originating from customer-side vulnerabilities. As a result, the bank saw a substantial reduction in fraud cases and an increase in customer confidence in its digital banking platforms.

The bank's proactive approach set a new standard for transaction security in the financial industry. It protected customers and positioned the bank as a leader in financial security, enhancing its reputation in the market. This case study exemplifies how integrating advanced technology with comprehensive strategy and customer education can create a resilient security environment in the financial sector.

Test Your Knowledge (Chapter 2)

Question 1: What is the primary purpose of implementing access control within an organization?

A. To monitor employee productivity

B. To ensure only authorized users can access certain resources

C. To increase the complexity of IT systems

D. To reduce the efficiency of network systems

Question 2: Which type of access control model assigns permissions based on roles within an organization?

A. Discretionary Access Control (DAC)

B. Mandatory Access Control (MAC)

C. Role-Based Access Control (RBAC)

D. Attribute-Based Access Control (ABAC)

Question 3: In data protection, what does the integrity aspect focus on?

A. Preventing unauthorized access to data

B. Ensuring data is not altered by unauthorized individuals

C. Making data available 24/7

D. Encrypting data

Question 4: Which of the following is not a typical component of identity management?

A. User provisioning

B. Data masking

C. Password management

D. Single Sign-On (SSO)

Question 5: What is the main benefit of implementing Multi-Factor Authentication (MFA)?

A. It simplifies the user login process

B. It provides a backup for user data

C. It enhances security by requiring multiple forms of verification

D. It decreases the time it takes to access systems

Question 6: Drag and drop the following components to match them with their respective data protection methods:

- Encryption
- Backup
- Watermarking

A. Prevents data tampering and unauthorized access

B. Ensures data availability in case of system failure

C. Tracks unauthorized distribution of data

Question 7: Which regulation requires businesses to protect the personal data and privacy of EU citizens for transactions that occur within EU member states?

A. HIPAA

B. GDPR

C. CCPA

D. SOX

Question 8 (Performance-based scenario): You are tasked with designing a security policy for your organization. List the steps you would take, starting from identifying risks to implementing the policy.

Question 9: True or False: Data minimization can help reduce security risks by limiting the amount of personal data collected and stored.

Question 10: Select all that apply. Which techniques are used to ensure data confidentiality?

A. Data encryption

B. Regular audits

C. Data masking

D. Multi-factor authentication

Question 11: What is the purpose of regular security audits?

A. To ensure all staff are satisfied with their IT systems

B. To check compliance with data protection laws

C. To update the organization's technology stack

D. To socialize new employees into security practices

Question 12: Which of the following is a critical reason for updating security policies?

A. Changes in technology

B. Changes in the brand logo of the company

C. Decreased number of IT staff

D. Lower budget allocations for IT departments

Question 13 (Drag and drop): Match the following elements of a secure network architecture with their descriptions:

- Firewalls
- Intrusion Detection Systems
- Encryption

A. Monitors network traffic for suspicious activity

B. Controls incoming and outgoing network traffic based on predetermined security rules

C. Secures data by converting it into a secure format

Question 14: Which type of access control uses policies defined by an organization's requirements, and permissions can be grouped by labels or tags?

A. DAC

B. MAC

C. RBAC

D. ABAC

Question 15: True or False: Teaching employees about security best practices are less important than having advanced technical security measures in place.

Please refer to the "Test Your Knowledge SYO-701 (Answers)" chapter for the answers.

CHAPTER 3

Threats, Vulnerabilities, and Mitigations

Malware, Network Attacks, and Common Threats

Understanding common threats is crucial for developing effective defense strategies in the ever-evolving cybersecurity landscape. This section provides a comprehensive overview of the primary types of cybersecurity threats that organizations face today, including malware, network attacks, and various other prevalent threats.

Malware, short for malicious software, refers to any program or file that is harmful to a computer user. Such software is crafted to infiltrate, damage, or disable computers, systems, networks, or mobile devices, often by taking partial control over a device's operations. Types of malware include:

- **Viruses**: These are malicious programs that attach themselves to clean files and infect other clean files. They can spread uncontrollably, damaging a system's core functionality and deleting or corrupting files.
- **Trojans**: Trojans are types of malware that disguise themselves as legitimate software or hide within legitimate software that has been tampered with. They tend to act discreetly and create backdoors in your security to let other malware in.
- **Ransomware**: This type of malware locks the victim's data, typically encrypting it, and demands payment to provide access to the files upon payment. Examples include WannaCry and Petya, which have had significant global impacts.
- **Spyware**: Spyware is software that secretly monitors user activity without permission and reports it to the software's author.
- **Adware**: Although often less malicious, adware can undermine security just to serve ads—which can be particularly disruptive if it infects your browser or computer.

Overview of Network Attacks

Denial-of-Service (DoS) and Distributed Denial of Service (DDoS) Attacks:

Mechanics: These attacks typically flood systems, servers, or networks with traffic to exhaust resources and bandwidth. As a result, legitimate user requests cannot be fulfilled.
Examples:
DoS: Involves a single attacking machine using one internet connection to flood a target with malicious traffic.
DDoS: Utilizes multiple compromised devices, often part of a botnet, to launch the attack, significantly increasing its scale and impact.
Prevention: Implementing rate limiting, using anti-DDoS hardware and software solutions, and maintaining robust network architecture can help mitigate these attacks.

Man-in-the-Middle (MitM) Attacks:

Mechanics: Attackers intercept and relay messages between two parties who believe they are directly communicating with each other.

Session Hijacking: Taking over a user session to gain unauthorized access to information or services in a system.

SSL Stripping: Downgrading a secure HTTPS connection to an unsecured HTTP connection, making the user's data accessible to the attacker.

Prevention: Use of strong encryption protocols, such as HTTPS for web applications, and educating users on secure practices, such as verifying URLs and not using unsecured Wi-Fi networks for sensitive transactions.

Phishing Attacks:

Mechanics: These involve sending fraudulent communications that appear to come from a reputable source, usually through email.

Examples:

Spear Phishing Targets specific individuals or organizations and is often more tailored and convincing.

Whaling: A form of phishing aimed at senior executives and other high-profile targets.

Prevention: Employee training to recognize phishing attempts, implementing advanced email filtering solutions, and using multi-factor authentication can reduce the risk of phishing.

SQL Injection:

Mechanics: The attacker exploits vulnerabilities in data-driven applications to insert malicious SQL statements into an entry field for execution.

Impact: This can allow attackers to read sensitive data from the database, modify database data, execute administrative operations, and potentially issue commands to the operating system.

Prevention: Use of prepared statements with parameterized queries, proper validation and sanitation of user inputs, and regular security testing.

Zero-day Exploits:

Definition: These are attacks that exploit vulnerabilities in software or hardware that are unknown to those interested in mitigating the vulnerability (including the vendor).

Impact: Since there are no existing patches, zero-day exploits can be particularly damaging.

Prevention: Implementing a robust patch management process, using intrusion detection systems, and employing security solutions that detect anomalous behavior.

Insider Threats:

Scope: Includes not just intentional sabotage or theft but also accidental breaches due to carelessness or lack of knowledge.

Prevention: Implementing strict access controls, conducting regular audits, providing ongoing security training, and employing data loss prevention (DLP) strategies can help mitigate these risks.

Understanding these threats is crucial for developing effective cybersecurity measures. By recognizing the signs and potential impacts of these common threats, organizations can better prepare their defense mechanisms to prevent, detect, and respond to malicious activities effectively.

Software and Hardware Vulnerabilities

In the realm of cybersecurity, vulnerabilities in software and hardware form the gaps that attackers exploit to gain unauthorized access or cause harm. Understanding these vulnerabilities is crucial for developing effective security measures to protect systems and data. This section will explain common software and hardware vulnerabilities, providing insight into how they can be identified and mitigated.

Software Vulnerabilities

Software vulnerabilities are weaknesses or flaws in software applications that, when exploited, can lead to unauthorized access, data leakage, or other malicious activities. They emerge from software bugs, design flaws, or the misconfiguration of systems. Understanding these vulnerabilities is crucial for developing effective defenses against cyber attacks.

Buffer Overflows: This occurs when a program attempts to write more data to a fixed-length block of memory, or buffer, than it can hold. This often results in corrupting or overwriting the adjacent data. Buffer overflow vulnerabilities can lead to the execution of malicious code, system crashes, and can compromise the security of the system. Techniques to prevent buffer overflow include rigorous code testing, the use of safe libraries, and adopting languages that enforce bounds checking.

Injection Flaws: These occur when untrusted data is sent to an interpreter as part of a command or query, tricking the program into executing unintended commands or accessing unauthorized data. Common examples include SQL injection, LDAP injection, and XML injection. To mitigate these risks, developers should use prepared statements or parameterized queries, sanitize user inputs, and employ robust authentication mechanisms.

Cross-Site Scripting (XSS): XSS attacks enable attackers to inject malicious scripts into content from otherwise trustworthy websites. These scripts run in the browsers of unsuspecting users and can steal cookies, hijack sessions, or deface websites. Preventing XSS requires encoding data, validating user inputs, and implementing Content Security Policy (CSP) headers that restrict the sources of executable scripts.

Insecure Deserialization: This involves an attacker manipulating the serialization data before it is read back by the application, leading to the execution of unexpected code, denial of service, or escalation of privileges. Mitigation strategies include using safe and secure APIs that do not allow arbitrary code execution, implementing integrity checks such as digital signatures on any serialized objects, and logging all deserialization exceptions and failures.

Use After Free: This vulnerability occurs when an application continues to use a pointer after it has freed the memory it points to, which can lead to arbitrary code execution or application crashes. Avoiding these issues requires the use of automated tools to detect and correct the use after free vulnerabilities during the software development lifecycle.

Race Conditions: A race condition emerges when a device or system attempts to perform two or more operations at the same time, but because of the nature of the device or system, the operations must be done in the proper sequence to be done correctly. Mitigation includes using locks to ensure that no other thread or process can access the critical section of code until the lock is released by the process or thread holding the lock.

Hardware Vulnerabilities

Hardware vulnerabilities arise from physical or logical flaws inherent in the components and architectures of computer systems. Unlike software vulnerabilities, which can often be patched with updates, hardware vulnerabilities typically require more substantial measures to mitigate, ranging from physical security enhancements to hardware replacements or firmware updates.

Firmware Vulnerabilities: Firmware is the low-level software that initiates hardware operations. Vulnerabilities in firmware can be particularly perilous because they operate beneath the operating system. Attackers might exploit these vulnerabilities to install rootkits or persistent malware that remains active even after system reboots. An effective mitigation strategy involves regularly updating firmware to the latest versions released by manufacturers, which often address known security flaws.

Side-channel Attacks: These attacks exploit the physical hardware of computers to extract sensitive information, such as cryptographic keys, without needing to breach the software directly. Examples include:

Timing attacks: These assess how long it takes for a device to encrypt data, which can reveal information about the encryption key.

Power-monitoring attacks: By analyzing power consumption patterns during the encryption process, skilled attackers can deduce the cryptographic keys.

Electromagnetic attacks: These involve measuring electromagnetic emissions during a cryptographic operation to find sensitive data. To defend against these sophisticated attacks, organizations can employ cryptographic techniques that are resistant to timing analysis, use hardware that normalizes power consumption, and shield devices to prevent electromagnetic leaks.

Physical Manipulations: Attacks based on physical access to hardware components like USB ports or hard drives.

Examples include:

- **Direct memory access (DMA) attacks via peripheral ports**: An attacker could connect a malicious device via a Thunderbolt or FireWire port that allows them to bypass operating system security measures to read and write system memory.
- **Cold boot attacks**: These occur when an attacker with physical access reboots a computer without properly shutting it down and uses a separate boot environment to read contents that persist in RAM, which might include encryption keys or other sensitive data. Mitigating these threats requires robust physical security controls such as locking down USB ports, using BIOS-level security to disable booting from external devices, and encrypting data stored in memory.

Supply Chain Attacks: These occur when a hardware device is tampered with at any point during its manufacture or delivery. This could involve the installation of a hardware implant or malicious modifications that create backdoors or vulnerabilities. To combat these threats, organizations should only purchase hardware from reputable vendors, use tamper-evident packaging, and conduct hardware integrity checks upon receipt and before deployment.

Having explored the range of software and hardware vulnerabilities that can expose organizations to significant risks, we are now equipped with the knowledge necessary to recognize and understand these threats. This foundational understanding is critical as we move into the next chapter, where we will focus on Threat Mitigation Techniques.

Threat Mitigation Techniques

Tools and Technologies for Threat Mitigation

To effectively defend against cybersecurity threats, organizations must employ a range of specialized tools and technologies. This expanded discussion covers the core tools that are pivotal in creating a robust defense against various cyber threats, offering detailed insights into their functionalities and best use cases.

Overview of Core Tools for Threat Mitigation

Firewalls:

Acting as a barrier between trusted internal networks and untrusted external networks, such as the internet, firewalls are crucial in preventing unauthorized access. Modern firewalls go beyond simple packet filtering; they include stateful inspections, which track the state of active connections and determine which network packets to allow through the firewall. They also may incorporate deep packet inspection (DPI), intrusion prevention systems, and the ability to act as a virtual private network (VPN) gateway.

Antivirus and Anti-malware Software:

These tools are essential for the detection, prevention, and removal of malware, including viruses, worms, and ransomware. They work by scanning the system for known threats and behaviors, often using heuristic and signature-based detection methods to identify harmful software. Updates are crucial for these tools as new malware variants are constantly developed.

Intrusion Detection Systems (IDS) and Intrusion Prevention Systems (IPS):

IDS are designed to passively detect and alert systems administrators of malicious activity and policy violations, while IPS actively blocks potential threats based on a set of predefined rules. Both systems use a variety of detection methods such as anomaly-based, signature-based, and stateful protocol analysis techniques to perform their functions.

Encryption Tools:

Encryption is the process of encoding data so that only authorized parties can access it. Tools that provide encryption can secure data at rest, in transit, and in use by converting sensitive information into unreadable code that can only be deciphered with the correct cryptographic key. Techniques vary from symmetric keys (the same key is used for both encrypting and decrypting) to asymmetric keys (two different but related keys are used).

Data Loss Prevention (DLP) Software:

DLP systems monitor, detect, and prevent data breaches or exfiltration from within the company. These tools classify and protect sensitive and critical information so that unauthorized end users cannot accidentally or maliciously share data whose disclosure could put the organization at risk.

Security Information and Event Management (SIEM) Systems:

SIEM systems aggregate and analyze log data from various sources within an organization, providing real-time analysis of security alerts generated by applications and network hardware. They help organizations to more effectively identify and respond to security threats by correlating collected events and identifying deviations from the norm.

Emerging Technologies in Threat Mitigation

The cybersecurity landscape is continually evolving, necessitating the integration of advanced technologies such as:

Artificial Intelligence (AI) and Machine Learning (ML):

These technologies enhance the capabilities of traditional security tools, improving the detection of novel and sophisticated threats by analyzing patterns and predicting malicious activities based on data analysis.

Blockchain Technology:

Known for its security features, blockchain can enhance cybersecurity with its decentralized nature that provides robustness against fraud, data tampering, and cyber-attacks.

Cloud-based Security Services:

These services offer scalable security solutions that include advanced security analytics and threat intelligence capabilities. They can provide a more flexible and cost-effective solution for managing security operations without the need for extensive on-premises infrastructure.

By deploying these advanced tools and technologies, organizations can create a comprehensive security strategy that addresses various aspects of cybersecurity. Each tool brings unique capabilities that, when integrated into an overall security framework, provide substantial protection against a wide array of cyber threats.

Proactive and Reactive Strategies

Effective cybersecurity management requires an intricate balance between proactive and reactive strategies. This dual approach ensures not only prevention and preparedness but also a dynamic response capability to incidents as they unfold. Here, we delve deeper into these strategies, highlighting advanced methodologies and tools that fortify an organization's security posture.

Proactive Strategies for Preventing Security Incidents

Proactive strategies in cybersecurity are essential for preventing incidents before they escalate into breaches or attacks. These strategies involve a multi-faceted approach, combining risk management, sophisticated technology implementation, employee training, and continuous improvement. Here's a detailed expansion on how organizations can develop and enhance their proactive cybersecurity measures:

Advanced Risk Assessments:

The first line of defense in a proactive strategy involves thorough and ongoing risk assessments. Organizations should utilize cutting-edge risk assessment tools that not only identify existing vulnerabilities but also predict potential future threats using predictive analytics and machine learning algorithms. These tools can analyze vast amounts of data from various sources to forecast threats based on trends and patterns. Regularly scheduled risk assessments ensure that the organization stays ahead of new vulnerabilities and can adjust its security measures accordingly.

Strategic Patch Management:

Effective patch management is critical to maintaining the security integrity of software and systems. Organizations should implement a strategic patch management system that automates the process of identifying, downloading, testing, and applying patches to their systems. This system should have capabilities to prioritize patches based on the severity of the vulnerabilities they fix and the criticality of the systems affected. By automating patch management, organizations reduce the window of opportunity for attackers to exploit outdated software, thus maintaining a strong defense against many common attack vectors.

Security Awareness and Training Programs:

An informed and vigilant workforce is a critical component of any proactive security strategy. Beyond basic security training, organizations should develop continuous learning programs that include regular updates on the latest cybersecurity threats and practices. Engaging training modules, gamified learning experiences, and regular security drills can help reinforce security best practices and prepare employees to respond effectively to potential security incidents. Additionally, conducting regular phishing simulations can train employees to recognize and report attempts at social engineering.

Threat Intelligence Integration:

To effectively anticipate and mitigate emerging threats, organizations must implement a dynamic threat intelligence system. This system should integrate real-time data feeds from credible external sources and internal monitoring systems to provide a comprehensive view of the threat landscape. By analyzing global security data, internal network traffic, and past incidents, threat intelligence platforms can help predict and prevent attacks before they occur. Organizations should ensure that the insights gained from threat intelligence are actionable and integrated seamlessly with other security systems to enable swift responses to detected threats.

Proactive Incident Response Simulations:

Regularly conducting incident response simulations can prepare organizations to handle real cybersecurity incidents efficiently. These simulations should test the effectiveness of communication channels, the decision-making process under pressure, and the technical capabilities of the response team. Learning from these simulations can highlight weaknesses in incident response plans and prompt necessary modifications to improve response times and effectiveness.

Reactive Strategies for Incident Management

Effective incident management is crucial for minimizing the impact of security breaches and restoring normal operations swiftly. Here's an expanded discussion on implementing robust reactive strategies:

Dynamic Incident Response Planning:

Create a flexible incident response plan that includes not only predefined procedures for various types of security incidents but also guidelines for adapting these procedures as incidents unfold. This plan should detail roles and responsibilities, communication protocols, and escalation paths. It should also incorporate automation tools that can respond to incidents in real time, such as automatically isolating affected systems or cutting off network access to compromised accounts.

Enhanced Disaster Recovery (DR) and Business Continuity Planning (BCP):

Develop comprehensive DR and BCP strategies that ensure minimal service interruption and quick recovery. This includes having redundant systems in place, especially for critical data storage and processing. Cloud-based disaster recovery solutions can provide flexible and cost-effective scaling during large-scale disasters, allowing for geographic redundancy. Regularly testing these plans through simulations will help identify potential gaps and prepare the team for actual recovery operations, making adjustments based on test outcomes to optimize the plans.

Forensic Analysis and Learning:

After a security incident, conducting a thorough forensic investigation is critical to determining how the breach occurred and who was responsible. Advanced forensic tools should be used to gather and analyze data logs, access records, and other relevant information. This analysis helps in identifying the attack vectors used and the extent of the damage. The lessons learned from these analyses should be documented and used to strengthen both proactive and reactive security measures. Sharing findings with the broader security community can also help others prepare for similar threats.

Regular Security Audits and Continuous Monitoring:

Implementing continuous monitoring systems that utilize machine learning algorithms can help detect unusual activities that may indicate a security breach. These systems should monitor network traffic, user activities, and system logs to provide real-time alerts. Additionally, regular security audits are essential to assess the effectiveness of both the proactive and reactive strategies in place. These audits can help identify weaknesses in the current security posture and suggest improvements.

Communication and Transparency:

During and after an incident, maintaining clear and open communication with all stakeholders, including management, employees, customers, and regulators, is vital. This communication should be carefully managed to provide all necessary information without causing unnecessary panic or revealing sensitive security details that could lead to further exploitation.

Post-Incident Review and Adaptation:

After managing a security incident, conduct a post-incident review involving all key stakeholders. This review should analyze the effectiveness of the incident response, identify any changes needed in security strategies, and update response plans accordingly. Continuous improvement in response strategies is crucial as cyber threats evolve and new vulnerabilities emerge.

Having explored a range of proactive and reactive strategies that fortify our defenses against cyber threats, it's clear that the foundation of any robust security strategy lies in its architecture. As we move forward, we will dive into the critical components of a resilient and comprehensive cybersecurity system. This chapter will discuss the importance of cryptography and data protection in maintaining the confidentiality and integrity of data, as well as the various aspects of network security architectures that protect organizational assets from emerging threats. By integrating the principles covered in previous chapters with strategic architectural decisions, organizations can create a fortified barrier against many cyber risks.

Test Your Knowledge (Chapter 3)

Question 1: What type of malware disguises itself as legitimate software to gain access to a system?

A. Virus

B. Ransomware

C. Trojan

D. Adware

Question 2: Which type of attack involves overwhelming a system with a flood of internet traffic?

A. Phishing

B. DDoS

C. SQL Injection

D. Man-in-the-middle

Question 3: In a cybersecurity context, what does the term 'phishing' primarily refer to?

A. Exploiting hardware vulnerabilities

B. Infecting computers with viruses

C. Deceiving individuals into providing sensitive data

D. Unauthorized access to physical devices

Question 4 (Multiple Responses): Which measures are effective for mitigating malware threats? (Select two)

A. Regular software updates

B. Installing a web application firewall

C. Enabling file sharing

D. Antivirus software

Question 5: Drag and Drop. Match the following tools to their correct function in threat mitigation:

- Firewall
- IDS
- Encryption tools
- DLP software

Functions:

- Blocks unauthorized network access
- Monitors data loss prevention
- Encrypts sensitive data
- Detects intrusion attempts

Question 6: What is the primary function of a SIEM system?

A. To encrypt data transmissions

B. To monitor and analyze security alerts in real-time

C. To prevent data exfiltration

D. To manage software patches

Question 7: What does 'Risk Assessment' primarily aim to achieve in a cybersecurity context? A. Identify potential security risks

B. Train employees on security protocols

C. Install security software

D. Monitor network traffic

Question 8: Which of the following is NOT a common feature of next-generation firewalls? A. Deep packet inspection

B. Traffic shaping

C. Adware removal

D. Application Awareness

Question 9 (Performance-based Scenario): Given a scenario where an organization is facing increased phishing attempts, list the steps you would take to mitigate this threat using a security framework or tool.

Question 10: What type of cybersecurity threat involves exploiting public key infrastructure (PKI)? A. Cross-site scripting

B. Buffer overflow

C. Man-in-the-middle

D. Ransomware

Question 11: What strategy involves decrypting data to prevent unauthorized access? A. Data obfuscation

B. Encryption

C. Tokenization

D. Authentication

Question 12 (Multiple Responses): Select the proactive strategies that help in mitigating cyber threats. (Select two) A. Installing antivirus software

B. Conducting a post-incident analysis

C. Regular security audits

D. Immediate incident response

Question 13: Which attack exploits the physical properties of computer hardware to extract data? A. Side-channel attack

B. SQL injection

C. Cross-site scripting

D. Trojan attack

Question 14: Drag and Drop. Arrange the following steps in the order they would typically occur in an effective incident response plan:

- Identification
- Eradication
- Containment
- Recovery

Question 15: What is the primary focus of Data Loss Prevention (DLP) software? A. To detect and prevent data breaches

B. To encrypt data in transit

C. To provide real-time traffic analysis

D. To facilitate secure software updates

Please refer to the "Test Your Knowledge SYO-701 (Answers)" chapter for the answers.

CHAPTER 4

Security Architecture

Importance of Cryptography and Data Protection

Cryptography is the cornerstone of modern data security, forming the foundation upon which safe data transactions and storage are built. It involves the practice of securing information by transforming it into a format that is unreadable to anyone except those with the key to decrypt it, ensuring both the confidentiality and integrity of data. This section delves into the different types of encryption used in cryptography and their roles in safeguarding data across various platforms and applications.

The Role of Cryptography in Data Protection

Cryptography protects information by ensuring it remains confidential and unchanged during transmission or while in storage. Only authorized users with the decryption key can access the original information by encrypting data, thus maintaining confidentiality. Additionally, cryptographic techniques such as hashing and digital signatures protect the integrity of data by verifying that it has not been altered from its original form.

Types of Encryption and Their Uses

Encryption is a vital tool in maintaining data confidentiality and integrity across various platforms and scenarios. Here's an expanded look at the main types of encryption and specific scenarios where each is most effectively utilized:

Symmetric Encryption

Overview: Symmetric encryption uses a single key to both encrypt and decrypt information. This shared key must be kept secret between the sender and the recipient, making key distribution a critical aspect of this encryption type.

Common Algorithms: Advanced Encryption Standard (AES), arguably the most secure and widely used symmetric algorithm, is known for its speed and security, making it suitable for encrypting large data volumes. Data Encryption Standard (DES) was once popular but is now considered less secure and largely obsolete, replaced by more robust standards.

Use Cases: Symmetric encryption is ideal for scenarios requiring high-performance and efficient encryption, such as encrypting data stored on a disk or transmitted over a secure internal network where key exchange has fewer risks.

Asymmetric Encryption

Overview: Asymmetric encryption, also known as public-key cryptography, involves two keys: a public key, which anyone can use to encrypt data, and a private key, which is kept secret by the owner and used to decrypt data.

Common Algorithms: RSA (Rivest-Shamir-Adleman) is one of the oldest and most secure public-key encryption methods, widely used for secure data transmission. Elliptic Curve Cryptography (ECC) is another form that offers stronger security with smaller key sizes, making it efficient and increasingly popular in mobile environments.

Use Cases: This type of encryption is crucial for secure communications over the internet, such as HTTPS, email encryption, and signing digital certificates. It ensures that data can be safely transmitted even over unsecured channels.

Hashing

Overview: Although not an encryption method per se, hashing is essential for maintaining data integrity. It converts data into a fixed-size hash value or hash code, which acts as a unique identifier. Any alteration to the original data results in a different hash value.

Common Algorithms: The SHA (Secure Hash Algorithm) series, including SHA-256, is extensively used for creating digital signatures and ensuring data integrity in blockchain transactions and software distribution.

Use Cases: Hashing is extensively used for secure password storage. By storing hashed values of passwords, systems ensure that even if the data is compromised, the actual passwords remain undecipherable. Hashing is also employed to verify the integrity of data transmitted over insecure networks, ensuring it has not been tampered with in transit.

Data Protection through Encryption

Layered Security: By combining symmetric and asymmetric encryption, organizations can leverage the strengths of both: the efficiency of symmetric encryption for bulk data handling and the security of asymmetric encryption for secure key exchange and communications.

End-to-End Encryption (E2EE): In messaging and communication platforms, E2EE ensures that data is encrypted on the sender's device and only decrypted on the recipient's device, preventing intermediaries from accessing the readable data.

Challenges and Considerations

Key Management: Effective encryption requires robust key management systems to protect and manage cryptographic keys. The security of encrypted data is directly tied to the security of the keys used.

Performance: Encryption, especially asymmetric encryption, can introduce latency and performance overhead. Balancing security and performance is crucial, particularly in environments with high throughput requirements.

By understanding and implementing these various types of encryption appropriately, organizations can significantly enhance their security posture, protecting sensitive data against unauthorized access and ensuring its integrity remains uncompromised.

Network Security Architectures

In today's rapidly evolving digital landscape, the demand for more sophisticated network security architectures has never been higher. This section delves deeper into the integration of cutting-edge technologies designed to not only defend against but also proactively predict and mitigate cyber threats, ensuring robust security across all network layers.

Exploration of Adaptive Security Architectures

Adaptive security architectures are not just about defending in real-time; they represent a dynamic approach to security that evolves continuously with the threat landscape. Unlike traditional static defenses, these architectures are characterized by their ability to:

Learn and Adapt: Utilize continuous monitoring data to learn from the network's behavior and automatically adjust policies and protections in response to new threats and anomalies.

Automated Orchestration: Integrate various security tools to automate response actions, reducing the time from threat detection to resolution and minimizing the reliance on manual intervention.

Zero Trust Network Access (ZTNA): Beyond the Perimeter

Zero Trust is predicated on the assumption that threats can exist both inside and outside of the network perimeters. Therefore, it mandates rigorous identity and device verification at all points of access, whether a user is inside the corporate firewall or not. Key aspects include:

Micro-segmentation: This technique enhances security by creating secure zones in data centers and cloud platforms, allowing organizations to isolate workloads from one another and secure data within a specific zone.

Least-privilege Access Control: Each access request is thoroughly evaluated, and permissions are strictly allocated based on the necessity for specific resources. This minimizes lateral movement possibilities for potential attackers within a network.

Applications of AI and Machine Learning in Security

Artificial Intelligence (AI) and Machine Learning (ML) are revolutionizing network security with their ability to predict, detect, and respond to threats with unprecedented speed and accuracy. They offer:

Behavioral Analytics: By establishing what normal behavior looks like for users and machines within a network, AI-driven systems can immediately spot deviations that might indicate a security incident.

Automated Threat Detection and Remediation: These systems can initiate responses to threats without human intervention, potentially stopping attacks in real-time.

Encryption Techniques for Robust Data Protection

As quantum computing advances, the need for *quantum-resistant cryptography* becomes more apparent. This next-generation encryption ensures that data remains secure against future threats that traditional algorithms can't withstand. Additionally:

Homomorphic Encryption: This revolutionary approach allows data to be processed while remaining encrypted, facilitating secure data analysis and processing without exposing sensitive information.

Blockchain Technology for Decentralized Security Management

Blockchain technology offers a novel approach to enhancing network security through its inherent characteristics:
Enhanced Integrity and Transparency: Each transaction is recorded in a nearly impossible way to alter, providing a verifiable and permanent record.
Decentralized Trust: By removing the need for a central authority, blockchain reduces single points of failure, distributing trust across a network of nodes.

Integrating SD-WAN into Network Security

Software-Defined Wide Area Networks (SD-WAN) not only optimize traffic and improve connectivity but also bolster security by:
Simplified Management: Centralized control over network traffic allows for easier implementation and management of security protocols.
Context-Aware Security Policies: These policies adapt based on the traffic's content, user identity, and application, ensuring that security measures are precisely tailored and responsive.

Regulatory Compliance Integration

In an era where compliance requirements are ever-tightening, automated tools play a crucial role in:
Continuous Compliance Monitoring: Real-time checks ensure that networks continually meet the security standards and regulations required.
Dynamic Compliance Reporting: Automated reports provide ongoing insights into compliance status, highlighting gaps and documenting adherence to regulatory standards.

By expanding the scope of traditional network security to include these advanced methodologies and technologies, organizations can not only defend against the threats of today but also anticipate and neutralize the cybersecurity challenges of tomorrow. This proactive and adaptive approach is critical in safeguarding digital assets in an increasingly complex cyber environment.

Mobile and IoT Device Security

Introduction to Mobile and IoT Device Security

In today's interconnected world, mobile and IoT (Internet of Things) devices are critical to organizational and personal networks. However, their widespread usage also introduces significant security challenges. These devices often process and store sensitive data, making them attractive cyberattack targets. This section explores the unique security vulnerabilities associated with these devices and discusses strategies for enhancing their security through effective policies and endpoint security software.

Challenges in Securing Mobile and IoT Devices

Securing mobile and Internet of Things (IoT) devices presents various challenges, each stemming from the unique characteristics and operational environments of these devices. Here, we delve deeper into the complexities involved:

Diverse Operating Environments and Fragmentation: Mobile devices such as smartphones and tablets run on various operating systems like Android, iOS, and others, each with distinct security measures and vulnerabilities. This diversity complicates the implementation of uniform security protocols. IoT devices further amplify this challenge due to the wide range of manufacturers and the lack of standardized security protocols across devices. This fragmentation makes applying a one-size-fits-all security strategy difficult and complicates the management of security updates and patches.

Physical Security Risks: The portability of mobile devices inherently increases their risk of being lost or stolen, which can lead to potential data breaches. For IoT devices, many of which are deployed in public or easily accessible locations (like public kiosks, street lights, or unsecured buildings), the physical security risks are significant. Unauthorized physical access can lead to tampering, compromising the device's functionality and the network's integrity.

Patch Management Difficulties: Many IoT devices have limited processing power and memory, which often cannot support traditional security software or regular updates. The situation is exacerbated by manufacturers who do not always provide ongoing product support or updates, particularly for cheaper or older devices. This leaves devices permanently vulnerable to exploits that target old vulnerabilities for which patches might exist but cannot be applied.

Scalability of Security Measures: As organizations increasingly adopt IoT solutions, the number of devices connected to a network can grow exponentially. This rapid growth can overwhelm existing security measures. Ensuring that each device adheres to security policies and is monitored effectively becomes a logistical challenge.

Mobile devices add to this complexity by frequently connecting and disconnecting from the network, often from various locations worldwide.

Inconsistent Security Updates and Support: Unlike PCs and servers that receive regular updates, many mobile and IoT devices suffer from inconsistent update cycles. Some devices may never receive updates after their initial release, leaving known vulnerabilities unpatched. This issue is particularly problematic with IoT devices, where the device's lifecycle can far exceed the period during which manufacturers provide software support.

Complexity of IoT Ecosystems: IoT devices often operate within complex ecosystems that integrate various technologies, protocols, and standards. The interoperability among these diverse components can introduce security gaps. For instance, data transmitted across different devices and platforms may be secured on one device but not on another, leading to potential data breaches.

Solutions for Enhancing Mobile and IoT Device Security

To effectively secure mobile and IoT devices within both personal and professional realms, a comprehensive strategy encompassing several security measures is essential. Here is an expanded look at the solutions to enhance the security of these devices:

Development and Enforcement of Robust Security Policies

- **Tailored Security Guidelines**: Organizations should develop security policies specifically designed for the unique challenges of mobile and IoT devices. These policies should cover acceptable use, password policies, encryption requirements, and security standards for connecting devices to corporate networks.
- **User Training and Awareness**: Regular training sessions should be mandatory to inform users about the latest security practices and threats. This training should include guidelines on how to use mobile and IoT devices securely, especially when connecting to public Wi-Fi networks or handling sensitive data.

Deployment of Advanced Endpoint Security Software

- **Comprehensive Security Suites**: Deploy endpoint security solutions that are specifically designed for mobile and IoT platforms. These solutions should offer traditional antivirus capabilities, app reputation services, web filtering, network scanning, and behavior-based anomaly detection to proactively identify and mitigate threats.
- **Remote Management Tools**: Use management tools that allow IT administrators to locate, lock, or wipe lost or stolen devices remotely. These tools can also install updates and manage software patches remotely.

Regular Updates and Efficient Patch Management

- **Automated Update Tools**: Implement tools that automate the process of updating software and firmware on mobile and IoT devices. Automation ensures that devices are always running the most current software versions, reducing the risk of human error and delay.
- **Vulnerability Scanning**: Regular vulnerability scans should be conducted to identify and remediate security gaps. Devices that cannot be updated or fixed should be isolated or removed from the network to mitigate potential risks.

Authentication and Access Control Measures

- **Multi-Factor Authentication (MFA)**: MFA is required to access sensitive applications and data on mobile devices. This could include something the user knows (a password or PIN), something the user has (a security token or app), and something the user is (biometric verification like fingerprints or facial recognition).
- **Role-Based Access Control (RBAC)**: Implement RBAC to ensure that users have access only to the data and functionality necessary for their roles. This minimizes the potential damage in case of a device compromise.

Data Encryption Practices

- **End-to-End Encryption for Data in Transit**: Use strong encryption protocols such as TLS for transmitting data to and from mobile and IoT devices. This ensures that data intercepted during transmission remains confidential and tamper-proof.
- **Encryption of Stored Data**: Encrypt sensitive data stored on devices using strong encryption standards. This protects the data if the device is compromised or physically accessed by unauthorized individuals.

Utilization of IoT Security Gateways

- **Security and Data Aggregation Gateways**: Deploy IoT gateways that can provide additional security measures, such as deep packet inspection, intrusion detection, and malware analysis. These gateways serve as the intermediaries between IoT devices and the network, adding an additional layer of security by filtering out potentially malicious data before it reaches the server or cloud.

Securing mobile and IoT devices is crucial for maintaining the integrity and confidentiality of personal and organizational data. Organizations can significantly mitigate the risks associated with these devices by implementing targeted security policies and utilizing advanced endpoint security software.

Patch Management and Updates

In the cybersecurity landscape, software updates and patching are critical defenses against vulnerabilities that can be exploited by cyber threats. Patch management is the process of distributing and applying updates to software. These updates are designed to patch vulnerabilities, improve functionality, or address other issues. This section explores effective strategies for patch management, emphasizes the importance of regular updates, and discusses tools that automate these essential processes.

The Importance of Regular Updates in Reducing Vulnerabilities

- **Closing Security Gaps**: Software updates often include patches for vulnerabilities discovered since the last iteration of the software was released. Regular updates close these gaps before they can be exploited by attackers.
- **Enhancing Software Performance**: Updates not only address security flaws but also enhance software's overall performance by fixing bugs and improving features, which can also indirectly improve security.
- **Compliance with Regulatory Standards**: Keeping software updated is frequently a requirement of regulatory standards, which can mandate that organizations apply critical security patches within a certain timeframe to remain compliant.

Strategies for Effective Patch Management

Effective patch management is essential for maintaining any organization's security and operational integrity. Here are more detailed strategies that can be implemented to ensure an effective patch management process.

Develop a Comprehensive Patch Management Policy:

Policy Framework: Create a detailed policy that outlines the procedures for regular patch assessment, approval, implementation, and verification. This policy should be formally documented and made accessible to all relevant staff members.

Roles and Responsibilities: Clearly define and assign responsibilities for each stage of the patch management process. This includes who is responsible for monitoring new patches, who approves them, and who is responsible for their deployment and testing.

Inventory of Assets:

Asset Management: Maintain an up-to-date inventory of all IT assets, including hardware, software, and associated data. Knowing what assets exist on the network and what software versions are running is crucial for effective patch management.

Asset Prioritization: Classify assets based on their criticality to business operations and the sensitivity of the data they handle. This helps prioritize patch deployment when vulnerabilities affecting critical systems are identified.

Automated Patch Management Tools:

Tool Selection: Choose patch management tools that best fit the organization's infrastructure and workflow. Consider factors such as compatibility with existing systems, scalability, ease of integration, and cost.

Automation Features: Utilize tools that automate the scanning, downloading, testing, and application of patches across the organization's network. Automation reduces the workload on IT staff and helps mitigate human error.

Risk Assessment and Patch Prioritization:

Vulnerability Assessment: Regularly perform vulnerability scans to identify weaknesses that attackers could exploit. This helps determine which patches are critical and should be prioritized.

Risk-Based Patching: Not all patches are equally critical. Assess the risk associated with each vulnerability (considering the likelihood of exploitation and the potential impact) and prioritize patching accordingly.

Testing and Validation:

Patch Testing: Test patches in a controlled environment before widespread deployment. This helps identify any issues that could affect system stability or compatibility.

Rollback Plans: Always have a rollback plan in place before updating systems. If a patch deployment goes wrong, systems should be quickly restored to their original state to minimize downtime.

Education and Training:

Staff Training: Regularly train IT staff on new technologies and practices related to patch management. This includes training on patch management tools and updates on new vulnerabilities.

User Awareness: Educate end-users about the importance of applying patches, especially for software that is not managed centrally by IT, such as personal devices and home computers used for remote work.

Compliance and Reporting:

Compliance Checks: Ensure that patch management processes comply with relevant industry standards and regulations. Regular audits should be conducted to verify compliance.

Documentation and Reporting: Maintain detailed records of all patching activities, including what patches were applied, when, and by whom. This documentation is crucial for audits, troubleshooting, and historical reference.

Tools That Automate Patch Management

Various automated tools can be deployed to enhance the efficiency and effectiveness of patch management within an organization. These tools simplify the process and ensure that patches are applied consistently and promptly across all systems. Here's a more detailed look at the types of tools available for automating patch management:

Patch Management Software

- **WSUS (Windows Server Update Service)**: Specifically designed for Microsoft environments, WSUS allows administrators to manage the distribution of updates released through Microsoft Update to computers in a corporate environment. This tool helps automate the download and installation of updates, which can be customized to fit the business's schedule and needs.
- **SCCM (System Center Configuration Manager)**: Also part of the Microsoft ecosystem, SCCM provides more comprehensive management capabilities, including patch management. It allows for deploying and securing devices and applications across an enterprise. SCCM can schedule updates, manage policies, and provide extensive reporting capabilities.
- **Third-Party Solutions**: Tools such as SolarWinds Patch Manager or Automox offer extended features that include support for multiple operating systems, easy integration with existing IT infrastructures, and enhanced reporting tools. These systems often provide more granular control over patch deployment, including vulnerability assessments and patch testing before full deployment.

Configuration Management Tools

- **Ansible**: An open-source tool that automates software provisioning, configuration management, and application deployment. Ansible can be used to automate patch management by scripting updates across distributed environments without significant overhead.
- **Puppet**: This tool focuses on keeping systems compliant and maintaining the desired state, as defined in Puppet's declarative language. It can be used to manage patching by ensuring that specific software versions are installed or by automatically applying updates to vulnerable packages.
- **Chef**: Like Puppet, Chef uses a master-agent model for configuration management but allows for greater customization of the scripting language. Chef can automate patch installation processes across both physical and cloud environments.

Vulnerability Scanners Integrated with Patch Management

- **Nessus**: While primarily known as a vulnerability scanner, Nessus can integrate with patch management systems to provide a holistic view of vulnerabilities and remediation actions. It can identify the patches needed to fix vulnerabilities, thus closing the gap between vulnerability detection and patch application.
- **Qualys**: This company offers integrated patch management in its cloud platform and provides continuous security and compliance solutions. Qualys automates the lifecycle of detecting vulnerabilities, prioritizing threats, and patching applications and systems across hybrid IT environments.

Effective patch management and regular updates are non-negotiable aspects of a robust security architecture. They protect against potential breaches by ensuring that vulnerabilities are promptly addressed. As organizations expand their digital infrastructure, the complexity of managing updates increases, making the role of automated tools and comprehensive patch management strategies more critical than ever.

Test Your Knowledge (Chapter 4)

Question 1: What is the primary function of a firewall in network security?

A. To monitor data usage on the network

B. To serve as a gateway for all incoming and outgoing network traffic

C. To filter incoming and outgoing network traffic based on predetermined security rules

D. To increase the speed of network traffic

Question 2: Which of the following are the benefits of using VPNs?

A. Encryption of data

B. Data loss prevention

C. Secure remote access

D. Performance optimization of the network

Question 3: Match the following types of encryption with their correct descriptions:

- **Types**: Symmetric Encryption, Asymmetric Encryption, Hashing
- **Descriptions**:
    - o   Encrypts and decrypts with the same key
    - o   Uses two different keys for encryption and decryption
    - o   Converts data into a fixed-size string to verify data integrity

Question 4: You are tasked with securing a mobile device. List the steps you would take to encrypt data at rest on this device.

Question 5: What role does segmentation play in network security?

A. It enhances the speed of the internal network.

B. It isolates network communication to improve security.

C. It simplifies network configuration.

D. It reduces the cost of network management.

Question 6: Which are common tools used for automating patch management?

A. Ansible

B. Nessus

C. WSUS

D. SNMP

Question 7: Organize the following network security tools into the correct category of use:

- **Tools**: Firewall, IDS, Anti-Malware, Data Loss Prevention (DLP)
- **Categories**: Threat Prevention, Threat Detection, Data Protection, Traffic Management

Question 8: Configure a firewall rule that blocks all incoming traffic from IP addresses that are known to be malicious.

Question 9: What is a primary security concern with IoT devices?

A. High cost

B. Complexity of use

C. Vulnerability to attacks

D. Energy consumption

Question 10: What features should a comprehensive endpoint security solution include for IoT devices?

A. Data encryption

B. Geolocation tracking

C. Real-time threat detection

D. Automatic software updates

Question 11: Match the following security measures with their appropriate technology implementations:

- **Measures**: Encryption at Rest, Secure Remote Access, Intrusion Detection
- **Technologies**: VPN, Disk Encryption, IDS

Question 12: Design a strategy to ensure compliance with GDPR using encryption and access control mechanisms.

Question 13: Which encryption standard is considered the strongest for data at rest?

A. AES

B. DES

C. SSL

D. RSA

Question 14: Which actions are critical when deploying a secure cloud architecture?

A. Regular auditing

B. Implementing physical security

C. Using a public-key infrastructure

D. Employing a zero-trust model

Question 15: Arrange the following steps in the correct order to form an effective patch management process:

- Steps: Assess vulnerabilities, Apply patches, Verify and test patches, Monitor for compliance

Please refer to the "Test Your Knowledge SY0-701 (Answers)" chapter for the answers.

CHAPTER 5
Security Operations

Security Operations Centers (SOC)

A Security Operations Center (SOC) is the cornerstone of enterprise cybersecurity, providing real-time analysis and monitoring to detect, assess, and respond to cybersecurity threats. This hub is crucial for maintaining the integrity of IT environments in the face of increasing cyber threats. This section explores a SOC's expanded functions and operational complexities and demonstrates its pivotal role in an organization's incident detection and response framework.

Core Functions of a SOC

Advanced Threat Detection: SOCs utilize various sophisticated tools to continuously monitor network traffic, endpoint behavior, and log data. Advanced detection techniques involve anomaly detection systems that leverage machine learning algorithms to identify deviations from normal behavior that could indicate a security threat.

Proactive Incident Response: Once a potential threat is identified, the SOC coordinates a swift response, which can involve isolating affected systems, deploying countermeasures, and, if necessary, conducting forensic analysis to understand the breach. Incident response teams work according to well-defined protocols to contain incidents and mitigate damage.

Security Information and Event Management (SIEM): At the heart of a SOC is its SIEM system, which aggregates and analyzes log data from various sources within the organization, providing a unified view of the security posture. SIEM systems are critical for correlating events and identifying potential security incidents.

Continuous Monitoring and Vulnerability Management: Beyond incident response, SOCs are responsible for assessing system vulnerabilities. This includes regular scans and the assessment of the security infrastructure to identify and rectify vulnerabilities before they are exploited.

Compliance and Forensic Capabilities: SOCs also ensure that an organization adheres to necessary data protection and cybersecurity compliance requirements. In the event of a breach, SOC teams perform forensic analysis to trace the origins of an attack, helping to prevent future incidents and ensuring legal compliance.

Operational Aspects of a SOC

24/7 Operations: Given that cyber threats can occur at any time, most SOCs operate on a 24/7 basis. This constant vigilance is supported by rotational shifts of cybersecurity professionals who monitor systems around the clock.

Integration of Cutting-Edge Technologies: SOCs integrate various technologies, including predictive analytics, threat intelligence platforms, and automated incident response systems. These technologies enhance the SOC's capabilities in detecting advanced threats and responding to them more efficiently.

Staff Expertise and Training: SOCs are staffed by experts in various domains of cybersecurity, including analysts, managers, and incident responders. Continuous training and development are crucial to keep pace with evolving cyber threats. Simulation-based training and regular cybersecurity drills help refine the team's skills and preparedness.

Strategic Use of Artificial Intelligence and Automation: Many SOCs are increasingly using AI and automation to handle high volumes of alerts, reducing the time to detect and respond to incidents. Automation in routine tasks allows analysts to focus on more complex analysis and decision-making.

SOCs are vital for robust cybersecurity, offering not just defense against attacks but also insights that drive security strategy and risk management. By effectively managing and optimizing the operations of SOCs, organizations can significantly enhance their ability to detect, respond to, and recover from cybersecurity incidents.

Incident Response Strategies and Emerging Technologies

In the rapidly evolving cybersecurity landscape, traditional incident response mechanisms often need to be supplemented with advanced strategies and the latest technological innovations. This section explores cutting-edge incident response strategies, focusing on how emerging technologies and methodologies reshape how organizations prepare for, detect, and respond to cyber threats.

Integration of Artificial Intelligence and Machine Learning

Automated Threat Detection: AI and ML are revolutionizing threat detection by enabling systems to identify patterns and anomalies at speeds and accuracies far beyond human capabilities. These technologies can analyze vast quantities of data in real time, spotting potential threats before they manifest into actual breaches.

Predictive Capabilities: Machine learning models can predict potential security incidents by analyzing trends and historical data. This proactive approach allows organizations to fortify defenses in areas most likely to be targeted in the future.

Utilization of Security Orchestration, Automation, and Response (SOAR)

Workflow Automation: SOAR platforms integrate with existing security tools to automate response workflows. By codifying response processes, SOAR ensures rapid and consistent action against threats, reducing the time from detection to resolution.

Incident Management and Collaboration: These platforms enhance the efficiency of security teams by providing tools that support incident management, from initial detection through response, investigation, and reporting. This centralized approach facilitates better communication and coordination across the security team.

Digital Forensics and Incident Response (DFIR)

Advanced Forensic Tools: New technologies in digital forensics offer more profound insights and faster analysis. Tools equipped with AI capabilities can sift through large datasets to extract relevant information much quicker than traditional methods.

Remote Forensics: Emerging tools now allow for remote forensic capabilities, enabling security teams to perform forensic investigations without needing physical access to the affected systems. This is particularly useful in complex network environments and in situations where quick response times are critical.

Blockchain for Incident Response

Decentralized Data Integrity: Blockchain technology can be employed to create immutable logs of all network transactions, providing a verifiable and tamper-proof record. In the event of an incident, these logs can be invaluable for tracing actions and understanding the scope of an incident.

Secure Information Sharing: Blockchain can facilitate secure, decentralized sharing of threat intelligence among organizations, enhancing collective defense postures without compromising the security of the participating entities' networks.

The dynamic nature of cyber threats necessitates a continual evolution of incident response strategies. By leveraging AI, ML, SOAR, advanced digital forensics, and blockchain technology, organizations can respond to incidents more effectively and anticipate and mitigate potential threats more proactively.

Disaster Recovery Planning

Backup Strategies and Data Recovery

In cybersecurity, recovering data after a disaster is as crucial as protecting it from threats. Effective backup strategies and data recovery techniques form the backbone of robust disaster recovery planning. They ensure that organizations can quickly restore operations with minimal loss, maintaining business continuity even in adverse situations. This section outlines various backup strategies and explains the significance of comprehensive data recovery techniques.

Understanding Different Backup Strategies

Backup strategies are essential components of a robust IT infrastructure, providing a means to recover critical data and maintain business operations after data loss incidents. Each backup strategy serves a unique purpose and is suited to different operational requirements and recovery objectives. Here's a deeper dive into various backup strategies:

Full Backups

Description: A full backup captures every file and folder in the system and is the most comprehensive type of backup. It creates a complete copy of the organization's data at a specific point in time.

Advantages: Full backups provide the simplest form of recovery since every piece of data has been stored. In the event of data loss, a full backup ensures that all data can be restored from a single dataset.

Challenges: The main drawbacks are the high storage requirements and the time it takes to complete the backup. Frequent full backups can also be resource-intensive, affecting system performance during the backup process.

Incremental Backups

Description: Incremental backups save only the data that has changed since the last backup, regardless of whether the last backup was a full or another incremental backup.

Advantages: This strategy significantly reduces the amount of data that needs to be backed up after the initial full backup, saving storage space and reducing the time required for subsequent backups.

Challenges: During recovery, data must be restored from the last full backup and every incremental backup taken since then, which can complicate the recovery process and increase recovery time.

Differential Backups

Description: Differential backups record all changes made since the last full backup, not just since the last differential backup. Each differential backup is larger than the last but smaller than running a full backup.

Advantages: Differential backups strike a balance between full and incremental backups by offering a more straightforward recovery process than incremental backups, as only the last set of full and differential backups need to be restored.

Challenges: They tend to grow in size and may require more storage space over time compared to incremental backups, as each backup contains all changes since the last full backup.

Mirror Backups

Description: Mirror backups create an exact copy of the source data in real time. This type of backup is often used in high-availability environments.

Advantages: Mirroring provides immediate recovery since the backup dataset is always up-to-date with the primary dataset. It also allows for real-time data access from the backup location.

Challenges: Mirrored backups do not protect against data corruption or file deletion, as these changes are immediately replicated in the backup. They also require significant storage capacity and bandwidth.

Choosing the Right Backup Strategy

The choice of backup strategy depends on several factors, including the criticality of data, recovery time objectives (RTO), recovery point objectives (RPO), and available resources for backup operations. For instance:

Critical systems where data needs to be restored quickly might benefit from more frequent full or differential backups.

Less critical data, where recovery time can be more flexible, might be suitable for incremental backups to conserve resources.

Organizations often employ these strategies to optimize their data protection efforts, balancing between comprehensive data coverage, resource utilization, and quick recovery needs. By understanding the strengths and limitations of each backup type, businesses can tailor their backup procedures to match their specific operational and recovery requirements, ensuring resilience against data loss incidents.

Importance of Backup Strategies in Disaster Recovery

Backup strategies are foundational to disaster recovery planning. They weave a complex tapestry of business continuity, compliance, and risk management into a unified defensive stance against data loss and system failures.

Ensuring Business Continuity Effective backup strategies are critical for minimizing downtime during disruptions, allowing businesses to swiftly restore critical data and system functionality. This rapid recovery capability is essential for maintaining continuous operations and mitigating the economic impacts associated with downtime. Regular and strategic backups ensure that businesses have multiple recovery points, providing the flexibility to select an optimal data state for recovery and thus enhancing operational resilience.

Safeguarding Data Availability and Integrity A robust backup system guarantees that vital data remains accessible even during system failures, which is crucial for sectors where immediate data availability is synonymous with operational functionality. Additionally, these strategies protect data integrity, offering a reliable method for restoring data to its pre-corruption state. This is particularly vital in environments susceptible to data corruption or malicious attacks, such as ransomware.

Regulatory Compliance and Legal Protection Many industries operate under stringent regulations that mandate stringent data retention and availability standards. Tailored backup strategies help organizations meet these legal requirements, thereby avoiding significant fines and penalties. Moreover, in legal and compliance scenarios, backups can serve as vital evidence, helping organizations demonstrate due diligence and adherence to regulatory standards. This aspect of backup strategies is crucial for legal defense and compliance verification, particularly in regulated sectors like finance and healthcare.

Risk Management Enhancement Implementing a backup strategy inherently involves a thorough risk assessment, identifying critical data that warrants protection, and determining the most effective means of safeguarding it. This proactive approach serves as a cornerstone of sound risk management, providing a cost-effective method for mitigating the potential impacts of data loss. While maintaining backups incurs certain costs, these are generally outweighed by the benefits of preventing significant data-related disruptions and losses.

Support for Scalability and Flexibility: As organizations grow, so too does the volume of data they generate and need to manage. Backup strategies must be scalable and evolving within the organization to accommodate increasing data loads without compromising recovery times or operational performance. Modern backup systems offer various recovery options, from traditional on-premises solutions to innovative cloud-based and hybrid models, allowing businesses the flexibility to choose solutions that best fit their immediate needs and future growth trajectories.

Data Recovery Techniques

Data recovery techniques are essential to the robustness of any organization's disaster recovery strategy. They provide the necessary tools to restore data quickly and minimize operational downtime following a disruption. This detailed discussion explores the various methods that can be effectively implemented.

Data Replication plays a crucial role in data recovery, ensuring data is copied to a secondary location. Synchronous replication ensures data is copied in real time, requiring confirmation from both the primary and secondary sites to complete a write operation. This method suits critical data needing instant recovery but can be costly due to high bandwidth requirements and the need for closely located replication sites. In contrast, asynchronous replication allows intervals between data copying, lessening the load on the primary system but increasing the risk of data loss during sudden failures.

Snapshot Technology is another pivotal method, offering point-in-time copies of data sets. These snapshots provide a recovery marker that doesn't disrupt the live environment and are particularly useful for systems requiring frequent backups, like databases and virtual machines. Continuous Data Protection (CDP) takes snapshots to another level by recording every data version as it is written. This allows organizations to restore data to nearly any point in time and minimizing potential data loss in dynamic settings.

Cloud-based recovery methods have become increasingly popular due to their scalability and cost-effectiveness. Many organizations now leverage cloud storage, which often includes built-in redundancy to ensure data availability even if one server or location is compromised. Disaster Recovery as a Service (DRaaS) simplifies the recovery process by outsourcing the management of disaster recovery operations, including data backups, storage, and recovery processes, which can be especially advantageous for organizations lacking the resources to maintain a comprehensive disaster recovery site.

Virtualization in Disaster Recovery includes techniques like virtual machine replication, which involves replicating the VM to an off-site location that can be rapidly activated in case the primary site fails. This replication includes the data and the entire virtual machine configuration, allowing for quick restoration. Virtual machine snapshots capture the complete state of a VM at a specific point in time, including its power state, memory contents, and machine settings, all of which can be restored quickly to recover from crashes or corruption.

Enhanced Techniques for Complex Systems, such as automated failover processes, provide high-availability environments with the ability to detect system failures and automatically switch to a backup system or site without human intervention. Hybrid data recovery approaches that combine on-premise and cloud-based solutions offer a balanced and robust recovery option, enabling businesses to optimize costs while meeting recovery objectives.

By understanding and implementing these data recovery techniques, organizations enhance their resilience against disruptions and ensure the integrity and availability of their data, thus maintaining continuous operations across various scenarios. This comprehensive approach protects data and strengthens the overall disaster recovery strategy.

Testing and Validation of Recovery Plans

Effective disaster recovery and business continuity plans are pivotal for any organization aiming to maintain resilience and operational integrity in the face of unexpected disruptions. However, these plans' existence is insufficient; regular testing and validation are crucial to ensure these strategies are actionable and effective when disaster strikes. This section delves into why regular testing and validation of recovery plans are indispensable and how to implement these processes effectively.

The Importance of Regular Testing

Identifying Gaps in Plans: Testing helps identify gaps in recovery plans before they are needed. This proactive approach allows organizations to address and rectify shortcomings, ensuring that when a real incident occurs, the plan functions as intended without significant obstacles.

Ensuring Plan Accuracy and Relevance: As organizations grow and evolve, so do their operational structures and technologies. Regular testing ensures recovery plans remain relevant and accurately aligned with the current organizational processes and IT infrastructure.

Training and Familiarity: Regular drills and testing scenarios ensure the staff remains familiar with their roles during an emergency. This training is crucial for reducing response times and improving the efficiency and effectiveness of the recovery process.

Validation Techniques

Several validation techniques are employed to enhance the robustness and reliability of disaster recovery and business continuity plans, each designed to test different aspects of the plans under various conditions. The validation of these plans is crucial to ensure they function as expected during an actual emergency and familiarize the response team with the protocols they need to follow, ultimately reducing recovery times and minimizing impact on operations.

Tabletop Exercises provide a theoretical environment where team members verbally walk through various disaster scenarios. This method is particularly valuable for assessing the decision-making process and clarifying roles and responsibilities within the recovery team. The discussions can help pinpoint areas where misunderstandings or lack of clarity could delay response times during an actual incident.

Walkthroughs and Drills take validation further by enacting the recovery processes through step-by-step checks or dynamic simulations. Walkthroughs allow the team to methodically verify each step of the plan in a controlled environment, ensuring that every procedure is actionable and practical. Drills, on the other hand, simulate real-life conditions, requiring the team to react as they would in an actual disaster, thus testing the plan's practical applicability and readiness to execute it.

Simulated Disasters offer the most realistic environment for testing the plans by mimicking the effects of a real disaster as closely as possible. This could involve cutting power, using backup systems, or activating off-site data centers. These simulations are crucial for understanding how the infrastructure and team will realistically react under stress. The insights gained from these exercises are invaluable for refining disaster recovery and business continuity strategies.

Automated Testing Tools are increasingly being integrated into the validation process, offering continuous, objective testing of the recovery systems. These tools can simulate network failures, data breaches, or full-scale system recoveries, providing regular feedback on the recovery time objectives and system resilience. Automation helps maintain a consistent testing regime and can highlight potential issues that may not be evident in manual testing processes.

Feedback Mechanisms and Continuous Improvement processes ensure that every test enhances disaster recovery and business continuity plans. After each test, detailed reviews are conducted to gather all stakeholders' feedback. This feedback is critical for identifying successful elements of the plan and areas needing improvement. Continually refining the plans ensures they remain effective and relevant amidst changing operational demands and emerging threats.

Automating Testing Processes

Automating the testing of disaster recovery and business continuity plans can significantly enhance the efficiency and reliability of these processes. By integrating technology into testing routines, organizations can ensure more consistent, comprehensive, and objective evaluations of their recovery strategies. Here's an in-depth look at how automation can be employed in the testing processes:

Benefits of Automation in Testing

Consistency and Frequency: Automated testing can be conducted more frequently and consistently than manual testing. Automation ensures that tests are performed the same way each time, eliminating human error and variability in how tests are conducted.

Real-time Monitoring: Automated tools can monitor systems and processes in real-time, providing immediate feedback when a component fails or does not perform as expected during a test. This capability allows for quicker adjustments and more dynamic testing environments.

Resource Efficiency: Automation reduces the need for extensive manual resources during testing, allowing team members to focus on more strategic tasks, such as analyzing test results and improving recovery plans.

Implementing Automated Testing Tools

Simulation Software: Advanced simulation tools are available that can mimic various disaster scenarios to test the resilience of IT infrastructure without impacting actual operations. These tools can model everything from cyberattacks to natural disasters, providing valuable insights into an organization's preparedness.

Virtualized Testing: Virtualization technology allows organizations to create virtual copies of their environment where recovery processes can be tested without affecting the live environment. This is particularly useful for testing the restoration of critical applications and services on virtual machines.

Automated Scripts: Scripts can be developed to automatically initiate and monitor the performance of specific disaster recovery procedures. For example, scripts can automatically back up data, switch operations to a backup site, and restore operations to the primary site after the test.

Integration with Existing Systems: Automation tools should be integrated with monitoring and management systems. This integration allows for a more seamless and comprehensive testing process that leverages real-time data from across the organization's infrastructure.

Challenges and Considerations

Complexity and Setup: Implementing automation requires initial time and resources to set up and configure the appropriate tools. The complexity of the organization's IT environment can significantly influence the extent and type of automation that can be implemented.

Regular Updates and Maintenance: Like any technology, automated testing tools require regular updates and maintenance to ensure they remain effective and secure. Organizations must keep these tools updated to handle new types of threats and changes in IT infrastructure.

Training and Expertise: Staff need to be trained to use automated testing tools and interpret the data these tools generate. Proper training ensures that the organization can benefit from automation by effectively analyzing and acting on test results.

Feedback and Continuous Improvement

Incorporating Feedback: After each test, gather feedback from all participants and use this information to refine the recovery plans. This feedback loop is essential for continuous improvement and adaptation to new organizational threats and changes.

Reporting and Documentation: Documenting the outcomes and lessons learned from each test is vital for tracking the evolution of the recovery plan and supporting compliance with industry regulations and standards.

Regular testing and validation of recovery plans are not just about compliance or theoretical readiness but about ensuring practical preparedness and resilience in the face of disruptions.

Test Your Knowledge (Chapter 5)

Question 1: What is the primary role of a Security Operations Center (SOC)?

A. To manage network performance

B. To conduct software installations

C. To monitor and respond to security threats

D. To handle customer service inquiries

Question 2: Which type of backup strategy involves copying changes made since the last full backup?

A. Full backup

B. Incremental backup

C. Differential backup

D. Mirror backup

Question 3: In a disaster recovery scenario, what is the purpose of using cloud-based recovery services?

A. To reduce the cost of hardware maintenance

B. To enhance physical security

C. To provide scalable and flexible recovery solutions

D. To increase data processing speed

Question 4: What does a firewall do in a network security architecture?

A. Monitors employee internet usage

B. Acts as a server

C. Filters incoming and outgoing network traffic based on security rules

D. Provides data storage solutions

Question 5: Which data recovery technique involves creating an exact point-in-time copy of data?

A. Data mirroring

B. Data replication

C. Snapshot

D. Cloud backups

Question 6 (Multiple Response): Which are essential features of an effective SOC? (Select all that apply)

A. Real-time monitoring

B. Automatic software updates

C. Threat detection and response

D. Sales and marketing analytics

Question 7: What type of backup is created by copying all changes made since the last incremental backup?

A. Full backup

B. Incremental backup

C. Differential backup

D. Snapshot backup

Question 8: Which scenario best utilizes synchronous data replication?

A. When immediate data recovery is essential

B. When data accuracy is not critical

C. When backup data can be several hours old

D. When reducing storage space is a priority

Question 9: What is the primary benefit of implementing automated patch management tools?

A. Enhancing email communications

B. Reducing the physical storage needed

C. Ensuring timely application of security patches

D. Decreasing energy consumption

Question 10 (Drag-and-Drop): Place the following incident response steps in the correct order:

A. Identification

B. Preparation

C. Recovery

D. Containment

E. Eradication

Question 11: Which statement best describes the purpose of forensic analysis in cybersecurity?

A. To upgrade software applications

B. To analyze data and identify how a security breach occurred

C. To market cybersecurity products

D. To train new employees

Question 12: What is the main function of encryption in securing data?

A. To speed up data access

B. To convert data into a secure format that is unreadable without a key

C. To serve as a password management tool

D. To create a backup of all system data

Question 13: Which recovery technique uses virtualization to enhance disaster recovery efforts?

A. Manual recovery

B. Physical replication

C. Virtual machine snapshots

D. Onsite data storage

Question 14: Why is it important to test and validate business continuity and disaster recovery plans regularly?

A. To ensure they work effectively under actual disaster conditions

B. To comply with international travel regulations

C. To increase employee productivity

D. To monitor daily task completion rates

Question 15 (Performance-Based Scenario): You are tasked with designing a test for a disaster recovery plan involving a simulated network outage. List the key components you would include in this test to evaluate the recovery plan's effectiveness.

Please refer to the "Test Your Knowledge SYO-701 (Answers)" chapter for the answers.

CHAPTER 6

Cybersecurity Governance

Implementing Security Frameworks for Organizational Compliance

In today's complex regulatory landscape, integrating established security frameworks such as NIST and ISO/IEC 27001 into organizational compliance strategies is essential for robust cybersecurity governance. This segment explores the pragmatic application of these frameworks, showing how they meet the dual needs of addressing technical security and fulfilling compliance obligations.

Strategic Alignment with Business Objectives

The integration of security frameworks into an organization must be intrinsically linked to its business objectives. This alignment ensures that the implementation of security measures not only bolsters business operations but does so without introducing unnecessary complexities or restrictions. The adaptation of these frameworks should be bespoke and tailored to meet the unique cultural, processual, and risk profiles of the organization. This customization ensures that the framework supports the organization effectively, making its application both practical and beneficial.

Leveraging Frameworks for Compliance

Security frameworks are often comprehensive, encompassing best practices that satisfy a broad spectrum of regulatory requirements. For instance, the control set provided by ISO/IEC 27001 can assist organizations in meeting the stringent demands of the GDPR for data security and privacy. Furthermore, the emphasis on continuous compliance monitoring within these frameworks helps organizations maintain an ongoing adherence to required standards. Organizations can proactively manage their compliance status by implementing systems that continually monitor compliance, identifying and addressing gaps more efficiently.

Leadership and Framework Enforcement

Successfully adopting any security framework relies heavily on the commitment and support of an organization's leadership. Leaders play a crucial role in championing the implementation of these frameworks, providing clear directions, allocating adequate resources, and ensuring continuous support for security initiatives. Additionally, fostering an organizational culture that prioritizes regular training and awareness is vital. By keeping security and compliance at the forefront of organizational priorities, employees become more engaged and proactive in their roles within the framework's processes. Moreover, establishing clear accountability within leadership roles and incentivizing compliance goals can significantly enhance organizational commitment and proactive engagement.

Operational Integration and Feedback Mechanisms

For security frameworks to remain effective, they must include mechanisms for continual feedback and improvement. Regular audits, employee feedback, and reviews of incident handling provide critical insights that help refine and optimize security strategies. Integrating these frameworks into the broader risk management strategy of the organization ensures that security measures are not only comprehensive but also dynamically responsive to the evolving risk landscape. Integrating security frameworks within organizational compliance strategies goes beyond mere regulatory adherence; it embeds robust security practices into the fabric of the organization.

Compliance and Internal Audits

Compliance and internal audits are critical components of effective cybersecurity governance. These processes ensure that an organization adheres to legal, regulatory, and technical standards necessary for protecting information assets. This section explores the detailed processes involved in conducting internal audits and compliance checks and highlights their role in strengthening cybersecurity governance within an organization.

Key Aspects of Compliance in Cybersecurity

Legal and Regulatory Compliance: This includes obeying laws and regulations that apply to cybersecurity within specific industries. For example, organizations handling health-related information must comply with the Health Insurance Portability and Accountability Act (HIPAA) in the U.S., which sets the standard for protecting sensitive patient data. Similarly, companies operating in or with the European Union must adhere to the General Data Protection Regulation (GDPR), which governs the processing of personal data.

Standards and Frameworks Alignment: Compliance also extends to voluntary standards and frameworks that are not legally mandatory but are considered best practices in the industry. These include the ISO/IEC 27001 standard, which provides specifications for an information security management system (ISMS) that enables organizations to manage the security of assets such as financial information, intellectual property, employee details, and information entrusted by third parties. Another example is the NIST Cybersecurity Framework, which provides a computer security guidance policy framework for organizations to assess and improve their ability to prevent, detect, and respond to cyber-attacks.

Risk Management Compliance: Beyond following laws and applying standards, compliance involves integrating risk management processes that identify, assess, and manage cybersecurity risks. This aligns with frameworks like COBIT, which provide comprehensive management and governance strategies that help organizations handle risks effectively.

Impact of Compliance on Organizational Security

Enhancing Security Posture: Compliance drives organizations to implement robust security measures that protect against a variety of threats. This often includes deploying advanced security technologies, adopting stringent security policies, and conducting regular security training for employees.

Building Trust with Stakeholders: Adhering to recognized compliance standards helps build trust with stakeholders, including customers, investors, and regulatory bodies. It reassures them that the organization is committed to maintaining high-security standards and protecting sensitive information.

Preventing Legal and Financial Penalties: Non-compliance can result in severe legal and financial consequences, including hefty fines, legal disputes, and damage to reputation. By ensuring compliance, organizations can avoid these penalties and protect their financial health and public image.

Facilitating International Operations: For organizations operating across borders, compliance with international standards and regulations is crucial. This facilitates smoother operations, helps in mitigating cross-border data transfer issues, and ensures alignment with global security practices.

Challenges in Maintaining Compliance

Evolving Legal Requirements: One of the significant challenges is keeping up with the changing legal landscape. As technology and data use evolve, so do the laws and regulations governing them, requiring organizations to stay informed and agile in their compliance strategies.

Integrating Compliance into Business Processes: Integrating compliance requirements into day-to-day business processes can be complex, particularly for large or global organizations with diverse operations.

Resource Allocation: Compliance often requires significant resources, including investing in technology, hiring skilled personnel, and ongoing training and audits.

Internal Audits - Process and Importance

Internal audits are essential mechanisms within an organization's cybersecurity governance structure, aimed at ensuring that security measures are both effective and compliant with established policies and external regulations. Here's a detailed breakdown of the internal audit process and its importance:

Planning and Preparation

- **Scope Definition**: Every audit starts with defining its scope, which details what will be audited, the departments involved, and the objectives to be achieved. This step ensures that the audit focuses on the right areas without overlooking critical aspects.
- **Resource Allocation**: Proper resources — including a team of skilled auditors and necessary tools — are allocated based on the scope. This also involves scheduling the audit at a time that minimizes disruption to regular business operations.
- **Risk Assessment**: Initial risk assessments may be conducted to prioritize audit areas based on their susceptibility to risks and past audit findings. This helps in focusing efforts where they are most needed.

Execution

- **Data Collection**: Auditors collect relevant information through interviews, system logs, configuration reviews, and security settings. Automated tools are often employed to gather detailed and accurate data.
- **Testing and Assessment**: Specific tests are performed to evaluate the effectiveness of security controls and policies. This might include penetration testing, vulnerability scanning, and simulation of attack scenarios.
- **Control Evaluation**: The effectiveness of existing controls is evaluated against the organization's policies and compliance requirements. This includes assessing administrative, technical, and physical controls.

Reporting

- **Findings Documentation**: Auditors document all findings, including deficiencies and areas of non-compliance. This documentation provides a clear record of what was found, supporting the transparency and accountability of the process.
- **Recommendations for Improvement**: Along with findings, auditors provide recommendations for how to address each issue. These recommendations are prioritized based on the risk and impact associated with the findings.
- **Review and Approval**: The audit report is reviewed and must be approved by senior management. This ensures that the leadership is aware of and understands the current security posture and necessary improvements.

Follow-up and Remediation

- **Action Plan Development**: Based on the audit report, a detailed action plan is developed to address each finding. This plan assigns responsibilities and deadlines for implementing improvements.
- **Implementation Monitoring**: The progress of remediation efforts is monitored to ensure that improvements are implemented as planned. Additional resources may be allocated to address any delays or complications.
- **Verification of Compliance**: After the remediation measures are implemented, a follow-up audit or verification process is conducted to ensure that the issues have been adequately addressed and that the organization is now compliant with the necessary standards.

Importance of Internal Audits

- **Enhancing Security Posture**: By identifying vulnerabilities and areas of non-compliance, internal audits help organizations enhance their overall security posture.
- **Driving Compliance**: Audits ensure that the organization remains in compliance with relevant laws, regulations, and standards, reducing the risk of penalties or legal issues.
- **Building Trust**: Regularly audited and compliant organizations can build and maintain trust among customers, stakeholders, and regulatory bodies, affirming the organization's commitment to security.

Automated Tools for Compliance and Auditing

The use of automated tools in compliance and auditing processes significantly enhances an organization's ability to maintain rigorous cybersecurity standards efficiently. These tools streamline complex processes, ensure accuracy, and save time by automating routine tasks. Here's a closer look at various types of automated tools that are integral to compliance and auditing in cybersecurity governance.

Governance, Risk Management, and Compliance (GRC) Platforms

Functionality: GRC platforms integrate governance, risk management, and compliance processes, centralizing control and visibility across all three domains. These systems are designed to ensure that organizational strategies are aligned with risk appetites and compliance requirements.

Benefits: They automate the collection and analysis of data from across the organization, making it easier to detect compliance gaps, manage risks, and adhere to regulatory frameworks. Examples include RSA Archer, MetricStream, and IBM OpenPages.

Security Information and Event Management (SIEM) Systems

Functionality: SIEM systems collect and aggregate log data generated throughout the organization's technology infrastructure, from network devices to servers to applications. They analyze this data to identify abnormal patterns or security incidents, aiding in rapid response.

Benefits: SIEM tools automate alerting and report generation, which are crucial for auditing processes. They help organizations respond to audits more quickly by providing detailed evidence of incident responses and security monitoring. Popular SIEM tools include Splunk, LogRhythm, and AlienVault.

Compliance Management Software

Functionality: These tools are specifically designed to help organizations comply with industry standards and regulations by automating compliance workflows, documentation management, and reporting.

Benefits: Compliance management software supports regular checks against compliance standards, automates the tracking of changes in compliance regulations, and helps in reporting for auditing purposes. This software is often critical in sectors heavily regulated, like finance and healthcare.

Automated Auditing Tools

Functionality: Automated auditing tools can perform network and system audits to check for vulnerabilities and non-compliance with established security policies.

Benefits: They provide detailed, actionable reports that help organizations focus their remediation efforts where they are needed most, ensuring that compliance and security postures are both up-to-date and effective. Tools like Nessus or Qualys are used widely for these purposes.

Continuous Monitoring Solutions

Functionality: These tools provide ongoing surveillance of an organization's network and systems to ensure that they remain in compliance with set policies and standards.

Benefits: Continuous monitoring solutions help in detecting compliance drift and security lapses as soon as they occur, enabling immediate corrective actions. This is essential not only for maintaining compliance but also for protecting against threats in real-time.

Integration Capabilities

Cross-Platform Functionality: Many of these tools are designed to work in concert with each other, providing a cohesive overview of governance, risk, and compliance activities. For instance, GRC platforms can integrate data from SIEM systems, compliance management software, and automated auditing tools to comprehensively view security and compliance status.

Effective compliance and internal audit practices are indispensable for robust cybersecurity governance. They ensure that an organization meets the required standards and implements best practices for securing its assets. As we transition to the next section, Risk Management, we will build upon the structured approach discussed here, focusing on how organizations assess, manage, and mitigate risks in line with their compliance efforts. This cohesive approach underlines the interconnectedness of compliance, internal audits, and risk management in creating a secure and resilient enterprise.

Risk Management

Risk Assessment Processes

Risk assessment is a fundamental component of an organization's risk management strategy. It involves a systematic process to identify, analyze, and prioritize risks to an organization's assets, including data, systems, and operations. This section details methodologies for conducting effective risk assessments, emphasizing the processes for identifying, analyzing, and prioritizing risks to enhance organizational security and resilience.

Methodologies for Conducting Risk Assessments

Identifying Risks: The first step in risk assessment is identifying the potential risks that could impact the organization. This involves gathering information about internal operations, external threats, and potential vulnerabilities. Techniques such as brainstorming sessions with various department heads, reviewing historical incident reports, and conducting system and network scans are essential to uncover a comprehensive list of risks.

Risk Analysis: Once risks are identified, the next step is to analyze their potential impact and the likelihood of their occurrence. This analysis can be qualitative or quantitative:

- **Qualitative Analysis**: Involves categorizing risks based on their severity and the likelihood of occurrence using descriptive scales such as high, medium, or low. This method is often used for its simplicity and speed of execution.
- **Quantitative Analysis**: Involves assigning numerical values to the impact and likelihood of risks. This may include calculating potential financial losses, estimating the cost of recovery, and using statistical methods to determine probabilities. Tools such as fault tree analysis (FTA) or event tree analysis (ETA) can be used for more detailed assessments.

Risk Prioritization: After analyzing the risks, the next step is to prioritize them based on their impact and likelihood. This helps organizations allocate resources and implement controls effectively. Risks that pose the greatest threat to organizational objectives are given the highest priority. Prioritization criteria often include factors such as potential revenue loss, legal repercussions, and impact on stakeholder confidence.

Tools and Techniques for Effective Risk Assessments

To conduct effective risk assessments that adequately identify, analyze, and manage potential risks, organizations can leverage a variety of tools and techniques. These resources enhance the ability to systematically address security vulnerabilities and threats, ensuring that risk management efforts are both comprehensive and effective.

Risk Assessment Tools

Automated Risk Assessment Software: These tools use algorithms to identify risks based on data input, making the process faster and more consistent. They can integrate with other IT management systems to pull real-time data and provide ongoing risk analysis. Popular software solutions like RSA Archer and RiskLens and GRC tools like LogicGate provide powerful platforms that automate risk identification, impact analysis, and reporting processes.

Threat Intelligence Platforms: These platforms provide up-to-date information about potential external threats, such as emerging malware, phishing schemes, and other cyber threats. By integrating threat intelligence directly into the risk assessment process, organizations can contextualize their vulnerabilities with real-time threat data, enhancing the relevance and timeliness of their risk assessments.

Traditional and Hybrid Techniques

Delphi Technique: This method involves a panel of experts who answer questionnaires in two or more rounds. After each round, a facilitator provides an anonymous summary of the experts' forecasts and reasons for their judgments. This process continues until a consensus is reached, helping to refine expert opinions on risk evaluations.

Bowtie Methodology: A visual tool for risk management, the bowtie diagram identifies and maps out potential causal relationships in high-risk scenarios. It illustrates paths from possible causes to preventive and mitigative controls and then to consequences, providing a clear overview of risk scenarios and management strategies.

Failure Mode and Effects Analysis (FMEA): This approach evaluates potential failure modes for processes and their likely effects on organizational outcomes, allowing businesses to prioritize risks based on their severity, occurrence, and detectability.

Innovative Approaches

Data Analytics and Predictive Modeling: Leveraging big data analytics and predictive modeling can significantly enhance the risk assessment process. By analyzing historical data, organizations can identify trends and predict potential areas of risk before they manifest into actual threats.

Scenario Analysis: This technique involves developing hypothetical scenarios based on possible events that could impact the organization. Scenario analysis helps in understanding the potential impact of complex events like cyber-attacks, natural disasters, or market changes.

Integration and Continuous Improvement

- **Continuous Monitoring Tools**: Software that provides continuous monitoring of network and system activities can feed real-time data into risk assessments, allowing for dynamic updating of risk status as the threat landscape changes.
- **Feedback Mechanisms**: Incorporating feedback mechanisms into the risk assessment process ensures that insights and data from past assessments inform future risk strategies. This continuous loop enhances the maturity and effectiveness of the risk management process.

The integration of these diverse tools and techniques into the risk assessment process not only enhances the ability to predict and mitigate risks but also aligns with broader organizational strategies for governance and compliance. By continually adapting and refining these tools, organizations can maintain a robust posture against an ever-evolving array of threats, ensuring resilience and sustainability in their operations. Effective risk management, supported by advanced tools and strategic methodologies, is essential for protecting an organization's assets, reputation, and long-term success.

Risk Mitigation and Acceptance Strategies

Effective risk management is not only about identifying and analyzing risks but also about implementing strategies to mitigate those risks and deciding when to accept risks that cannot be economically or practically mitigated. This section explores the various strategies organizations can employ to mitigate identified risks and the criteria used to determine when risks should be accepted.

Strategies for Mitigating Identified Risks

Risk Avoidance: This strategy involves altering plans to sidestep potential risks entirely. It is often the most straightforward approach but can also lead to missed opportunities. Organizations typically use this strategy when the potential loss from the risk far outweighs the potential gain from the risky activity.

Risk Reduction: Implementing controls to reduce the likelihood or impact of a risk is known as risk reduction. This can involve adding new technologies or processes, enhancing security protocols, or conducting rigorous training programs to minimize the potential for risk.

Risk Sharing: Sometimes, risks can be shared with other parties, which can involve outsourcing certain functions to third parties who can manage the risk more effectively. Insurance is a common method of risk sharing, where the financial impact of certain risks is transferred to an insurance provider.

Risk Transference: This strategy involves shifting the risk to a third party who is willing to accept it, typically through outsourcing or through contracts. For example, a company might require a contractor to assume liability for certain types of damages that occur on a project.

Criteria for Risk Acceptance

Cost-Benefit Analysis: Risk acceptance often involves conducting a cost-benefit analysis to determine if the costs of mitigating risk would exceed the benefit derived from that mitigation. If the cost of prevention is higher than the potential impact, accepting the risk may be justified.

Risk Appetite and Tolerance: Each organization has a defined risk appetite and tolerance that dictate the level of risk they are prepared to accept. These thresholds are set based on the organization's strategic objectives, financial capacity, and industry standards.

Legal and Regulatory Requirements: Some risks may involve legal or regulatory requirements that cannot be ignored. In such cases, risk mitigation must be prioritized to ensure compliance, regardless of cost or other factors.

Operational Capacity: The organization's capacity to manage and mitigate certain risks effectively without compromising its operational efficiency can also influence risk acceptance decisions.

Implementing and Reviewing Risk Mitigation Strategies

Regular Reviews: Risk mitigation strategies should be reviewed regularly to ensure they remain effective and relevant to the organization's operations and external environment. This includes reassessing risks periodically to account for new threats and organizational changes.

Feedback Loops: Effective risk management requires continuous improvement. Implementing feedback mechanisms to learn from past incidents and refine risk strategies is crucial for evolving an organization's risk posture.

Integration with Broader Risk Management Processes: Mitigation strategies should be integrated with the organization's broader risk management and governance frameworks to ensure alignment and support from senior management.

Risk mitigation and acceptance are critical components of comprehensive risk management. Organizations can safeguard their assets and ensure long-term sustainability by understanding and implementing effective mitigation strategies and establishing clear criteria for risk acceptance.

Test Your Knowledge (Chapter 6)

Question 1: What is the primary purpose of implementing security frameworks within an organization?

A. To ensure that employees are satisfied with their IT equipment

B. To increase the company's stock price

C. To manage cybersecurity risks effectively

D. To advertise the company's products

Question 2: Which international standard is known for providing a framework for information security management systems (ISMS)?

A. ISO/IEC 27001

B. ISO 9001

C. NIST Cybersecurity Framework

D. COBIT 5

Question 3: Which of the following is NOT a typical component of a Governance, Risk Management, and Compliance (GRC) platform?

A. Risk assessment automation

B. Financial management

C. Compliance tracking

D. Policy management

Question 4: Choose all that apply. Which roles are typically involved in enforcing cybersecurity frameworks?

A. CEO

B. Cybersecurity Analyst

C. Marketing Manager

D. CISO

Question 5: In the context of risk management, what does the term 'risk appetite' refer to?

A. The amount of risk a company is financially capable of handling

B. The level of risk an organization is willing to accept before action is deemed necessary

C. A new catering business for corporate events

D. The metrics used to measure risk in the IT department

Question 6: Drag and drop the correct order of steps for a typical risk assessment process.

1. Analysis
2. Identification
3. Prioritization
4. Review

Question 7: What type of risk management strategy involves transferring the risk to a third party?

A. Avoidance

B. Reduction

C. Sharing

D. Transference

Question 8: Fill in the blank: _____ is a proactive approach that uses machine learning to detect potential security threats based on patterns and anomalies.

A. Predictive modeling

B. Manual monitoring

C. Retrospective analysis

D. Historical trend mapping

Question 9: In a Zero Trust security model, which aspect is considered most crucial for determining access?

A. The location of the user

B. The time of day

C. The user's job title

D. Verification of the user's identity and device security

Question 10: Which approach is best for a company that wants to handle risk by using insurance to cover potential data breach costs?

A. Mitigation

B. Acceptance

C. Avoidance

D. Transfer

Question 11: Which type of audit provides real-time analysis of security alerts and logs within an organization?

A. Financial audit

B. Compliance audit

C. Operational audit

D. IT security audit

Question 12: True or False: Regular reviews and updates of disaster recovery plans are unnecessary if the company has not experienced any significant changes in operations.

Question 13: Select all that apply. What outcomes are expected from conducting effective internal audits?

A. Enhanced cybersecurity posture

B. Increased employee turnover

C. Identification of non-compliance with laws

D. Improved product quality

Question 14: What does the acronym SIEM stand for in cybersecurity governance?

A. Significant Information Every Minute

B. Security Information and Event Management

C. Simple Internal Evaluation Metrics

D. Systematic Investigation of Enterprise Malfunctions

Question 15: Scenario-based: If an organization is faced with a cybersecurity threat that could potentially shut down production, which risk strategy involves accepting the threat due to high mitigation costs?

A. Risk Avoidance

B. Risk Reduction

C. Risk Acceptance

D. Risk Transfer

Please refer to the "Test Your Knowledge SY0-701 (Answers)" chapter for the answers.

CHAPTER 7

Preparing for the Exam

Planning Your Study Schedule and Resources

Embarking on the journey to pass the CompTIA Security+ SYO-701 exam requires a strategic approach to studying. The right plan and resources are crucial to not only grasp the vast topics covered but also to apply them effectively in the exam and your future cybersecurity endeavors. This section provides detailed guidance on organizing your study time and selecting the best materials to prepare efficiently and effectively.

Creating a Structured Study Schedule

Assessment of Available Time: Start by realistically assessing how much time you can dedicate to studying each week. Consider your personal and professional obligations and carve out consistent, focused study periods. The key is consistency rather than duration.

Set Specific Goals: Break down the exam content into manageable sections and set specific goals for each study session. For example, dedicate certain weeks to specific domains of the SY0-701 exam, ensuring that you cover all material in a structured way.

Incorporate Review Sessions: Regular review sessions are critical to reinforce learning and ensure information retention. Schedule weekly reviews of what you've studied to solidify your knowledge and identify areas that need more attention.

Choosing the Right Study Materials

- **Supplementary Textbooks**: Consider supplementary texts from recognized authors in the cybersecurity field. These can provide different perspectives and deeper insights into complex topics.
- **Online Courses and Videos**: Engage with interactive online courses and video tutorials, which can be particularly helpful for visual learners. Platforms like LinkedIn Learning, Cybrary, or Udemy offer specialized courses that align with Security+ objectives.
- **Practice Tests**: Regularly taking practice tests can help you gauge your readiness and familiarize yourself with the exam format. Check the Bonus section; inside, you will find complete Practice Tests.

Leveraging Technology and Tools

Study Apps: Utilize study apps that offer flashcards, quizzes, and the ability to track your progress. Apps like Anki or Quizlet can be customized to focus on Security+ exam content and are excellent for studying on the go.

Online Forums and Study Groups: Participate in online forums and study groups. Engaging with peers can provide moral support, diverse insights, and explanations of difficult concepts that can enhance your understanding and retention.

Engaging with Content

Interactive Learning: Engage actively with the material. This can include teaching the content to someone else, discussing topics with peers, or even writing blog posts about what you've learned. Teaching is often the best way to solidify your grasp of the subject matter.

> **Regular Updates**: Keep your study materials updated, especially in fields as dynamic as cybersecurity. Ensure that your resources reflect the latest industry trends and exam requirements.

Planning your study schedule and carefully choosing your resources are fundamental steps toward success in the SY0-701 exam. By setting clear goals, using diverse and reliable materials, and engaging actively with the content, you can build a solid foundation of knowledge and go into your exam with confidence. Remember, the journey to certification is not just about passing an exam but also about preparing to handle real-world security challenges effectively.

Memory Techniques and Learning Aids

Mastering the content of the CompTIA Security+ SY0-701 exam requires more than just understanding the material; it involves retaining that knowledge long enough to apply it effectively in an exam setting. This section explores various memory enhancement techniques and learning aids that can significantly boost your ability to remember and recall crucial information during your study sessions and beyond.

Effective Memory Techniques

Mnemonic Devices: Mnemonics are tools that help you remember information by associating it with words, sentences, or imagery that are easier to recall. For example, using the acronym "CIA" to remember the three key principles of information security: Confidentiality, Integrity, and Availability. Creating vivid, unusual images or sentences can make the association stronger and the information more memorable.

The Method of Loci: Also known as the memory palace, this ancient technique involves visualizing a familiar place and associating items you need to remember with specific locations within this place. For instance, while trying to remember different network security protocols, you might imagine placing each protocol in different rooms of your house.

Chunking and Organization: Breaking down large pieces of information into smaller, manageable chunks can enhance information retention. Organizing these chunks into categories that make logical sense helps in creating mental connections that facilitate easier recall.

Learning Aids to Support Memory

Practice Tests: Regularly taking practice tests can significantly boost memory retention by reinforcing the material and helping you recall information under exam conditions. Practice tests also help identify areas where your recall is weak, allowing you to focus your studies more effectively.

Flashcards: Using flashcards for key terms, concepts, and definitions can be a very effective repetitive learning tool. They are particularly useful for memorizing ports, protocols, and security settings. Digital flashcards available on platforms like Anki or Quizlet can include multimedia elements to enhance learning.

Study Apps: Apps that employ spaced repetition algorithms can help in scheduling review sessions based on how well you have learned the information. This technique adjusts the frequency of review based on your mastery of the material, ensuring that information is reviewed right before it is likely to be forgotten.

Interactive Learning Techniques

- **Group Study and Discussion**: Engaging in discussions with peers or study groups can help reinforce learning and uncover new insights or perspectives. Explaining concepts to others is a powerful way to enhance your own understanding and retention.
- **Teaching Sessions**: If possible, try to teach the material to someone else. The preparation required to teach ensures a deep grasp of the subject matter, and the teaching process itself can uncover gaps in your own understanding.

Utilizing these memory techniques and learning aids will prepare you to pass the SY0-701 exam and retain the knowledge as you progress in your cybersecurity career.

Types of Questions and Approaches

The CompTIA Security+ SY0-701 exam tests your knowledge and skills through a variety of question formats. Understanding these question types and how to approach them effectively is crucial for maximizing your score. This section breaks down the common types of questions you'll encounter and provides strategic advice on how to tackle each.

Types of Questions

Multiple-Choice Questions (MCQs): These are the most common question types, where you are required to select the correct answer(s) from several options. Questions may ask for a single answer or multiple correct answers.

Strategy: Read each question carefully to understand what is being asked, especially in questions that require multiple answers. Use the process of elimination to narrow down choices, and look for keywords or phrases that are absolute (such as "always," "never," and "only"), as these can often guide you to or away from the correct answer.

Performance-Based Questions (PBQs): These questions assess your ability to solve problems in a simulated environment. You might be asked to configure network security settings, implement a firewall rule, or identify security vulnerabilities within a scenario.

Strategy: Before starting, spend a moment to plan your approach. Understand the scenario fully and prioritize tasks. Often, PBQs can be complex and time-consuming, so managing your time efficiently is key.

Drag-and-Drop Questions: In these questions, you need to match or place items in a specific order or configuration.

Strategy: Familiarize yourself with concepts that often require ordering (such as incident response phases or layers of security). Practicing these types of questions beforehand can significantly improve your speed and accuracy.

Effective Strategies for Answering Questions

Time Management: Allocate your time wisely. Begin by answering the questions you find easiest to build confidence and secure quick wins. Save more time-consuming PBQs for later, as these can drain your time if tackled first.

Reading Comprehension: Read each question carefully to understand exactly what is asked. Misunderstanding a question can lead to incorrect answers, especially when the wording is designed to test your attention to detail.

Use of Practice Tests: Regularly engaging with practice tests can help you become familiar with the question formats and exam timing. This practice also aids in identifying areas where your knowledge may be lacking, allowing for focused study sessions.

Reviewing Answers: If time allows, review your answers before submitting the exam. This can be particularly useful for multiple-choice questions, where your first instinct may not always be correct. Revisiting questions with a fresh perspective might reveal insights you missed initially.

Career Opportunities with CompTIA Security+

Typical Roles and Employment Sectors

The CompTIA Security+ certification is recognized globally as a vital credential for cybersecurity professionals, validating foundational skills necessary to perform core security functions. This certification paves the way for various career opportunities in numerous sectors. Here, we explore the typical roles and sectors where a Security+ certification is highly valued, offering insights into the diverse pathways that certification holders can pursue.

Common Job Roles for Security+ Certified Professionals

Security Analyst: Security analysts are responsible for monitoring and defending networks against security threats. They analyze security breaches and implement solutions, often collaborating with other departments to establish organization-wide best practices for digital security.

Systems Administrator: While primarily responsible for managing, operating, and maintaining a company's computing infrastructure, systems administrators with a Security+ certification also ensure that these systems are secure against internal and external threats.

Network Administrator: Network administrators with a Security+ certification focus on the security aspects of network configurations. They are tasked with installing and supporting network systems, including local area networks (LANs), wide area networks (WANs), network segments, intranets, and other data communication systems.

IT Auditor: IT auditors assess and evaluate an organization's information technology infrastructure, policies, and operations. They ensure compliance with laws and regulations, helping to maintain data integrity and operational efficiency of secure IT systems.

Penetration Tester: Often known as ethical hackers, penetration testers simulate cyberattacks to identify and fix vulnerabilities in security systems before they can be exploited maliciously.

Employment Sectors That Value Security+

Government Agencies: Many government positions require Security+ certification due to its focus on compliance and operational security. It is particularly valued in the defense and intelligence sectors, where security is paramount.

Financial Services: Banks and other financial institutions invest heavily in cybersecurity to protect sensitive financial data and comply with industry regulations like PCI-DSS.

Healthcare: With stringent compliance requirements such as HIPAA, the healthcare industry values Security+ certified professionals to help protect patient information and critical medical data.

Education: Educational institutions use Security+ professionals to protect student information and safeguard their systems against breaches, which are increasingly common in academic environments.

Technology and Consulting Firms: As the backbone of digital solutions, tech companies and consultancies seek Security+ certified professionals to craft robust security frameworks for their projects and services.

Earning the CompTIA Security+ certification is just the beginning of a career in cybersecurity. Professionals are encouraged to continuously learn and gain additional certifications to advance in specialized areas such as cyber forensics, ethical hacking, and security architecture. Pursuing advanced certifications and roles can lead to more strategic positions like Security Manager or CISO (Chief Information Security Officer).

The CompTIA Security+ certification opens up a world of opportunities across various sectors. Whether you are starting your career or looking to advance, it provides a solid foundation in cybersecurity principles and practices that are crucial in today's digital world. As you move into more specialized roles, the skills acquired from achieving Security+ certification will serve as a stepping stone to more advanced positions, underlining the importance of lifelong learning in the ever-evolving field of cybersecurity.

Career Advancement and Further Certifications

Achieving the CompTIA Security+ certification is an important milestone for professionals in the cybersecurity field. However, it is just the beginning of a pathway to deeper specialization and higher responsibilities within the industry. This section discusses the avenues for further certification and career advancement after obtaining your Security+ credential, providing a roadmap for continuous professional development.

Paths for Further Certification

Advanced CompTIA Certifications: After Security+, many professionals choose to pursue more specialized CompTIA certifications. CompTIA Cybersecurity Analyst (CySA+) focuses on behavioral analytics to improve security; CompTIA Advanced Security Practitioner (CASP+) caters to those interested in staying in hands-on technical security roles rather than managerial paths.

Vendor-Specific Certifications: Depending on your career goals and the technologies used by your employer, vendor-specific certifications can be highly beneficial. Certifications from Cisco (like CCNA Security), Microsoft (like Microsoft Certified: Security, Compliance, and Identity Fundamentals), or AWS (like AWS Certified Security – Specialty) can make a significant difference in roles that utilize specific technologies.

Specialized Security Certifications: For those looking to specialize further, certifications such as Certified Information Systems Security Professional (CISSP), Certified Ethical Hacker (CEH), or Certified Information Security Manager (CISM) offer advanced knowledge and skills in particular areas of cybersecurity like ethical hacking, information security management, or architecture.

Strategies for Career Advancement

Skill Enhancement: Continuously update your skills with the latest technologies and practices in cybersecurity. Participate in workshops, webinars, and other educational opportunities. Stay abreast of new threats and innovations in the field to remain competitive.

Networking and Professional Associations: Engage with professional associations such as ISACA (ISC)^2 or the Information Systems Security Association (ISSA). These organizations offer networking opportunities, resources, and conferences that can enhance your knowledge and professional visibility.

Leadership and Management Skills: As you advance in your career, soft skills, particularly in leadership and management, become as crucial as technical abilities. Consider courses in project management, communication, and leadership to prepare for roles that involve team leadership or strategic oversight.

Hands-On Experience: Nothing substitutes for the real-world experience. Seek out projects and roles within your current employment that stretch your abilities and expose you to new challenges. Consider roles in different aspects of cybersecurity to build a well-rounded skill set.

I want to extend my heartfelt thanks to you for your dedication and hard work in navigating the complexities of cybersecurity with this guide. Congratulations on completing a significant step towards mastering the skills necessary for the CompTIA Security+ exam and advancing your career in cybersecurity.

Your journey doesn't end here. I encourage exploring the bonus section, where additional quizzes and exam tests await. These resources are designed to test your knowledge and sharpen your skills, providing you with the practice needed to approach your certification exam with confidence.

Thank you once again for choosing this book as your companion on this educational path. Remember, every step you take in learning and preparation brings you closer to achieving your goals in the ever-evolving field of cybersecurity. Good luck, and I look forward to helping you succeed on your journey to certification and beyond.

Test Your Knowledge
SY0-701 (Answers)

Test Your Knowledge (Chapter 2)

Question 1: B. To ensure only authorized users can access certain resources

Question 2: C. Role-Based Access Control (RBAC)

Question 3: B. Ensuring data is not altered by unauthorized individuals

Question 4: B. Data masking

Question 5: C. It enhances security by requiring multiple forms of verification

Question 6:

- A. Encryption - Prevents data tampering and unauthorized access
- B. Backup - Ensures data availability in case of system failure
- C. Watermarking - Tracks unauthorized distribution of data

Question 7: B. GDPR

Question 8: (Performance-based scenario; there is no right or wrong answer as it depends on the individual's proposed steps based on the guidelines in the chapter)

Question 9: True

Question 10: A, C, D (All techniques that help ensure data confidentiality)

Question 11: B. To check compliance with data protection laws

Question 12: A. Changes in technology

Question 13:

- A. Intrusion Detection Systems - Monitors network traffic for suspicious activity
- B. Firewalls - Controls incoming and outgoing network traffic based on predetermined security rules
- C. Encryption - Secures data by converting it into a secure format

Question 14: D. ABAC

Question 15: False

Test Your Knowledge (Chapter 3)

Question 1: C. Trojan

Question 2: B. DDoS

Question 3: C. Deceiving individuals into providing sensitive data

Question 4: A. Regular software updates, D. Antivirus software

Question 5:

- Firewall - Blocks unauthorized network access
- IDS - Detects intrusion attempts
- Encryption tools - Encrypts sensitive data
- DLP software - Monitors data loss prevention

Question 6: B. To monitor and analyze security alerts in real-time

Question 7: A. Identify potential security risks

Question 8: C. Adware removal

Question 9: [Performance-based; requires a list of steps based on the scenario provided.]

Question 10: C. Man-in-the-middle

Question 11: B. Encryption

Question 12: A. Installing antivirus software, C. Regular security audits

Question 13: A. Side-channel attack

Question 14:

- Identification
- Containment
- Eradication
- Recovery
  Question 15: A. To detect and prevent data breaches

Test Your Knowledge (Chapter 4)

Question 1: C. To filter incoming and outgoing network traffic based on predetermined security rules

Question 2: A. Encryption of data C. Secure remote access

Question 3:

- **Symmetric Encryption**: Encrypts and decrypts with the same key
- **Asymmetric Encryption**: Uses two different keys for encryption and decryption
- **Hashing**: Converts data into a fixed-size string to verify data integrity

Question 4:

- Enable full-disk encryption in the device settings.
- Use secure container apps for sensitive data.
- Ensure the encryption algorithm used is up-to-date and robust, like AES.

Question 5 B. It isolates network communication to improve security.

Question 6: A. Ansible C. WSUS

Question 7:

- **Firewall**: Threat Prevention
- **IDS**: Threat Detection
- **Anti-Malware**: Threat Prevention
- **Data Loss Prevention (DLP)**: Data Protection

Question 8:

- Access the firewall configuration panel.
- Specify the known malicious IP addresses or ranges.
- Set the rule action to "block" or "deny."
- Apply and save the configuration.

Question 9: C. Vulnerability to attacks

Question 10: A. Data encryption C. Real-time threat detection D. Automatic software updates

Question 11:

- **Encryption at Rest**: Disk Encryption
- **Secure Remote Access**: VPN
- **Intrusion Detection**: IDS

Question 12:
- Implement strong access controls.
- Encrypt personal data.
- Regularly update and review access permissions.

Question 13: A. AES

Question 14: A. Regular auditing D. Employing a zero-trust model

Question 15:
1. Assess vulnerabilities
2. Apply patches
3. Verify and test patches
4. Monitor for compliance

Test Your Knowledge (Chapter 5)

Question 1: C. To monitor and respond to security threats

Question 2: B. Incremental backup

Question 3: C. To provide scalable and flexible recovery solutions

Question 4: C. Filters incoming and outgoing network traffic based on security rules

Question 5: C. Snapshot

Question 6 (Multiple Response): A. Real-time monitoring, C. Threat detection and response

Question 7: C. Differential backup

Question 8: A. When immediate data recovery is essential

Question 9: C. Ensuring timely application of security patches

Question 10 (Drag-and-Drop):

Answer:
1. B. Preparation
2. A. Identification
3. D. Containment
4. E. Eradication
5. C. Recovery

Question 11: B. To analyze data and identify how a security breach occurred

Question 12: B. To convert data into a secure format that is unreadable without a key

Question 13: C. Virtual machine snapshots

Question 14: A. To ensure they work effectively under actual disaster conditions

Question 15 (Performance-Based Scenario):.

Notification and Communication: Ensure all team members are promptly notified of the outage and establish communication lines.
- **Role Assignments**: Confirm that all team members know their responsibilities during the outage.
- **Implementation of Response**: Activate the disaster recovery procedures to mitigate the outage.
- **Data Accessibility**: Check data accessibility to ensure critical data is still available or recoverable.
- **System Recovery**: Implement steps to recover the main system operations.
- **Time Measurement**: Record the time taken to respond and recover from the outage.
- **Evaluation and Feedback**: After recovery, evaluate the effectiveness of the response and gather feedback for improvement.

Test Your Knowledge (Chapter 6)

Question 1: C. To manage cybersecurity risks effectively
Question 2: A. ISO/IEC 27001
Question 3: B. Financial management
Question 4: A. CEO, B. Cybersecurity Analyst, D. CISO
Question 5: B. The level of risk an organization is willing to accept before action is deemed necessary
Question 6: Correct order: 2. Identification, 1. Analysis, 3. Prioritization, 4. Review
Question 7: D. Transference
Question 8: A. Predictive modeling
Question 9: D. Verification of the user's identity and device security
Question 10: D. Transfer
Question 11: D. IT security audit
Question 12: False
Question 13: A. Enhanced cybersecurity posture, C. Identification of non-compliance with laws
Question 14: B. Security Information and Event Management
Question 15: C. Risk Acceptance

BONUS

Scan the QR code to claim your exclusive bonus and access to Audiobooks, Quizzes, Mock exams and more to enhance your knowledge.

I want to express my gratitude for your selection of my book.

Your review on Amazon would be invaluable and greatly appreciated.

Thank you.

Made in United States
Orlando, FL
02 April 2025

60098886R00131